Muscle

Jon Hotten is the author of *Unlicensed: Random Notes From Boxing's Underbelly*. He has also written for the *Guardian*, the *Sunday Times*, *Esquire* and *Punch*.

For more on *Muscle*, visit www.musclethebook.com

By the same author

Unlicensed: Random Notes from Boxing's Underbelly

Muscle

*A Writer's Trip through a
Sport with no Boundaries*

Jon Hotten

YELLOW JERSEY PRESS
LONDON

Published by Yellow Jersey Press 2005

2 4 6 8 10 9 7 5 3 1

First published in Great Britain in 2004 by
Yellow Jersey Press

Yellow Jersey Press
Random House, 20 Vauxhall Bridge Road,
London SW1V 2SA

Random House Australia (Pty) Limited
20 Alfred Street, Milsons Point, Sydney,
New South Wales 2061, Australia

Random House New Zealand Limited
18 Poland Road, Glenfield,
Auckland 10, New Zealand

Random House (Pty) Limited
Endulini, 5A Jubilee Road, Parktown 2193, South Africa

The Random House Group Limited Reg. No. 954009
www.randomhouse.co.uk

A CIP catalogue record for this book is available from
the British Library

ISBN 0–224–06967–5

Papers used by Random House are natural, recyclable products made
from wood grown in sustainable forests; the manufacturing processes
conform to the environmental regulations of the country of origin

Typeset by SX Composing DTP, Rayleigh, Essex
Printed and bound in Great Britain by
Cox & Wyman Ltd, Reading, Berkshire

For Lily and Ruby

Contents

'Everyone wants to be big.
No one wants to lift no heavy-ass weights . . .'

Ronnie Coleman, Mr Olympia

1

Andi Redux (i)

He went to the stage as hard as a bagful of nails. He looked like the Eighth damn Wonder of the World up there: seventeen stone of muscle and bone and not much else. He was huge and dense and cut. He had twenty-one-inch arms, a fifty-eight-inch chest and enough junk in his bloodstream to kill a horse. It was certainly killing him. He lived in agony. If he'd still had the will to turn his head to the left, he would have seen other men like him, Godzillas of the iron game. To his right, the same. They looked barely human. They looked like a sub-strain, a spin-off, a genetic joke.

He was so dry that his lips kept sticking together. His body was arid. He was parched. The last of his sweat rolled slowly down him, streamed by his deep striations. It left light streaks in his tinned tan. Andi fixed his feet harder into the floor and squeezed his unsteady muscle one more time.

The other guys still had some zap and heft and zing left in them. Kevin Levrone, 'The Maryland Muscle Machine', was ripped and zipped; Kenny 'Flex' Wheeler was as austere and as beautiful as a Greek statue; Paul Dillett had a chest by

Jackson Pollock, splattered with fat chunks of vein; Vince Taylor brought out his galactic shoulders; Shawn Ray ran as thick as a bull, front to back. It was a war of the strangest kind. Huge men in spangly thongs shovelled each other aside so that they could hit muscleman poses. There were four thousand people watching them do it, and they were going off while they did. The Veterans' Memorial Arena was a mushroom farm of jumping muscle. Most of the crowd were bodybuilders of a sort themselves – there were women sitting around who could've beaten the living crap out of you.

Andi already knew that the game was up. This was the final round of competition, the posedown; a concocted crowd-pleaser. It existed mainly to allow the judges time to verify the scores. Levrone, Ray and Dillett jumped from the stage and walked into the stalls so that the fans could see them close up. They posed for photos. They gripped and grinned. Andi held on at the edge of the platform. There, perhaps one more judge might catch the final nuances of his development. Perhaps one more judge might move him up by one more place. Perhaps Arnold Schwarzenegger himself would look up from his seat in row two and understand that Andi's head had blazed with his name for twenty years. Perhaps then he would finally get his due and perhaps it would tip the balance of his life. His name was Andreas Munzer. For a decade, he had been the greatest bodybuilder in the German-speaking world.

The head judge was a man named Wayne DeMilia. He was from Queens, New York, and he sounded like it. He called the last six competitors back into line. Arnold Schwarzenegger had vacated his seat in row two and stood in the wings ready to present the prizes. Arnold had not been a bodybuilder for a long time, it had been sixteen years since he was Mr Olympia 1980, but he remained the talisman of muscle. The Arnold Classic was a contest named after him and promoted by him and dedicated to his glory.

In professional bodybuilding events, results were announced in reverse order. Andi would die soon, but he wouldn't die wondering.

Wayne DeMilia said: 'Sixth place . . . winning five thousand dollars . . . from Austria . . . Andreas Munzer . . .'

Andi picked up a slim cheque and a joke trophy. The applause was thin and slow. The crowd already had Munzer sixth. This was how things often were at the top shows. The consensus of years informed results. The judges had muscle memory too.

Fifth: Shawn Ray, no surprises there, either.

Fourth: Vince Taylor – obviously.

Third: Paul Dillett and his terrifying vascularity. Those blossoming blood vessels had got the crowd's blood up, too. They hooted and yelled.

Two were left, Kevin Levrone and Flex Wheeler. The Maryland Muscle Machine beamed and squeezed. There was some Italian in Levrone and it showed: he glowed with *la dolce vita*.

Flex, though, was drawn with orbs and ellipses. The lines of his body flowed like water. At the elbows and wrists, at the waist and knees and ankles, Flex was a regular joe. But from these bone junctions, he curved outwards like a bow. Genetics – there was no drug invented that could overcome them. Flex had kidneys that were on the blink. They only had a few years left. But he had genetics from heaven and they made him hard to beat.

The separation fell to DeMilia. At least he was quick: 'Second place, winning forty-five thousand dollars . . . Flex . . .'

The 'Wheeler' was inaudible, carried off by the cheers and screams of the fans. The Muscle Machine had won the Arnold Classic, $100,000 and a Hummer car.

At that moment, Andreas Munzer had the sixth-best body in the world. His problem was, he was competing against the top five.

Some days later, Andi sat on a plane feeling like death. Flight attendants looked at him. Passengers checked Andi out. He was a rare thing in the rare air; a colossus at 30,000 feet. The passengers were the usual crew. They had mortal bodies. They were smokers, drinkers, faddists, bloaters, bingers, deniers, dieters. They sagged. They slumped. They slouched. They were units working at half speed, at exhaustion rate. They were mundane, everyday. And some day their bodies might up and surprise them, give out with little notice. Others would fold more slowly. One way or another, their bodies would let them have it. Andi's body, though, hurtled along like the plane that presently contained it. It sped towards its ugly implosion, each painfully won gain hastening the end. No one could tell, except Andi. His beef appeared implacable, irresistible. His muscle looked like it meant business, and in Andi's business, the look was everything. To look as he did, you had to believe, at least in part, in your own invincibility.

So Andi had his secrets, and he kept them to the end.

*

There was a truism in bodybuilding: be born black or German. These were the favoured genetic lines. Through them, muscle thrummed down generations. It thrummed through Andi, a monumental mesomorph, born blessed. Andi's people were farmers, 'simple with weather-tanned faces' as the press would later describe them. They lived a

4

mile or so from the Modriacher Stausee reservoir near a village called Pack in rural Austria. They ran a dairy business that just about kept them afloat. Andi absorbed their ethic of stoic self-improvement. He was a quiet boy, a hard worker. Andi paid his dues in the fields. He liked to play the trumpet in a local band, a *Musikkapelle*. During the summer he played football. During winter, he skied. Andi was a fast skier. He fizzed down the pistes too easily. He built jumps, to challenge himself.

Andi was hired as a toolmaker in Flach, a town ten kilometres from the farm. He didn't have a car so he took the bus. Between finishing work and catching the bus home, Andi had a two-hour wait. 'To loaf about and drink beer was not his thing,' Andi's father Killian said. Andi joined a gym instead. Passing time waiting for a bus home, he connected with his strange fate.

Andi got big quick. The weight hooked up with those juiced-up Germanic genes. Ethics of work and sacrifice ran deep in Andi too. Strange quirks, random connections sparked. The fluke combination of desire and suitability lay within him. His muscles began to haul him out of obscurity.

When he was nineteen years old his pals pushed him to pose. He entered a local competition: the *Steirische Meisterschaft* in the junior section, for novices of '80 kg and under'. Andi weighed 176 lean and clean pounds. He came second. It was a big result. Andi wasn't pumping for fun any more. He was no longer lifting to kill time waiting for a bus. First he won the junior class at the championships of Austria, and then later the senior title, too.

Andi's God was Arnold Schwarzenegger. Arnold was Austrian. Moreover, Arnold was Styrian. Arnold came from Thal. Andi was from Pack. Arnold took up bodybuilding after seeing a muscleman working out by a mountain reservoir. Andi grew up by one. Arnold became the greatest bodybuilder in the German-speaking world. Andi was striving towards that end. Arnold was a seven-time Mr Olympia. Now he was a movie star.

Arnold, who once said he'd eat a kilo of shit if it gained him a pound of muscle. Arnold, the planet's most driven man.

Killian Munzer remembered that Andi found success 'automatically'. Andi's sister, Maria Klement, said: 'Body-building became his life.' In 1986, Andi's employer went to the wall. Andi wasn't a toolmaker any more. He stayed in Flach and opened a fitness club. It had a name that reeked of a small town's big dreams: he called it 'Fitnessclub Florida Flach'. Now he could pump iron full-time. In 1987 and 1988, in Madrid and Brisbane, Andi was placed third in the World Amateur Championships. For his age – twenty-two and then twenty-three – Andi was something exceptional, a man apart.

Albert Busek got a look at Andi in the world champs. Busek was the kingmaker in German bodybuilding, and he knew a prince when he saw one. He'd known it when he looked at Arnold Schwarzenegger back in '68, and he knew it when he looked at Andreas Munzer, too. Busek put Andi on the cover of *Flexs Digest* magazine. He called him 'a potential world champion'. The cover of *Flexs Digest* made everything worthwhile for Andi. 'It is worth so much more than winning the championships,' he said.

The Fitnessclub Florida Flach was falling apart. Andi could either pay for the renovations or close it down. He closed it down. Andi had outgrown Austria, as Arnie once had. He was twenty-four years old and on the cover of *Flexs Digest*. And Albert Busek had offered him a job, as he had Arnold twenty-four years before.

Andi moved to Munich to work for Busek. He was employed as a trainer in one of Busek's gyms. Albert Busek was an operator: he had gyms, he ran *Sportrevue* magazine, he was honorary chairman of the DBFV and a vice-president of the International Federation of Bodybuilders, the IFBB, controlled by Joe and Ben Weider. *Der Spiegel* newspaper said of him: 'He is to bodybuilders what Ron Hubbard is for Scientologists'.

Then Andi won the World Games in Karlsruhe, south of Heidelberg. The win gave him an IFBB professional card. It was 1989.

In the gyms, everyone was juicing. To succeed in professional bodybuilding, you had to. But you had to do many other things too. If winning pro shows was as easy as taking steroids, every loser iron-junkie, every tragic muscle rat would be Mr Olympia.

Somehow, somewhere, at some point, Andi joined in. He had no choice. In chess, there is a position called 'zugzwang', where you must make a move, even though that move will cause you to lose. Drugs were Andi's zugzwang. Drugs were bodybuilding's zugzwang.

But first Andi took a ride on the upward curve of life, passage on which is reserved for the special, the few, the chosen. He stayed in shape all year round, a Sisyphean ordeal. Andi looked liked he was wearing his muscles on the outside. His condition became his USP. He was a shy boy, a clunky poser who disliked the show stage. But when he was up there, there was no one more ripped, no one more shredded. Andi stayed brutally hard. His muscle was glued to his skin, and his skin was as finely grained as ricepaper.

In the gym, he was driven, obsessed. 'It's as if you own a Ferrari,' he said. 'Only very few people do.'

Maria Klement said: 'To Andi, bodybuilding was like a trance.' It was. It consumed him: his job, his time, his conversation, his life. He ate six times a day (no fat, no junk, no dead calories), he slept for twelve hours and more, he didn't drink, he didn't smoke, he didn't mix with non-bodybuilders. He was stoic, determined, principled. He was Albert Busek's poster boy. In *Sportrevue*, readers learned about 'The Mysterious Munzer Monster'. He laid out his gym routines for them, coached them on his diet. He kept a heavy schedule of public appearances: guest poses, night-club gigs, gymnasium seminars and competition. He was a rigorous and dedicated pro. He was going somewhere.

Through the IFBB and its representatives, through its publications and journals, through the public utterances of its athletes, bodybuilding operated an *omertà* on drug use. Albert Busek instructed his gym staff to report any suspicions they had. In *Sportrevue*, he produced editorials against steroid use. He accused his accusers, too: 'Sensationalist journalism proliferates like a cancerous ulcer.'

Andi became used to the annual cycles that dictated his life; the boom and bust of bulking up and dieting down. It was binge and purge, governed by the need to grow bigger each year, and then to shed body fat in order to display the hard-won gains in competition. While he did, he worked in the gym. Andi was quiet, modest, but his size and demeanour discouraged casual approaches. Aspirant lifters came from miles away to work out where Munzer worked out, in the gym owned by Busek. 'Just like every Indian has to take a bath in the Ganges, every real bodybuilder has to exercise there,' said one.

Andi kept his love life in-house, too. He started seeing Elisabeth Schwarz. They made a hell of a couple. Sissy was also a bodybuilder. Perhaps Andi looked at Sissy and saw himself. Perhaps Sissy did the same. They began living together in a flat in Munich. Andi told Sissy he would marry her when she was world champion. It was a bodybuilder's deal, a bargain that they both understood. Sissy was runner-up in the IFBB World Amateur Championship in 1994 and 1995. They remained unmarried.

Andi had the girl, the blue Toyota sports car, the apartment. Andy was a good son and a good man. He was the 'Mysterious Munzer Monster', the greatest bodybuilder in the German-speaking world. And Andi had his secrets, too.

After Andi's death, a young guy identified just as Ralf came forward. He had a story about Andi, and about Albert Busek's gym. He had begun training there at nineteen, with the notion of treading the footsteps of Teutonic champs. He worked hard and made gains. Then he hit the wall. He stopped growing. Ralf's life became all pain and no gain. A serious bodybuilder might face the wall several times in a career, and there were two methods of dealing with it: get round it or go through it. Ralf asked Andi what he should do. Andi took him aside, somewhere quiet, behind the bar. Andi reviewed his training and his diet. He stressed the importance of supplements. He put Ralf on to a steroid cycle. He jump-started his muscles with synthetic juice.

Ralf says he signed up to Andi's plan. He gained 44 lb of processed muscle. He blew straight through the wall. The testosterone gave him unbearable erections. He had his girlfriend 'twice or three times a day'. His hard-on became unbearable for her too; she left him. He masturbated every morning before college. Buoyed by his beef, Ralf stayed on his steroid cycle. His temper grew exponentially. He beat up two men in discos and was hauled up in front of the magistrates. Ralf wasn't bothered. Within three months, he was doing well in regional competitions.

At the gym, Ralf realised two things: everyone was juicing, and no one was talking about it. From watching Andreas Munzer, he learned how to behave in public.

Busek promoted Andi as a clean athlete, 'one of the greatest ambassadors of our sport'. And he was. Andi had his secrets, but he was honest and hard-working. He wasn't screwing all day, he never had a fight. When he went home to Styria to visit the farm, he was a modest son; he never mentioned his achievements.

His body was evidence enough. If the family sat down to eat pork knuckle, Maria Klement remembered, Andi would cook something else for himself, turkey and rice, maybe. Andi would not allow his other life to intrude on theirs. He played with his nephews. He helped with the hay harvest. He'd go to a lounge bar in Pack, the Kirchenwirt. There he was met with quiet pride and a pleasing indifference; this was Pack. This was home.

Just as Andi had doubled his size, he doubled himself. Back in Munich he was the big man without a past. Acquaintances knew only that he came from 'somewhere in the proximity of Graz'. Few mentions were made of the coincidence of birth, the genuine closeness of Andi's origins to Arnie's. If Andi yearned one day to return to Styria and to its simple life, he did not make it known. At home in Pack, Andi was the oldest son, with all of the honours of that office. In Munich he was a king of a different kind. It carried obligations not of birth but of his own making and it was a high-maintenance gig. Yet Styria had formed Andi too completely for him to divorce its influence when he was away. He was known as one of the nicest men in a sport mostly populated by meatheads, narcissists, egoists, attention-seekers, over-compensators and the terminally aggrieved. It was a sport that demanded extremity, so it attracted extremists. Andi was no such thing.

But he had made the deal. The Munich Andi would play the zugzwang. He hit some heavy cycles: he injected two ampoules of testosterone a day; he took the oral steroids Halotestin and Anabol; he combined them with Masteron and Parabolan; he used between four and twenty-four units of the growth hormone STH.

Andi 'had tremendous know-how', acknowledged by the experienced gym junkies. Steroids aided muscle repair and general recovery; they allowed him to train with greater intensity. He combined different steroid types to maximum effect. He found that STH, the synthetic growth hormone, mimicked human growth hormone; it made everything grow – muscles, bones, organs, tissues. He ate between six and eight thousand calories a day to nourish his muscles. He used insulin to stimulate his metabolism and churn the calories more quickly; he used at least five aspirin tablets each morning to thin his blood and help with the pain of training; he used ephedrine and Captagon to increase his intensity on the weights.

Fifteen weeks or so from competition, he would begin a rigorous diet designed to reduce his body fat. He'd come down to two thousand calories a day. In the days and hours before a show he used Aldactone and Lasix, both diuretics, to rid himself of the last of his water.

Most pros would get close to competition shape once or twice a year. Anything else demanded too much; Andi maintained a reputation for always being in shape, or close to it.

Andi's life in Munich was expensive. It came at a cost, split three ways. The bill for the physical cost came in pain:

11

he had a pain ledger at the gym, and he paid in full, every day, year upon year. The mental cost – the price of living two lives – was met by Andi's unyielding Munich persona. The financial cost, prosaic by comparison, was nonetheless an imperative. Andi might spend DM10,000 a month on the upkeep of that body.

It would have been simple for Andi to offset his expenses – growing, as he was, all the time, endlessly – by guiding men like Ralf towards the juice and then supplying them. It would have been easy for Andi to deal in steroids and growth hormone and insulin and diuretics. Andi refused to. Andi had already made his losing move. There was no reason to make another. Instead, Andi looked to his body as his product, as his USP. He'd fed it, and so it must feed him. Andi stayed in shape throughout his cycles. He piled on chemical muscle but he did not gorge and grow fat. Andi kept close to contest condition, or at least close enough to deceive the amateur eye. His body remained remarkable enough to earn its keep year-round. At gyms and seminars, in clubs and discos, forty times a year, Andi would do his thing for money. For DM2,500, he'd pose for pay, he'd flash for cash.

His friend Michael would drive him around. Michael worked as an undertaker. Everyone called him Grufti. Most often, Andi would pose before knowledgeable crowds, other bodybuilders. But sometimes he would go on at provincial discos and clubs, an alien attraction. Here, ordinary people could encounter something sublime. Andi worked for his cash. He amped up his arms. He prised apart his pecs and dicked around with his delts. He striated his stomach and carved out his calves. He squished his nuts into a posing pouch. He oozed oil all over. He hardened himself up. He checked himself out. Andi understood that the people would not know that they were in the presence of greatness. That out of the six billion bodies on the planet, they were sharing a room with one of the top ten. He had read Schwarzenegger's words on the subject. Arnie had laid it down straight: 'I have a good sense of my body in a bathing suit around people who appreciate what I'm doing, like a contest. Then I'm proud. But on a beach, most people are not experts. The general public does not know how to look. How proud can you be when they don't even know what they're looking at?'

He'd wait for the music to begin and for the dry ice to clear. He'd appear, gleaming, in the lights and mist. Andi would come out smokin' and swingin'. First his back, in all its broad glory. Then the thighs that he dreamed were cut from Styrian oak. Next he'd pop the real crowd-pleasers: the front double biceps, the front lat spread, the most muscular. One of the world's top ten bodies in a small provincial discothèque. The crowd would cheer and laugh. They would stare at his crotch and wonder. Women screamed and screeched. Men leered and shouted. They copied his poses. They clucked and gurgled and took the piss. He would detach himself. Andi would take the money and let Grufti drive him back to Munich.

The stomach pains had begun some months before Andi went to Columbus, Ohio, for the 1996 Arnold Classic. At first it was just more pain, and pain was the currency of muscle. Andi paid it little heed. It dug in and nestled down with all the other pain: the agonies of training, the banal deprivations of dieting down, the pulls, nicks, strains, jags and twists of the gym. But it kept coming back and its payload was different. A connoisseur of pain like Andi would soon have been able to tell. He would have been able

13

to recognise it and rank it as something special in the pain game, something more exotic than the stuff he usually bore. He began to mention it to friends at the gym. He tried some health cures that would strengthen his stomach lining. Perhaps if Andi had quit training then, if he'd turned away from the withering deprivations of another round of competition and stopped juicing he might have survived. Instead, the boy from Pack made himself ready to compete in front of the boy from Thal, his hero. Andi got granite hard and shrink-wrapped. There might be bigger men onstage in Ohio, but there would be no one who was shredded quite like Andi. He was a walking, talking anatomical textbook; he was curious and weirdly beautiful, an abstract, set apart.

After his sixth place at the Arnold Classic on 2 March, Andi's mood remained low. 'Man, why don't you laugh?' one of the German officials had said to him. 'You're the best white guy behind five Negroes.'

Andi was never going to laugh at that. Best white guy. Best German speaker. All of the pain and deprivation, all of the gym seminars and pain-filled nights for those worthless epithets.

Andi and Elisabeth Schwarz flew into California to shoot some magazine photos while Andi's condition held. He'd entered the San Jose Pro Invitational on 9 March. It was a popular stop-off after the Arnold, as the pros looked for some extra cash while they were able to hold on to their contest shape. Kevin Levrone, Paul Dillett and Vince Taylor, three of the men who had beaten Andi in Ohio, were competing; so were two Germans that Andi had beaten there; Roland Cziurlok, who had finished seventh, and Gunter Schlierkamp, a new pro who had come in eleventh at his first attempt. Levrone cleaned up again for his second

14

win in a week. Dillett took second, Vince Taylor third. And Roland Cziurlok took Andreas Munzer out; he finished fourth while Andi struggled to seventh. Schlierkamp pushed Andi too, finishing ninth. The San Jose Pro was a minor show, but suddenly Andi's 'best white guy, best German speaker' tag was more tenuous. He was thirty-one years old. He was never going to be Arnie after all. The San Jose Pro was his last contest.

Andi arrived home in Munich on 12 March. He stopped by the gym. Without his tinned tan, he looked pale. He called his parents' house in Pack, but spoke only to his six-year-old nephew Markus. He told the boy that he would be coming home for the Easter holiday. They'd have some fun then.

On the morning of 13 March, Andi's stomach pains became intense. His gut was swollen and hard. His bill had come in. He was fairly sure that this time he couldn't meet it. The debt was too big. The agony grew. Andi had a fifteen-year relationship with pain. Pain was an old pal of his. He thought that he knew pain pretty well by now. Pain had thrown a lot at him and he'd taken it. Pain meant change. Pain meant growth. It meant strength. Andi was a king of pain.

Sissy called for a doctor. Andi tried to ride it like he'd ride the hardest reps, to use pain as joy. Inside the bulging horror that began under his ribcage artificial testosterone had docked on to the receptors of the muscles. Once there, it instructed the production of proteins which thickened the muscle walls. The blood vessels, already strained, could no longer withstand Andi's blood pressure. They ruptured. Under the dense gut muscle, Andi was bleeding to death.

The doctor could do nothing for him. Sissy took him to hospital. Doctors there diagnosed the bleed, but could not

15

prevent it continuing. He was transferred to the University Clinic. At 7 p.m., surgeons decided to operate to stop the bleeding inside Andi's stomach. Andi came through the operation, but his problems had multiplied catastrophically. His blood was viscous and slow-moving. His potassium levels were excessively high. He had been dehydrated by the diuretics he used in the days before his last competitions. His liver was melting. A post-mortem would find that it had dissolved almost completely. Andi's body went into shock. After his liver failed, his kidneys did too. He was offered a blood transfusion, but it was too late. Andi's heart held out for a while – he'd always had a big heart – but by morning it had folded and Andreas Munzer joined the ranks of the bodybuilding dead.

His implosion had been awesome, and inevitable and sad. Grufti drove Andi home from Munich to Pack. Arnold Schwarzenegger sent a wreath from Hollywood to Andi's grave in Styria. The message was simple. It read: *A last greeting to a friend.*

2

Mr Universe and the Meaning of Everything

I only knew one bodybuilder. His name was Grant Thomas. He lived in a breeze-block rabbit hutch in the backstreets of Cardiff. We had met first on the day after Princess Diana died. I wanted to write a newspaper piece about him. I'd called to make sure the meeting was still on. It was. He didn't seem to think it was any reason to cancel. Neither did I. I drove to Cardiff. The roads were quiet. On the radio, all the talk was about cars and tunnels, booze and conspiracy. All the talk was about bodies. The grief fascists hadn't yet asserted their grip. No one seemed to know what to do.

Cardiff was hot under a big sky. It looked about as good as it was ever going to; green squares on a blue planet. The city centre was all show. The real Cardiff hung around behind it, groaning, in the hills. The real Cardiff, the one Grant Thomas wanted out of, was a sulking and sagging smallsville.

Grant answered his front door. He was short, wide and

orange. We shook hands and went inside. Everything about the house was small, except for Grant. He sat on the sofa, all covered up. He was a few weeks away from a competition, the famous Mr Universe. His routine consisted of two gym sessions and six meals. The rest of the day he sat on the sofa, sipping from a bottle of deionised water.

Grant had a girlfriend called Kimberley and a baby called Kyle. They were betting on him. His body was a way out of the real Cardiff for all of them. Grant laid out the world of bodybuilding, for an amateur like me. This is how it was:

You had to have semi-reasonable genetics. He pointed at my wrist. 'Not like that.' My wrist was girlishly slim. The radius and ulna were close together. My body type was ectomorph – long and thin. All were wrong. Grant held up his arm. His wrists were thick. His palms were square. His fingers were short. God had spoken. Me, and millions like me, were out before we started.

But even the genetically talented had to begin somewhere. In his Year Zero, Grant Thomas weighed ten stone. He hit the gym. He asked questions. He watched and learned. At school, he'd had no qualifications. At the gym, he was enrolled on a crash course in the human body. He broke his muscles down with big black weights. A few heavy reps to tear the fibres apart. A few days rest to let them knit and grow. Lesson one was: break it down to build it up. His body changed quickly. He moved it on to a fast track.

The gym was a place of work, of science, and in it, you divided up your body into six: back, shoulders, chest, arms, mid-section, legs. Each group was alternately worked and rested, broken down and built up with resistance training. Each body part was examined dispassionately, with a cold eye in the long gym mirrors. The bodybuilder sought size, but with symmetry and proportion. Grant Thomas grew and grew. He learned another lesson: men as big as he was becoming quickly leave the ordinary world behind. Grant accepted his rarity. People began to notice his freakishness. He became more serious. He manufactured a new psychology. He no longer weighed ten stone.

Grant began to understand the real rules of muscle. Muscle grew through failure. Stressed to exhaustion, it responded by becoming larger. But muscle was contrary and it had a mind of its own. If you stressed it too often, it would shrink. If you stressed it too little, it would shrink. If you failed to nourish it, it would shrink. If you failed to rest it, it would shrink. If you over-nourished it, it would hide. If you left it alone for too long, it would atrophy. If it didn't get what it wanted, when it wanted it, muscle would not do very much at all.

Grant and I sat and talked for a few hours. We watched some tapes of his shows. I wasn't expecting too much from him, or from bodybuilding. I'd found a quote about body-builders from Wayne DeMilia, the guy who ran the IFBB pro division and who was usually head judge at the big shows.

Wayne recounted a story about an American bodybuilder who in just a short time had won a whole boatload of money. 'But what did he do?' Wayne went on. 'He went out and bought a car that cost $80,000. That's their mentality. They get money and then it's, "Well, I gotta go to the gym in a cool car!" They don't have a grasp that this will not go on for ever. If people tell you all day long you look great, you're fantastic – it affects your head. The sexual aspect – male, female, whatever, saying, "I want you" – it's a big head trip. Then you have to live the part . . .

'We were in Germany on tour,' he went on, 'and four or five of them are looking at one of those white-blonde gym girls. There was talk of a gang bang. I said, "I don't want to know about it. I think you're all nuts. If she takes on three or four of you at once, how many hundreds of others has she had? You're willing to take that risk?" One guy says, "A hard-on has no brains."

'That's how a bodybuilder takes life,' Wayne said. 'Very lightly.'

Grant listened to the quote and said: 'No bodybuilder likes another. They're worse than women. They'll always find a way to slag you off.'

This was his world. He told me more about it. Once he had understood the brutal truths of the gym, he'd heard nuances in what his muscle had to say. For muscle to take priority on his body, it screamed for an intense and finicky regime, more demanding than any baby. It needed attention, 24/7. It wanted total subjugation to its whims and whimpers. Muscle was selfish and moody and spiteful. The food it craved wasn't the kind of food you wanted to eat: the blandness, the expense, the sheer *amount* of it . . . It needed supplements, too, and vitamins, hours of rest and sleep.

Then there were the things it didn't need. It didn't need a full-time job messing with its schedule. Late nights out disagreed with it. It really didn't need any alcohol. It was pretty much opposed to other forms of exercise or sport or entertainment. It wasn't a fan of fun.

If you took all this on board, though, and played ball, you might end up looking how Grant looked. It wouldn't take long, either. Only say, *ten years* . . . It had a timeframe like rearing koi or breeding pandas. Muscle was just as rare and as difficult.

Grant described how much bigger he was going to get. If he won the Mr Universe title, he would be able to turn professional. He was, he said, too small to make a mark in the pros as he was. He would take a year off, maybe two, and load up on muscle. When he debuted as a pro, he would be a different man. But he couldn't obsess about that yet; he had to obsess about getting there first. So his thoughts of becoming Mr Universe obsessed him. Particularly, he said, he thought about the judges, and how they would look at him. Whether, after all that he had been through, they would just like some other guy's muscles better.

Kimberley came home. She seemed tired. She looked at Grant, at the still body on the sofa that used up all of their money and on which they were relying, and her emotions were impossible to judge. Grant ate twenty-one chickens a week. He ate thirty eggs per day (only the whites – he threw the yolks out). He ate forty tins of tuna a week, too, and most of a tub of whey protein powder, that cost £70. The fake tan he wore for competitions cost £35 per tin, and he used ten tins a year. To help a little, he'd organised a deal with the local butcher. But it was hard, harder than lifting weights. All of their money went on feeding Grant. He couldn't work, so he mostly just sat. He trained and slept. He waited. He waited for muscle. They all did.

Grant had a hero. Everyone with muscle or dreams of it had a hero. His name was Dorian Yates. Grant was big, but he was small compared to Dorian Yates. Everyone on earth was small compared to Dorian Yates. Dorian came from Birmingham. He was a five-time winner of professional bodybuilding's greatest title, Mr Olympia, the first and only non-American to take it since Arnold Schwarzenegger had won for the final time in 1980. Dorian made hundreds of thousands of dollars a year. He had his own gym. He was on the covers of all of the muscle mags. He had a big house and more cash than he could spend. He had the life Grant wanted. He was known as 'The Shadow' – this was after his habit of remaining in seclusion in his gym for eleven months of the year, and then emerging to win Mr Olympia, each time by a greater margin, each time with even more muscle. I asked Grant if he had a nickname yet. He looked at Kimberley. ' "The Welsh Beast",' he mumbled.

As a sidebar to the piece I had to write on Grant, and for a bit of fun, we looked at a picture of Dorian and I asked Grant to tell me what was so great about him. To me, he looked just like Grant. In my notebook I wrote:

Symmetry: The left and right sides of his body and the upper and lower halves have excellent symmetry despite his bulk. The judges look for symmetry (for example, that the circumference of the thighs when together is double that of the waist and so on).

Proportion: His muscle groups correspond in size. For example, his biceps are proportioned with his triceps and then in turn with his shoulders (there's no point in having huge thighs if your calves are skinny).

Muscle size and density: His muscles are huge and dense; years of training have filled and shaped them correctly. The muscle bellies are full and rounded.

Definition: Yates is totally 'ripped' – his body carries virtually no fat, only 4–5 per cent, so that the muscles cling to his skin and punch out. The striations or 'cuts' in them are apparent. As well as being 'cut', he has great separation between the muscles. He's very vascular – his veins are close to the surface of his skin. The bulging veins demonstrate his lack of fat.

Skin: It's not loose anywhere. Very few blemishes.

Back: Yates is known throughout bodybuilding for the size of his back – his best feature.

Posing: Yates is noted for his power posing. His size prevents him from moving freely to the music, but he overcomes that with his mind-blowing physique.

X-factor: His size and swaggering confidence give him charisma. He blows the others offstage. Gives him an indefinable edge with most judges.

While we did this, Grant sat trembling. He held the bottle of deionised water. He could not drink from the tap. He was six weeks out from the Mr Universe show. His diet was kicking in hard now. His metabolism was permanently provoked. Grant churned up his calories in the gym and on the sofa. He tinkered with a precarious equation, reducing his nourishment to rid himself of fat while still taking enough in to maintain his muscle size and hardness. He would not know until the day of the contest whether he had found the answer. Then he would fill the muscles with his newly sugared blood and pray that they bloomed for him. On the Mr Universe stage, he hoped to reap their harvest. But as the processed protein sustained his bulk, his brain cells were departing with his body fat. They were starving away, dying in their millions. It was hard to concentrate, tough to think straight for any length of time. He was sluggish and quiet, loaded with ennui. The gaps in our conversation grew longer. Grant fiddled with the bottle of water.

He didn't like leaving the house, he said. He didn't enjoy people looking at him. 'The thing I always get is: "Yeah but it's all steroids, isn't it?" They don't think, "Maybe he's eating right, perhaps he's weighing his food".'

Grant said that he didn't use steroids. He didn't have anything against them, particularly. Money was tight and he just couldn't afford them, at least not the proper ones. The others, the ones that got offered to him at the gyms, might come from anywhere, Bulgaria, Kazakhstan, and have anything in them, aspirin, chicken-shit, who knew? Grant had heard all sorts about them. Besides, they were testing for drugs now, even in the pros. Guys had been dropping dead: Benaziza back in '92, Munzer last year. At the last Mr Olympia, Wayne DeMilia had brought in an IOC accredited lab to find the guilty blood. Even Dorian Yates had looked smaller. At one time judges had been instructed to disqualify competitors who were exhibiting the visible symptoms of use. Grant figured he could live without them, at least for now. At least until he needed even more muscle.

Kimberley took Kyle upstairs for his nap. Grant watched them go. Arranged to one side of his television set were some of his trophies. They were almost taller than Grant was, five-foot-high gold plastic things that featured distorted models of bodybuilders pulling poses while set on Greek-style colonnades; they were wearing wreaths and garlands, they were attended by bikinied women holding plates of fruit, they sat atop pewter discs with lettering so ornate you could barely read the title that they bore for their holder. They were ridiculous. I asked Grant if he had heard the theory that the bigger the trophy, the smaller the prize. He laughed. 'That's bodybuilding,' he said. 'You get fuck all else, so you might as well have a big shiny cup.'

'Mr Universe, though,' I said. 'Everyone's heard of that.'

'Yeah, but it means fuck all to them . . .'

Grant was right, too. The title seemed like an anachronism, a throwback to the 1950s, to the days of strongmen on the beach and of Charles Atlas ads in the backs of boys'

24

comics. It was a title from a spent time. It was, nonetheless, probably the only psychic connection the ordinary man could make with bodybuilding. Grant was counting on a bit of its buzz and its magic rubbing off on him. It was just an amateur contest and it had been surpassed by others of more prestige for many years; it was staged in a small hall before a few hundred people and run by an organisation called NABBA, the National Amateur Bodybuilding Association. Yet the Mr Universe title offered Grant a further chance at a precious payload: an IFBB pro card. The pro card offered entry into professional contests, the European Grand Prix shows, the regional American shows, and then perhaps even the big three: the Night of Champions in New York, the Arnold Classic in Ohio, the Mr Olympia in Las Vegas. The pro card was the bridge between one world, in which we sat, and another, better one, in which men like Dorian Yates resided. That was the modern value of being Mr Universe.

*

In the early 1900s there was a colossus of a kid called Eugene Sandow who performed feats of strength and who possessed an astonishing physique. He had been discovered by a famous vaudevillian called Louis Atilla, whose own performances were so amazing he was chosen from all of Europe's strongmen to appear at Queen Victoria's jubilee in 1887. Louis Atilla had a rival, another strongman named Charles Samson, who Atilla considered to be a braggart and a show-off. Samson claimed to be the world's strongest man. At the end of his show, he would issue a challenge to all-comers to get onstage and try to lift the same weights as him.

Atilla trained Eugene Sandow until he became sure that Sandow could defeat Charles Samson. They travelled

25

together to London to confront him. When Samson reached the end of his act, Louis Atilla jumped onstage.

'You're going to challenge me?' Samson asked.

'No, not me,' Atilla replied. 'Him.' He introduced his protégé and the crowd gasped when Sandow, who had a soft and gentle face, revealed his iron torso. For its time, Eugene Sandow's body was as rare and extraordinary as Dorian Yates's. Among the strongmen and the carny performers and vaudeville acts, Sandow was the very first freak of them all. He had constructed a body to echo the classic idyll. He looked at Greek and Roman sculptures. He shaped himself to those standards. He was so successful that he would sometimes cover himself in white powder and become a 'living statue' to astound onlookers.

Sandow looked as though he should be more powerful than the squat, pot-bellied strongman, and it turned out that he was. He defeated Charles Samson, and he became a sensation. A rematch was arranged, and Sandow won again. He began a craze for feats of strength. Strongmen travelled from across Europe to London for a piece of the action. Lots of them were stronger than Eugene Sandow, but none had his verve or his charisma, and they didn't have his body. They didn't understand that people wanted a show, or that Sandow offered his audience a glimpse of the possible with his heavenly physique.

A company from New York took Sandow to America but they weren't sure how best to exploit him, and so they sold his contract to Florenz Ziegfeld at the Chicago World Fair in 1893. Ziegfeld knew exactly what to do with Sandow. He put on a show called 'Sandow's Trocadero Vaudevilles', in which he promoted Eugene as the Strongest Man in the World. Because Sandow had the body that he had, the public believed the claim. They got a load of Eugene and they thought: 'Well, no one could beat *him*. He looks just like a *god* . . .'

In that way, and in others, Eugene Sandow became the father of all of the Mr Universes and Olympias and so on. Sandow didn't just display himself. He would perform many stunts – he was photographed with a board on his back that held nineteen people and a dog; he carried a pony across the stage under one arm – but he had established some of the tenets of modern bodybuilding. He had proven that people liked to look at an exceptional physique, and he had shown that the best-looking body might not be the strongest one. Seven decades before Arnold Schwarzenegger's jacked-up genes kick-started an exercise revolution in America, Eugene Sandow's muscle persuaded a generation of men to buy dumb-bells and work out.

Physique contests became a fad. A man named Al Treloar won a thousand dollars and the title The Most Perfectly Developed Man in America. The competition was organised by a wrestler called Bernarr 'Body Love' Macfadden, and took place at the old Madison Square Gardens in New York in 1903. Bernarr Macfadden was arrested after the contest for 'having a number of toothsome women walking around the stage in their underwear'. Macfadden didn't care about that. The stunt had helped to promote his magazine, which he called *Physical Culture*. The contest ran for several decades. 'Body Love' became the first of a series of men who would control bodybuilding by means of a promotion and publishing operation. Nineteen years after Al Treloar won Macfadden's title, Charles Atlas won it too.

Atlas, who was actually an Italian immigrant named Angelo Siciliano, really did get sand kicked in his face as a young man. It happened on a beach in Coney Island, New York, and his physique became his revenge. Atlas began to sell his training methods, which he named Dynamic Tension, by using the sand-kicking story to shame young men into working out. '*Are you fed up with seeing the huskies walk off with everything?*' his newspaper ads asked. '*Sick and tired of being soft, frail, skinny or flabby – only HALF ALIVE?*' He scared around 70,000 of the half-alive per year into buying his course, and he became very famous, even though his body barely qualified as being built, with its nondescript abs and smooth legs.

The really big guys started to come soon, though. In 1939, the American Athletic Union regionalised body-building contests and sponsored one overall national event, which they called Mr America. The first champion was Roland Essmaker. He was followed by one of the greatest, John Grimek, and then by Steve Reeves, who became a movie star, and then Reg Park, who was Schwarzenegger's first idol and also a movie actor, and Clancey Ross and Bill Pearl, and then Larry Scott, the first Mr Olympia.

Soon there were hundreds of Mr Men, as various organisations slugged it out and sanctioned titles in the same way that boxing became splintered. In 1973 Jimmy Morris, Lou Ferrigno and Chris Dickerson all held the title Mr America, each awarded it by a separate sanctioning body. In the same year, Roy Duval, Boyer Coe and Ken Waller were all Mr World. And none of them were the best bodybuilder in the world, because that was Arnold Schwarzenegger, who was Mr Olympia. Slowly, the Weider brothers, Joe and Ben, assisted by Wayne DeMilia, gained control of the sport and the business of bodybuilding, and their organisation, the IFBB, and its greatest title, Mr Olympia, superseded all of the competition. Mr America and Mr Universe hung around as amateur titles, as stepping stones to the big time and the money of the IFBB.

The Weiders and DeMilia imposed a rigid structure on the contests, too. Each consisted of four rounds. The first round involved the competitors performing four compulsory poses, the second round seven compulsory poses. During the first and second rounds the judges would call out three or four well-matched men at a time to compare them against each other. Together, these two rounds were known as prejudging. This was a misnomer – they were the rounds where most of the judging was done. They were called prejudging because the public weren't admitted to watch them, or at least they weren't until Wayne had figured out that they could become a popular part of the show for which he might sell a separate ticket. After the prejudging came the free-posing round, in which the competitors could perform their own routine to music of their choice for up to three minutes, followed by the final comparisons round, in which just the top six competitors at the end of round three took part. Here, the judges stood the men together in various combinations and compared them against one another in the seven compulsory poses used in round two. Wayne divided the biggest contests into afternoon and evening events, with prejudging in the afternoon and the final two posing rounds in the evening, and he found better and better venues for the shows, and increased their production values until they looked like rock concerts and generally took them back towards the sort of vaudeville glamour they'd had when Eugene Sandow had stepped up and dropped his robe and made the society crowds coo and gasp.

Things hadn't worked out too well for Eugene Sandow. He married a beautiful woman called Blanche Brookes and had two daughters. He was appointed personal fitness instructor to King George V and became an advocate for sanitary inspections in restaurants, free school meals for underprivileged children and prenatal examinations for pregnant women. He continued to travel, which placed a strain on his marriage because he was constantly approached by both men and women in thrall to him. He began a long affair with a man named Martinus Sieveking, who was a composer. They even lived together for a while in New York. Sandow died soon after rupturing a blood vessel as he lifted an automobile out of a ditch. His health had been compromised by syphilis. Blanche, vengeful and betrayed, had him buried in an unmarked grave in 1925. His name survived though. The trophy awarded to Mr Olympia each year is called the Sandow in his honour.

*

I was writing a lot of offbeat feature stories: prison football, unlicensed boxing, Olympic shooting, macho stuff about male cultures. I was writing about Don King, Roy Shaw, Mike Tyson; about a guy who made his living filming bare-knuckle bouts, another who would fight pit bulls for money. These were men who sought to impose themselves on a formless and hostile world; I was a frequent flyer to those chaotic places. Grant, or perhaps Grant's life, didn't appear as weird to me as it should have. He seemed like just another guy overcompensating for his circumstances. It was a straightforward 'Rocky' narrative; the best part was the divorce between his world, with its free chicken deal and the struggle to afford tinned tan, and Dorian Yates's, with its international travel and its six-figure prize money. I wrote the story, and sent it in. The paper did a nice job on it. The headline was, BEAST SEEKS HIS PLACE IN BUILDING SOCIETY. There was a picture of Grant working out, and another of him holding Kyle. There was a shot of Dorian Yates, too, next to the dissection of his body that Grant had provided.

Dorian hit a pose with his hands behind his head. His lats flared out like bat wings. His abs were stone cubes, laid like paving next to one another. The tops of his thighs seemed to explode from his trunks under high pressure. They spread outwards in all directions. Grant was right: next to Dorian Yates, he was small.

In the interval between the piece being written and published (more prolonged than usual: Di's ugly demise; the endless grieve-up; gathering rumours of conspiracy, all eating newsprint), Yates had won his sixth successive Mr Olympia title. A week or so after this, Grant Thomas won Mr Universe. Dorian Yates got $110,000. Grant got his IFBB pro card at the British Championships. A few people phoned me about the piece. A magazine picked it up and ran it again. I rang Grant and congratulated him on his win. He had already started getting bigger, right there in his small house. The Mr Universe trophy was parked by the TV with the others.

But Mr Universe still lived in a nondescript place on a rough estate in south Wales. Most of the neighbours didn't even realise that Mr Universe was right next door. Mr Olympia, though, lived as a man called Mr Olympia should: in a large house with surrounding land, distantly flanked by other rich and successful people, revered and feared. Even Mr Universe wanted to be Mr Olympia. Actually, Mr Universe *especially* wanted to be Mr Olympia, with its money and its prestige, with its tasteful trophy named after Sandow (a bespoke one-off sculpture of the perfect man, each year subtly different, as a real body would be) and with its heavy symbolism; with all of its muscle.

Mr Olympia's life *was* Olympian, in a way. It was ascetic and aesthetic, or at least it was supposed to be. It was the perfect title for a bodybuilding title. Mr Universe wasn't though. The world of Mr Universe was a very small one and it held no mystery. Grant wanted to break out of it, quickly.

The words that Grant had used to describe Dorian Yates hung around him: 'freaky' . . . 'unreal' . . . 'inhuman' . . . They described the state that Mr Universe must achieve if he wanted a shot at real bodybuilding.

It had been done. Arnold Schwarzenegger was Mr Universe in 1967 and had won Mr Olympia seven times; Frank Zane had held both titles, Mr Universe in 1970 and the O from 1977 to 1979; Chris Dickerson, Mr Olympia in 1982, had been Mr Universe in 1973. Two great pros who had never won the O but might have done had been Mr Universe: Ken Waller in 1971 and Bertil Fox in 1977. Poor Bertil. His world had become unreal, too. He was in the Basseterre prison on St Kitts, convicted of double murder, banged up for life.

Schwarzenegger had gone from Universe to Olympia the fastest, in three years – but he was Schwarzenegger. Zane had taken seven. Dickerson had taken *nine*. As always, muscle had taken its time. Even the great Yates was not exempt. He was British champion in 1988, Mr Olympia for the first time in 1992. Grant would have to wait and eat and grow. He was Mr Universe, but his life was not immediately different. Kimberley might hold on to Kyle and look at her man and know he was Mr Universe. Then she could examine the dimensions of her world and wonder exactly what the meaning of the Universe was, for all of them.

3

The Shadow, The King

Three years later, two things had happened: Dorian Yates had won the Mr Olympia contest for the final time, and bodybuilding had got big on the Internet.

An online muscle mag called *Testosterone* used an anonymous source to compile a bizarre Dead Pool, a top ten of the most likely bodybuilders to die within the next twelve months. The *T* mag boys had tried to protect themselves by giving a false name to every person on the Dead Pool list, but it wasn't hard to guess who was who in their scurrilous speculation. Dorian Yates was in the *T* mag Dead Pool, number two with a bullet. *T* mag didn't like his chances. Anonymous wrote:

Byron Peterson

Perhaps it's jealousy that's caused [the rumours of why he's] so successful in pro bodybuilding. Maybe it's because he's isolated in Europe, and our American imaginations run away with us as to what 'The Ghost' is doing in his dungeon of a gym in Northern Europe. Whatever the reason, I have heard absolutely insane rumors of the drug practices of Byron. The nuttiest one claims that each night, Byron withdraws a certain amount of blood, then mixes it with growth hormone. This is left refrigerated overnight, then re-injected every morning. Yuck! Another rumor claims that Byron takes 2 iu's of growth hormone every two hours, every day. True? Nobody but Byron knows for sure. But we've all seen this man grow bigger, uglier, and blockier since his first Olympia. (Over 30 pounds bigger, to be exact.) And to see him in the off-season, with dark bags under his eyes, you would think you were looking at the bloated face of a 50-year-old alcoholic, not the man who's supposed to represent a pinnacle of health and fitness. If Byron is one of our sport's top represent-atives, it's amazing anyone wishing to live to a normal old age would ever take up bodybuilding.

However unlikely, however *impossible* it sounded, remov-ing your own blood, mixing it with growth hormone and refrigerating it didn't qualify you for the number-one spot in the Dead Pool, though. Not even that was good enough. [What was good enough was a potentially fatal intake of diuretics, drugs designed to reduce water retention within the body.] So number one in the Dead Pool went not to 'Byron Peterson' but to 'Luke Deters':

Many know about this bodybuilder's famous 'freeze' during the prejudging of a recent contest. His entire body cramped so painfully that three men had to carry him offstage like a statue.

Only one bodybuilder had 'frozen' onstage: the vast Canadian Paul Dillett. He'd had so little water in his body,

34

he'd locked up, right there during prejudging at the Arnold Classic in 1994. He was in a front double biceps pose at the time. Some men had walked onstage, tilted Dillett into a horizontal position and walked off with him under their arms, still holding his front double biceps pose. Later he would claim to have urinated for an hour straight before going on stage. But he recovered to compete successfully again. The Dead Pool had been dead wrong.

It had been dead wrong about Dorian Yates, too. Even as 'Anonymous' – hardly an intrepid correspondent – filed his (or, slim chance, her) egregious Dead Pool copy, Yates was preparing to announce his retirement from pro body-building. The story that would emerge from the last defence of his Mr Olympia title in 1997 would be a ripe melodrama, packed with suffering. But it would have nothing to do with growth hormone, blood doping or having the face of a fifty-year-old alcoholic. Dorian Yates left bodybuilding as he had arrived: from afar, from the shadows.

There were other rumours about Dorian Yates. In competition, the sight of his body had provoked speculation about how it had become what it became. In retirement, which had arrived in 1997 after six big Mr O titles, more speculation began, because his body no longer appeared onstage as evidence of his condition. Somewhere out on the wild frontiers of the Internet message boards I read that he 'weighed no more than thirteen stone now'. Someone else suggested that he 'had the face of a wizened old man'. One guy had posted some snatched photos of his back taken in a nightclub. They said he had a 'steroid head', whatever that was. They said he 'liked to party'.

There was plenty more along the same lines. Dorian's story kept pricking at me; it was intriguing. I often thought about the day with Grant Thomas, the Mr Universe next door, and the contrast between his life and Dorian Yates's. There was something else, too: for six years, the British had had a champion that we knew nothing about. We had suffered dreadful iniquities during that time. Our sportsmen couldn't win, and not only could they not win, they seemed to find ever more extravagant and egregious ways of losing. There was a countrywide malaise, a flaw in the national psyche. We were losers. And yet here was a champion, an undefeatable behemoth, a winner, and we knew nothing about him at all. He could walk down the streets undisturbed. He could open the newspaper after his victories and not read one word about himself.

He still owned his gym, the Temple, in Birmingham, and he wrote a column about training for *Flex* magazine. He had gone into business producing nutritional supplements. I wrote to Kerry Kayes, who was his partner in the supplement company. Kerry said he'd meet me at the Wembley Plaza hotel. He was about to begin work promoting the British Grand Prix, right next door at the Wembley Conference Centre. It was British bodybuilding's biggest show. Although, officially, nobody ran pro bodybuilding in Britain, Kerry ran bodybuilding in Britain. Through him, officially or unofficially, almost everything happened. In the small, square white book that he had kept for many years, and which had pages falling out of it every time he opened it up, were the numbers of anyone who was anyone; practically anybody who had picked up a weight, or thought about it, in the last twenty years. There were Weiders and Schwarzeneggers and hundreds of Mr Men: Olympias, Universes, Americas, Britains, Englands, North-Wests, South-Easts and more; Hungarys, Czechs and the rest. Kerry had them all in his little white book. Kerry Kayes had bodybuilding's number.

It hadn't always been that way. For a while, he thought he'd been cursed. He'd got into the weights when he was a lad working on building sites in Manchester. 'Some people do it because they've had some terrible experience,' he said. 'Something that they're compensating for. I just wanted big arms.' He lost his first wife in a road accident a couple of months after they'd got married. Their car had been hit by a vehicle driving on the wrong side of the road. The guy in it had only been in the country for a day. The doctors told Kerry that the fact he was a bodybuilder had saved his life.

For many years he'd been employed by Yorkshire television, as a technician. He was working as an electrician in Guyana wiring a bridge when the Jonestown Massacre happened right in front of him. Then he was there in the players' tunnel at Bradford City football ground when the Main Stand caught fire and fifty-six people died. He'd tried to help but was forced back by the infernal heat. 'I saw an old man sitting right in front of me. He put his hand out towards me, and he just . . . caught light . . .' Then he'd been rigging up York Minster with broadcast equipment for the coronation of a bishop when he found a body on the roof.

He left Yorkshire television and his luck turned. He opened a gym, Betta Bodies in Manchester, and got a start in the supplement business. He began to do very well for himself. Kerry was the classic overachiever. He would set himself a goal – becoming Mr Britain, getting a karate blackbelt, learning to fly a helicopter – and not rest until it was accomplished. His first partner in Chemical Nutrition was Paul Borresen, a huge guy, obsessed with the macho weights cult. He was a maverick figure who revelled in the excess of it all. He was also something of a steroid savant, a

37

renegade chemist pursuing just one goal: extreme size. He wrote a book called *Anabolic Edge* about what he termed 'the big three – food, drugs and supplements'. Even *Testosterone* marvelled at the amount of gear Paul Borresen had ingested. The partnership with Kerry ended. Problems, both personal and business, mounted. Borresen attempted suicide by jumping out of a window, badly injuring his back. He began another supplement company called Biohazard. In October 2000, the Biohazard website was featured on a BBC television programme called *Crime Squad*. On 31 January 2001, Borreson was dead, killed by an accidental overdose of the painkillers he used for the back injury. He was thirty-eight.

Kerry had become partners with Dorian Yates on Yates's retirement. Together they were producing a line of supplements under the banner 'Dorian Yates Approved'. The company was going well. They'd won a Small Exporter of the Year award; they were getting big in America. He knew now that he hadn't been cursed: it was just life, sometimes lucky, sometimes not.

Kerry's story was a good one, told so well that we'd talked for a few hours in the hotel bar and I hadn't asked him about Dorian Yates. Did he weigh thirteen stone? Was he a wizened old man? Could he tell me?

Kerry said: 'I can do better than that,' and as he said it, he flicked a hand at the entrance to the bar at the moment that Dorian Yates walked in. He wore a loose T-shirt and jeans. He moved with the slightly rolling gait of a man whose legs were forced apart by their size. His feet pointed slightly outwards. He took short steps. He arrived at his own speed.

'All right?' he said, and shook hands with a gentle grip.

He wore a thick gold bracelet decorated with flag

emblems. Around his neck hung a tiny golden replica of the Sandow statue, the prize for winning Mr Olympia. Underneath the statue, it said DORIAN in gold capital letters. He had on a big Rolex watch, highlighted with diamonds.

There was something else about him too: Dorian Yates was huge. He had no grim history. His size mocked the rumours about him.

He and Kerry were on their way to one of the seminars that they gave in local gyms, along with another pro bodybuilder called Ernie Taylor. Ernie was Britain's new number one. He came and joined us in the bar, too. Ernie had on a big white warm-up suit and all sorts of jewellery: chains, bangles, necklaces. Ernie went bling bling when he moved. He came from Birmingham, like Dorian. He was a few months out from the Mr Olympia show and then the British Grand Prix. I asked Dorian if he missed moments like these, getting in shape for big contests.

'First two years were very hard,' he said. 'I don't mind it now. I like going along to shows. I like not having to diet for sixteen weeks . . .' But, he said, he no longer had the single-mindedness he'd had during his career. As soon as he'd lost that, he'd begun to examine the rest of his life. His marriage had broken up and many things had changed. He was in business, not just with Kerry, but as a promoter, too. He was putting on a Grand Prix show in Holland a week after the British one. He had a new girlfriend, a dark and fiery Italian called Lily who owned a hotel in Amsterdam and who was co-promoting the Grand Prix with him.

'If you wanna know about bodybuilding,' he said, 'come over. I'll give you Lily's number.'

We sat around and shot the breeze. It was fun. Ernie was a full-time bodybuilder. He had contracts with Dorian Yates Approved and also with the British edition of *Flex*. He was into fighting, too. He'd trained in a couple of martial arts and then he'd become an Ultimate Fighter. He had a great tactic for his ring entrance. He would wear a baggy, long-sleeved T-shirt until he got inside the cage, and when he was sure his opponent was watching and couldn't get out, he pulled the shirt off and let everyone get a load of his body. 'Freaks 'em right out, it does,' he said. He'd had two fights so far, undefeated.

We tried to think up a good nickname for Ernie. I liked 'The Bodysnatcher' – there had been a ferocious boxer called Mike Maccallum who'd had that ring name, too.

'What's your nickname at the moment?'

'Er, E.T.,' Ernie said.

I began to spend more time with Kerry and Dorian and Ernie. I went to their seminars. We did a couple of prison visits, where Kerry and Dorian would talk about nutrition and training and then Ernie would come out and guest pose for the prisoners.

Dorian spent half of the week in England, and then he'd fly out to Amsterdam to see Lily at the weekends. He got invited to lots of other places, too, to gyms and expos and shows all over America and Europe. Being Dorian Yates was a full-time job.

Kerry ran Chemical Nutrition and his gym and the British Grand Prix and loads of other things, too. Whenever we went anywhere, to a seminar, or a prison visit or some such, Kerry would always arrive hours early. We'd be there, waiting for Dorian and Ernie, who'd travelled together from Birmingham. They would always get lost, without fail, despite the complex instructions Kerry faxed over for them. The call would come as we stood outside prisons or gyms or in car parks and they went barrelling down the wrong motorway in a big car: Dorian's Beamer or Ernie's Land

Cruiser. 'Where are you . . . ?' Kerry would ask. 'Fooking hell, you're *miles* off . . . Turn round and put your foot down . . .'

'See, they're bodybuilders,' Kerry would say. 'Always the same . . .'

He was right. Ernie, for example, had to remember two things for the prison visits, his posing trunks and a CD to perform to. He usually brought with him an enormous black holdall. When he opened it up on one occasion, all that was inside was a cuddly rabbit that his baby daughter had given him, and a lunchbox, the contents of which he'd already consumed.

'Fookin' hell . . .' Kerry would say. '*Bodybuilders* . . .' Ernie had come out to pose in his boxer shorts, which he'd rolled up and tucked in, to make them look more like posing trunks.

I went to visit Dorian at his gym, the Temple, where he and Ernie trained. From there, Dorian had won his six Olympias. I got to know him better. I told him about Grant Thomas and the differences between their lives, about the gulf between Universe and Olympia. I began to understand what it took to bridge that gap, how you might move from one world to the other. Over time, Dorian laid it out for me, the true story of all of his muscle.

*

Sometimes he'd felt so strong he thought he could lift the whole gym up. He would load the leg press with 1,045 lb and knock over a couple of sets of twelve reps as warm-ups. Then he'd up it to 1,300 lb and do a full set of twelve with perfect form. That was almost 30,000 lb on one exercise on one day. He would use another 1,300 lb for his standing calf raises. He'd do sets of ten hack squats with 660 lb. On back days he'd deadlift 405 lb eight times after warming up with

310 lb eight times. He'd do barbell curls with 140 lb over and over for his biceps, and he'd do incline barbell presses with 425 lb for his chest. He worked out four times per week; he would lift every weight in the gym. He would use every machine. He would pick the whole gym up, every week. On shoulders and abs day, he lifted a combined 29,080 lb. On back day, he lifted 37,875 lb. On chest and arms day, he got through 24,690 lb. On leg day, it was 92,430 lb. In an average week, Dorian Yates lifted 184,075 lb. He trained fifty weeks per year: 9,203,750 lb. He was a pro bodybuilder for nine years: 82,833,750 lb. He wore all of that weight like a suit. He was bigger, heavier, harder, thicker, drier, more dense than anyone had ever been. He had redefined his sport, rethought what was possible. Arnold Schwarzenegger had been the last man to do that. Arnold was six feet two inches tall, and competed at a weight of 224 lb. Dorian was five feet eleven inches tall. He competed at a weight of 270 lb. Forty-six extra pounds, more than three stone of beef on a frame three inches shorter. And each year, there was more of him. He was multiplying, expanding. When he had started training seriously, he weighed 180 lb. Out of competition, properly hydrated, he ended up 100 lb heavier. He had made himself almost 60 per cent bigger.

This was how: After breakfast (oatmeal, eggs) and an hour and a half before his workout, he would go into his study. He would review his training diary, which he kept religiously in closely printed handwriting, analysing his last relevant workout. He'd begin to question himself: '*Do I feel strong today?*' '*Am I gonna do forced reps?*' '*Am I a little tired?*' He would visualise himself completing the exercises. He'd see the plates on the bar and feel the weight and how heavy it was going to be. He'd imagine the bar bending and envisage how hard he was going to have to push to shift it. He would ask himself if he had recuperated from his last workout. Sometimes (rarely), when the answer was no, he would abort training at that point, without guilt. If the decision was to train, a further ritual began. He had a carbohydrate drink, to boost his glycogen reserves. He wore particular clothes depending on the day: he always wore a hat on days he trained his chest; he wore the same top to a delt workout every time; for the more explicit agonies of leg day, he always wore his 'leg pants'. He drove to the gym. It took twenty minutes. During that time, he became more focused. The rest of the world slipped away. When he walked in, he acknowledged no one. Regulars knew better than to try and catch his eye. Newcomers might try, but he wouldn't allow them the buzz of contact. If, in their enthusiasm, they managed it, they would be met by the game-face of the biggest man in the world. Silently, he would prepare all of the machines and free weights that he was planning to use. He'd take a particular heavy metal tape – on leg day, it was Guns N' Roses; back day, Aerosmith; Delts day, Pearl Jam – remove whatever music anyone else was playing and turn his up loud. He'd stretch and warm up. This was the last point at which he might pull the plug and back out. Once he gave himself the green light, it was on. He communicated with his training partner with short sentences, or, where possible, with a nod. If he spoke it would be to give simple commands: 'Put another twenty on'; 'Give me two forced reps when I ask.' All of the pre-set targets were hit, and then he walked away. It took forty-five minutes four times per week to cook up all of that beef.

He had the gym just the way he liked it. It was right in the middle of Birmingham, near New Street station. But it was down a back alleyway and in a cellar. It squatted under the city, a mad old scrapyard filled with alien-looking contraptions. These were chipped and dented; unpainted; hard and unyielding cold things. They clanked and jangled in their own mad language. The weights themselves were so dull and blunt they might have been filled with mercury. The machines and weight racks stood on old carpet the colour of wet wood that deadened the thumps that the weights made when dropped. The internal walls bowed inwards, shaped by other weights from above and below. Some were unfinished stone, others had cheap fake wood panels on them. Some by the stairs and entrance were covered with pictures of Dorian Yates. The air had a vague damp quality to it. Even the air was heavy; even the air had some weight behind it. You had to work a little to suck it into your lungs. It was a place that encouraged awesome effort and a swift exit. It was not a place where he was likely to be disturbed or spied upon. Dorian Yates could walk down the stairs at the Temple gym and know that each time he did, he was coming home.

He'd got banged up when he was seventeen. It was the night of the Birmingham riots. He was a punk rocker. Sid Vicious was his god. He had a British bulldog tattooed on his arm. He worked in a slaughterhouse, cleaning out the blood trays. It was OK once you got used to the smell and the noises that the animals made when they realised what was going to happen to them. He and a pal were going to a party. They walked past Dunne & Cc., a gentlemen's outfitters. Someone had outfitted the window with a brick. Dorian and his pal nicked a couple of tweed suits and put them on. It would get a laugh at the party, two punks in fancy clobber. They got arrested as they stepped out of the broken shopfront. He found it funny until he got six months in a detention centre. While he was there, one good thing happened to him. He discovered he could train harder than anyone else, even the tough boys. One of the prison warders wrote down the name of a power-lifting gym and told him to go there when he got out. He never did, but he liked it that someone had shown some faith in him. He got a job on an industrial cleaning gang and he found a place of his own.

His oldest friend Chocky had taken one look around the flat and said: 'Fucking hell, Dorian. This is the sort of place where you hang yourself . . .' It had a naked bulb, damp walls, a sink slumped in the corner. He had a bed and a cooker. No TV. He went out drinking every night, just to get out of the room. Then he thought: 'I just can't do this any more.' He was a natural loner. He was a rebel without a clue. He decided to take up bodybuilding. He thought that he might one day become Mr Birmingham. For three weeks, he didn't touch a weight. He didn't go near a gym. He went to a library. He lifted some books. He read everything he could about bodybuilding. He prepared himself properly. He did things right, just like a potential Mr Birmingham should.

Chocky noticed that he wasn't seeing much of Dorian. He worked, ate, trained, slept, over and over. He had entered another realm. He wanted a different life. He didn't want to live in the sort of place where you'd hang yourself. He became interested in the technique of a bodybuilder called Mike Mentzer. Back in the seventies, Mentzer had a physique that was years ahead of its time. He was rugged and thick and full. He looked like a peeled rhino. He'd got that way by inventing a method of training called 'Heavy Duty'. He'd theorised that the muscle simply needed a short, hard shock to failure in order to stimulate the growth response, followed by the appropriate rest. Mentzer experimented with low reps, high poundages delivered in brief periods of savage intensity. Steve Michalik, the notorious Mr America, was training just as heavy. But he trained for five times as long as Mike Mentzer: seventy-five to a hundred sets of reps per body part in a system he'd named 'Intensity or Insanity'. It had built him a bitchin' bod all right. It had also taken him into the room next to death. Yet after a while, Mike Mentzer's body looked just as good as Michalik's.

Mentzer moulded some mental muscle on to Heavy Duty, too. He had become obsessed with Ayn Rand's philosophy of objectivism, a cult of the individual about which she had written gigantic novels like *Atlas Shrugged* and *The Fountainhead*. Objectivism spoke to Mike Mentzer. It told him that he must accept reality as an absolute, regardless of his perception of it. It told him to place faith in his ability to reason. Most of all, it told him that his body was a sovereign thing, an end in itself. The pursuit of his own happiness could become the high moral purpose of his life. For these things to be so, he needed principles, both physical and moral. In this long-winded way, Mentzer destroyed bodybuilding orthodoxy. He became the philosopher prince of muscle. To prove his success, he had simply to remove his shirt. By 1979, he'd won the 200 lb and over class at the Mr Olympia.

For Dorian Yates, about to build a body that made Mike Mentzer's look like a school project abandoned halfway through lack of interest, Heavy Duty offered all of the excuses he needed to transform himself. He could break down his body parts under the weights and wait for them to re-form themselves bigger, greater. Everything about Heavy Duty appealed to him: the effort, the deferral of pleasure, the individuality, the science. He was a lone obsessive and his body became his means of expression. He was a singular force, an individual taking hold of his destiny. He was alone in the world, and he withdrew from his past. His father was dead. His mother and sister had moved away. His mates went out and lived the life that he wanted to escape from. They drank, they partied, they chased women. They lived for today. Dorian Yates lived for another day entirely. His friends would ask him when that day might be, what he was trying to do. He didn't know. All he could tell them was that he felt that something good would become of him. He kept detailed diaries of his training. In his steady printed hand he noted every session; splits, reps, sets, durations, recoveries. More than that, he noted feelings, emotions, repercussions. He rested more than he trained. He studied nutrition. He weighed out his food and ate it at such regular intervals that he no longer needed to wear a watch. He could tell what time it was by how his stomach felt. He met a woman who could understand his life. Her name was Debbie. Although they lived apart at first, they had a son named Lewis. By the time he was twenty-five, he owned the Temple gym.

His era began in the unlikeliest of places. Morecambe in Lancashire in 1985 was a dead town. It had the Irish Sea right in its face, giving it hell twice a day. The pubs and clubs and shops on the front looked as though they'd had a gutful of it. They stood about like pissed old squatters, too shagged out and knackered to move on. The wind was a sullen old thug. It knocked Morecambe about, too.

A bodybuilding show was just another C-list attraction to go with the clapped-out singers and the comedians waiting for panto to roll around. Only one man in town realised that Elvis had just entered the bodybuilding. Peter McGough watched Dorian Yates win the intermediate class of the West Coast Championships on 12 July. Yates weighed 210 lb. He had size, shape, quality and a terrible haircut. He had been training for two years. McGough estimated that the rank novice had misjudged the standard of his condition. He wasn't quite right for the West Coast intermediates. In the shape he was in, he would have won the British Heavyweight Championship. McGough wrote: 'Journalists dream of being there the day a star is born. Dorian's day at Morecambe was also my day.' Dorian Yates had found his Boswell. Peter McGough was running his own bodybuilding magazine, just him and an art director. It was a cut-and-paste job, all soft pics and mushy print, but it was something. As Dorian Yates rose, so would Peter McGough.

Dorian Yates freaked Morecambe out. Even as he packed up his gear into a duffel bag backstage, body-building officials were insisting he joined the England amateur team for the World Games. The show was the following week at the Wembley Conference Centre. He allowed the big time to beckon him down South, but as he pumped up pre-show, he understood that he'd misjudged it. His condition had slipped in seven days. He'd allowed his head to be turned by all the fuss. He would never make that mistake again. The World Games were a pivotal experience for him. He finished in seventh place. It was to be the lowest position he would ever occupy in a body-building contest. He brooded on it and went home to Birmingham. He stayed there until November 1986, when he went back to the Wembley Conference Centre for the British Championships. He won the heavyweight class. In the overall, he was placed second behind a light heavy-weight called Chris Oskys. It was a dog of a decision. The crowd almost lost it. McGough waited backstage, expecting Yates to blow his cool. Dorian uttered one sentence, which was 'I'm pissed off with that result', and never spoke about it in public again. Now he understood what it took to come first in big events. He needed to place all subsequent contests beyond doubt. He would win not by inches but by miles. He went back to Birmingham again, and no one in bodybuilding saw him for two years. Peter McGough began calling him 'The Shadow'.

On 13 November 1988 he won the British Championship by a margin bigger than anyone could remember. McGough wrote: 'The rest of the line-up had as much chance as a one-legged man in an ass-kicking contest.' Yates had an IFBB pro card. He also had what McGough called 'a controlled ferociousness' that McGough had also identified in Lee Haney, who was then Mr Olympia. Once more, Yates returned to Birmingham. He stayed there for another eighteen months.

All of this time his family had been making their small sacrifices to muscle. He was spending money that they might spend. He was eating food that they might eat. He lived inside a viciously rigid paradigm of his own construction, and so did they. He entered the Night of Champions in New York in May 1990. He swore to Debbie that if he failed to finish in the top three he would quit bodybuilding for ever. Nobody in America knew who the hell he was. They hadn't even seen his picture. They thought he was black; all of the best British bodybuilders – Albert Beckles, Bertil Fox – had been.

Wayne DeMilia was promoting the show. Dorian got him on the phone. He told Wayne that he and Debbie would be needing somewhere to stay in New York. DeMilia was an operator. He wasn't about to lay out bread for some guy he'd never seen. Night of Champions always had a big field, at least thirty competitors. Wayne wasn't going to make any money if he was paying for hundreds of hotel rooms. He phoned around the muscle gyms until he found someone willing to put up the Yateses for a week.

They arrived at JFK. A driver picked them up and took them to an apartment somewhere on the Lower East Side. He dropped them outside. It looked like downtown Baghdad on a wild night.

'They're all right on the inside,' the driver said, gesturing up at the busted building. And then he drove off. Dorian and Debbie lugged their cases up to the top floor. Dorian had left nothing to chance. He'd even brought his own cooker. Some faggy guy owned the apartment. He showed Dorian his room. It was a curtained-off corner. The guy had tacked up gay muscle pictures around the walls.

Dorian looked at the guy.

'We're not staying here,' he said.

'Why not? It'll be OK. You can pull the curtain . . .'

'Sorry, mate. It's just not suitable. Give me your phone.'

It was late. Dorian got Wayne DeMilia on the line.

'You need to put me in a hotel now. I don't care where it is.'

It wasn't the gay porn. He didn't mind about that – he hadn't thought twice about the muscle groupie putting them up. He just knew that he couldn't prepare himself properly for the Night of Champions here.

He harangued Wayne DeMilia some more. Soon, a cab showed up. It took them to the Chelsea Hotel. As he walked into the foyer, Dorian realised that it was the place where Sid Vicious, his first hero, had killed Nancy Spungeon in Room 100.

Peter McGough had tried to PR the Shadow a little before his arrival. He had spun them a nice line about the silent giant from a broken-down city. It hadn't worked, they wouldn't bite. Someone from *Flex* magazine told him: 'We don't want anything from Britain.' When Yates walked on stage on 19 May, he weighed 228 lb. Someone said 'Dorian who?' as he came out. They stuck him right on the end of the line-up, almost in the wings. The Shadow was in shadow. It didn't matter. The crowd had paid to see some muscle. They got one look at him and started chanting his name: 'DOR-I-AN' in three-syllable bursts. An hour or so later, he'd finished second behind Mohamed Benaziza. He won $7,000.

Momo Benaziza would be dead within two years, and Dorian Yates would be king before it happened.

In bodybuilding, Dorian discovered, there were tigers and there were lambs. Most of the lambs were onstage next to him. Most of the tigers encircled them. He was neither. He was more like a shark, something that had to keep moving forwards or else it would die.

Joe Weider, the man who ran a $250 million industry built around his muscle magazines and protein supplements, and his brother Ben, who controlled the IFBB, had pro bodybuilding sewn up. When Arnold Schwarzenegger came to America in 1968, Joe had given him a gig lumping boxes around one of his warehouses. Every Mr O, every Mr America, every Mr Universe, every musclehead with any dream of making a living went through Joe Weider, and if he didn't go through Joe, he went through Ben. Joe Weider was not going to miss out on Dorian Yates, or, later, on the man who had discovered him. Immediately after the Night of Champions, the Shadow flew to California at Joe Weider's expense, for seven days of shoots for *Flex* and *Muscle & Fitness* magazines.

It was exciting, but once he was back in Birmingham, he still only had what was left of his $7,000 winnings once he'd paid for the trip to New York. He had no money, but he also had no weak-mindedness, no abrogation of responsibility. He redoubled his efforts in the gym. He pinned a picture of Mohamed Benaziza's back up by the cable fly machine. He kept another copy of it at home. He brooded on its deep striations. He planned twelve months of preparation for a return to the Night of Champions. He was six months into them and his body was reaping its rich harvest when a bodybuilder named Tom Platz rang him.

Tom Platz was one of his heroes, along with Mike Mentzer. He had the same kind of iron physique that Yates was shooting for: raw and rugged. Platz wanted him to come to New York to meet a man called Vince McMahon. Platz laid it all on: first-class flights, flash hotels, some nice exes. This time a limo met him at JFK. He went to upstate New York where he met with Platz and Vince McMahon's wife. McMahon was a former wrestler who had invented the World Wrestling Federation. He'd blurred sport and entertainment in an absurdist theatre, a Grand Guignol trailer-trash extravaganza worth millions of dollars. Now McMahon and his wife wanted to set up the World Bodybuilding Federation. It would go right up against the IFBB. He'd told all of the bodybuilders it was going to be a big threat to the Weiders. He already had Tom Platz signed up. He had approached another golden boy called Bob Paris. McMahon's wife and Tom Platz gave Dorian

Yates the hard sell. They told him it was still going to be a sport, but it would be a sport that had stars, and it would be an organisation that made its stars rich. They offered him a two-year contract at $125,000 per year. A week or so later, the man who had won $7,000 in twenty-four months as a pro rang Tom Platz and said thanks but no thanks.

Peter McGough hammered away at the WBF in *Pumping Press*. The *Press* was an inky weekly that he'd started himself. He ran it with his girlfriend, Anne Byron. While *Flex* and *Muscle & Fitness* took months to print show reports because of their lead times, *Pumping Press* was written by Saturday and on the streets by Tuesday. It was an out-and-out newspaper, running on information and gossip. The section that got everyone talking was a column called 'Ripping Yarns'. McGough was small-time but he was thinking big. Every week he personally mailed copies to everyone in the IFBB and everyone in the WBF. Joe Weider was calling Ben and saying 'Have you read this?' Vince McMahon was getting a business partner called Jonathan Flora to ring McGough and scream at him. McGough didn't care. He knew a good target when he saw one. 'To be blunt,' he said, 'the previous year, it could have been the IFBB.' All of the other squares sat on the fence as a little paper from England put Vince McMahon to the sword. McGough and Byron redoubled their efforts. Hacks on Joe Weider's *Flex* magazine, which was based in California, used to ring McGough in Nottingham to ask for hush-hush stuff about bodybuilders who lived twelve miles up the road from the *Flex* offices. After *Pumping Press* had been running for ten issues, Joe Weider had had enough. He rang McGough and offered him a job. By the time he and Anne took up the offer and moved to Woodland Hills, Dorian Yates had won the

1991 Night of Champions and finished second to Lee Haney at the Mr Olympia.

Haney had picked up the Mr O eight years on the spin. He'd gone past Schwarzenegger. He'd gone past everyone. Statistically he was the greatest of all time. After eight, Haney had nothing left to prove. Fresh in his mind was his final posedown with Dorian Yates, onstage at the Walt Disney Dolphin hotel in Orlando, Florida. By now, Yates weighed 240 lb. Haney was 248 lb, his biggest ever. It was usual to call three competitors out for final comparisons. The judges called just two. The crowd sensed that history was at hand, whichever way the result went. They caused mayhem over all that muscle. The place went into melt-down. The seven compulsory poses took more than four minutes to complete. When the scores were passed down, Yates had actually defeated Haney in one of four categories, the muscularity round.

For Lee Haney, as big as he was ever going to get, the portents were clear. He was the last of the regulation freaks, the last man that a normal man might feel existed as a part of the same species. The really freaky freaks were coming now. The Shadow was just the first. In the big, bad muscle game, things were about to go galactic. Things were about to get genuinely freaky. Haney took the hint. He had held on this time, but Dorian Yates was a king in waiting, a champion elect.

It was harder than Dorian had imagined, becoming the chosen one. One night, out of the blue, he'd said to Debbie, 'The best bodybuilder in the world . . . Could that be me?' He addressed the weakness in the question himself, immediately: 'It has to be someone,' he said out loud. 'Why shouldn't it be me?' But he knew too that the question had been asked.

The title Mr Olympia had been contested twenty-seven times since 1965. Nine men had won it. Chris Dickerson and Samir Bannout were flukes rather than freaks; one-off winners in transitory years. Larry Scott, the first Mr O, and Franco Columbu, who had competed during the era of Schwarzenegger, had each won twice. Frank Zane and Sergio Oliva had won three times, each consecutively. Arnold Schwarzenegger had won seven times, six of them consecutively and one other five years later on, just because he could. Lee Haney had won eight times, all of them consecutively.

No one holding the title Mr Olympia had been beaten at a bodybuilding competition other than the Mr Olympia. Mr O either retired or was deposed onstage by another Mr Olympia. Except for the brief gap between the reigns of Schwarzenegger and Haney, the title changed hands rarely.

These were among the doubts that visited the Shadow. Somebody had to be the best, it was true. But they had to be the very best, they had to be the man of not just the year, but of the era. Was that him? Perhaps. Or maybe it was Vince Taylor, who had finished third behind Yates and Haney at the O. He had then taken out the entire European tour and followed that by winning the Arnold Classic. Perhaps it was Shawn Ray, a fizzing new star, small but utterly perfectly formed. It might be him. Or it could be Kevin Levrone, another new boy with a swinging chassis and a winning smile. In a year or two it could be Kenny 'Flex' Wheeler, a kid with unimaginably perfect genetics and muscles that grew like potatoes in dirt.

Dorian buried his doubts under tons of iron at the Temple gym. He was made favourite for the title, and he took the news with equanimity. He prepared immaculately and travelled to Helsinki for the show.

Something entirely unexpected happened to him three days before the Mr O: he fell into a state of calm. He felt the opposite of nervous anticipation. He had to remind himself constantly that his moment was at hand. It wasn't until the press conference where he got a look at the other competitors that the one-track mind got back on track.

What was bothering him was this: there was no bogeyman any more. There was no Lee Haney up ahead. Momo Benaziza's striated back no longer haunted his dreams. There were no dodgy judges or political decisions. There was just the title, and the need to step forward to the plate and make it his.

Before the contest, which was held at an ice rink, got started something freaky happened. Vince Taylor got flicked in the eye by a luggage strap on his suitcase and had to compete wearing a patch. He looked odd, and must have felt odd, as he faded down the field. Lou Ferrigno, a fearsome throwback to the *Pumping Iron* days who had fashioned a subsequent career as the Incredible Hulk on an American TV show, was making a comeback. But only Arnie could do comebacks. Ferrigno fell apart as soon as he walked onstage. Dorian blew away Momo Benaziza's ovenready rear with a back as broad as a barn door. He overwhelmed Shawn Ray's killer cuts with his insane size. He ended Lee Labrada's hopes of ever holding the O. Poor Lee. He had lived through Lee Haney's time. Now he must compete in the Shadow's shadow. Finally, there was just Kevin Levrone, coming up on the blind side as Yates had twelve months before. There were some confusing call-outs. Mismatched men stood together for comparisons. Dorian suffered two bouts of cramping, but by then it was pretty much over. He was Mr Olympia, 1992.

He was the tenth man to hold the title; the first Englishman; the first non-American or non-naturalised American since Sergio Oliva, who came from Cuba; the first Mr O to be living outside of the US when he won. He took the Sandow back home two days later, where he walked the British Grand Prix in front of two thousand screaming lunatics in Peter McGough's home town of Nottingham.

Once he became a champion, everything about his life made sense. He realised that he was not a natural underdog, however well he had exploited that state. Instead, he was an alpha male, an *Übermensch*, a man that demanded an era of his own. He understood that the difference between him and the rest was not physical but mental. He had the best body because he had the best mind. His mind really gave his body a hard time. His body had all the muscle, but his mind had all the strength. If he flagged under the weights, his mind might come up with an image of Shawn Ray driving his Ferrari around Los Angeles. 'Look at that flash bastard,' his mind said. 'He's out there in the sun. You're in Birmingham in the pissing rain. That's why he can't beat you.' Or he might think about Kevin Levrone or Flex Wheeler, trying to take the food from his table. They were going to hurt Debbie and Lewis. They wanted to ruin his life. That was how his mind spoke to his body.

He thrived on confounding the expectations of others. He heard what they were saying about him: that he was a one-off Mr O, like Dickerson or Bannout. He was some Limey joke, keeping the thing warm for the real deal – who would be an American. His mind worked all of this up for him, and it turned it into hatred and fear and ferocity. He focused like a laser on the 1993 Mr O. He had never forgotten the lesson of losing the 1986 British Championships to Chris Oskys. It wasn't enough just to win, he had to win by miles, not by inches. He needed to triumph definitively. To do this, he would have to redefine the sport.

He went to New York three months before the Mr O. He appeared at a local contest as a guest poser. He showed off his 269 lb of glistening beef. He allowed the shock waves from that to spread concentrically outwards while he went home and boiled down the remaining body fat and excess water. At 2 p.m. on 11 September 1993 he walked out onstage at the Civic Auditorium in Atlanta, Georgia. He weighed 257 lb. His skin looked as if it had been painted directly on to his muscle. He was stone hard and grainy. Every detail of every body part punched out into the first ten rows. No man had ever looked quite like Dorian Yates looked that day: he looked *big*. He looked *bad*. He looked *sick*. There *was* no Mr Olympia contest. The judges saw no need to call him out for comparisons during the muscularity round.

'I knew then,' he would say, ten years later, 'that I was either first or last. And I wasn't fucking last.'

Eventually Wayne DeMilia asked him to step forward between Shawn Ray and Flex Wheeler, just so that the audience could marvel at him some more. Samir Bannout looked at the three of them and said: 'Dorian is first, second and third.'

He was the biggest Mr Olympia ever, the first to weigh over 250 lb on show day. He had more than simply won. He had taken bodybuilding into a new age; into the Era of the Freak. By 1996, six of the Olympia top ten would weigh more than 250 lb onstage.

Sometimes Dorian hated lugging all that muscle around. In the off-season when he was eating big and training heavy and gaining mass, he felt the pull of his burden. Walking

58

down the streets in Birmingham, he was not cosseted by the fame a champion might enjoy. No one knew who he was, and therefore, no one understood why he looked as he did, twenty stone of primo beef, six feet in all directions.

He viewed his body as a product. He liked to think of himself as a sculptor. He would look at his muscle in the long gym mirror like it wasn't really him. He'd think: 'Right, a bit off here . . . a bit more on there . . .' Then he would set about himself with all that weight, and make it happen. He would make sure that his vision of himself was fully realised.

By February 1994 he was 295 lb and lean enough at the weight. He was ready to eclipse 1993, to leave it in the shadow of the Shadow. His frame was still taking muscle. Then in March he tore a ligament near the rotator cuff in his left shoulder. In April he tore the vastus muscle in his left thigh. In July he tore his left biceps muscle while doing barbell rows. In less than five months his body had turned sinister on him. For a two-week period he considered withdrawing, not defending his title. There were nine more weeks until the show. The best he could hope for was to work out enough to prevent any more deterioration to his physique, and to train light enough to avoid any other injuries. He booked an operation on his shoulder for the month after the Mr O. The beast who did barbell curls with 140 lb in each hand was reduced to doing concentration curls with 10 lb weights.

Three hundred and sixty-four days after he launched the Era of the Freak, he flopped over the line as a three-time Mr O. He had been so far ahead, he was able to win minus half a year's training. He'd posed cleverly onstage. He'd hidden the injuries as best he could and he'd accentuated the best of what remained. He'd learned something important, something that British athletes didn't often learn: he'd learned how to win.

The real world occasionally noticed Dorian: one year, two *Sun* journalists were flying to America to cover a title fight. The plane was rammed with muscle. 'What are you lot going over for?' one of them asked. 'We're going to see Dorian, mate . . .' 'Who's Dorian?' The *Sun* boys couldn't believe that there was a planeload of people travelling four thousand miles to support a man they'd never heard of. When they got into town, they rang Wayne DeMilia and asked if they could come and watch the Mr O.

Dorian was asked to appear on TV chat shows. But the invitations came with a kicker: 'Will you take your shirt off?' or 'Will you come out in posing trunks?'

His answer was always no. You wouldn't invite Maradona on and ask him to kick a ball around in his kit. So he'd offer to turn up and do an interview, and provide film of himself competing that they could air. Their answer was always no, too. He'd had it with them now. He'd had it with all the people who said he didn't do enough to represent the sport, too. Schwarzenegger had made some snide comments in an interview. He asked why Dorian Yates didn't wear 'proper clothes, like Armani'. Sometimes, Arnold could be a two-faced bastard. Dorian wasn't going to take any shit from him. Schwarzenegger knew nothing about modern body-building. He turned up in Ohio for two days a year at the Arnold Classic, let everyone kiss his ass for forty-eight hours and went home again. Dorian told him so.

What Dorian hadn't told Arnold about was the time he was walking through Central Park with Kerry Kayes, and two policemen on horseback had stopped them and asked him for autographs, not just for them, but for the boys at the station, too. In America, it was strange, different to Britain. In America, he had all sorts coming up to him, women for sure, but also doctors, pilots, professional people, all stopping him and asking for signatures or photographs or training tips. He got recognised everywhere. Dorian and Arnold got face to face at the Arnold Classic. Arnie was as nice as pie. He had nothing to say about Dorian's clothes, or about anything else. There was some needless resentment in Schwarzenegger, though. Not just towards Dorian, but towards modern bodybuilding. It was as if he didn't like anyone else taking out an old girlfriend he no longer wanted for himself.

Dorian Yates represented something, too. He carried a particular symbolism: that the age of Arnold and his mythic body was in the past and must be viewed through the prism of Yates's own greatness.

He had them now, and he knew it. After 1994, he healed up and went to war. He had a fat contract with Joe Weider to appear in his magazines. He had career winnings approaching half a million dollars. He could charge $5,000 for a guest posing spot that lasted ten minutes. It could have made him soft. Instead, it made him harder. It drove him further into himself. He was transgressive, too. Unlike the others, he had no ego with the weights. He didn't care about the poundages he was lifting. He only cared about the effect that they had. He ran his body like it was a multinational company. He was ruthless with it. He made cuts where they were needed. He invested in it wisely. When people asked him what he bench-pressed, he'd reply: 'It doesn't matter.' And to him, it didn't. The product was all. He was a one-off, a wizard, a true freak in body and mind.

The rest of them, though, they were nutters. No wonder they couldn't beat him. If Dorian Yates had the genetics of

Flex Wheeler, for example, the Shadow might have used them to fashion a body that would never have been defeated. Instead, Flex Wheeler had the genetics of Flex Wheeler. He also had the brain of Flex Wheeler, and that wasn't necessarily a good thing. Flex was an almost heroic failure. He almost killed himself in a car crash; he almost killed himself with diuretics and steroids. He ran a sex life that would have crippled Casanova. He'd go out of the house to buy food and come back with a new car. He'd go out to buy a new car and come back with a new house. He was pissy with his fans (one told him he'd put Flex's picture on his fridge to stop him cheating on his diet. Flex had said: 'A picture of me won't stop you eating crap.'). He was a fighter and a fornicator. When he got it together he could beat anyone. He had won the USAs, the Ironman, the Night of Champions, the Arnold. When he was at his best, he looked beyond human. He was the Sultan of Symmetry. No one knew how he did it. Unfortunately, he didn't know how he did it, either. Once, he was chatting with Dorian about his contest prep. He'd said: 'I wanna look how I looked last year.'

So Dorian said: 'Well, what was your prep last year?'

Flex said: 'I can't remember . . .'

By his own admission, he was a lost soul. And things were only going to get worse for him.

Then there was Kevin Levrone. Levrone was the Muscle Machine from Baltimore. He was a great mix of ethnicities, part Afro-Caribbean, part Italian; he had the best of both worlds. He was a very handsome guy blessed with great athletic talent. He could run track; he would have made a great wide receiver. He just had to amp up that natural muscle and he had a body built for bodybuilding. He was 5'9", 240 lb, with shoulders for miles, a tight waist and a winning smile. He had charisma, too; not the glowering presence of the Shadow but a song-and-dance man's zap. Crowds went nuts for him. But he only trained for half the year, sometimes less. The rest of the time, he withered down to 200 lb. Then he'd jack himself back up three months before pay day by using crazy poundages in the gym. His head was all over the shop, too. He used his four or five months off to play in a band and 'have fun'.

Like Flex, he'd won the Arnold and the USAs. He'd also won Grands Prix in Spain, Britain, Germany, Finland and the Czech Republic. Compared to Dorian Yates, though, he was a part-timer.

Chris Cormier was something else, too. With Chris as a barometer, Flex Wheeler and Kevin Levrone came across like Zen ascetics. Everything Chris did was approximate. He looked like Evander Holyfield, or at least a version of Evander Holyfield that hadn't spent fifteen years being punched in the face. He called himself 'The Real Deal', just like Commander 'Vander, too. Chris lived the woozy southern California life. He liked to party. Women loved Chris and he loved them right back. At any given moment, he may or may not have been where he should have been, where he may or may not have been doing what he should have been doing. Everything was approximate, including his physique. When he was good, it was spectacularly beautiful, like a giant, muscled letter X. But when he was bad, he got beaten in his head. The other competitors got in there and they wouldn't get out. Everything was approximate, and often he had nothing solid to grip on to.

Dorian Yates ran him down like roadkill.

The man Yates respected most, the one he'd call 'mentally tenacious' if pushed to call him anything, was Shawn Ray. Shawn was a terrific bodybuilder. He was a prince of proportion, a demon of definition. He was a lightning rod for show crowds. He posed and preened in the California sun; he was as handsome as Eddie Murphy and he aspired to the superstar life. He brought some pizzazz to proceedings. He could back it up with his body, too. He was lissom and lithe: the Shadow lumbered by comparison. But he was also small. He weighed 215 lb. Yates outmuscled him. He threw three surplus stone of beef at Shawn Ray and Shawn Ray receded into that vast shadow.

Paul Dillett *was* big. In fact, Paul Dillett was enormous. In the off-season he crashed around Canada at more than 330 lb. They called him the Freakazoid or Freakzilla. He might be able to match Yates's size, but he could never present such condition. He was lumpy where the Shadow was ripped raw. Then there was the famous diuretic freeze-up at the Arnold Classic in 1994, when he was carried off stage like a cardboard cut-out. Dillett was just as erratic in his opinions. He held that the judges were racist, biased against black guys. But then he'd claim that he had the best-paid Weider contract, even though Yates was Mr Olympia.

Nasser El Sonbaty had the gene pool stuff nailed. He was born in Germany. His father was from Egypt and his mother was from Yugoslavia. He had muscle, too, and stacks of it, piled on. He took a freaky picture, especially when he wore his glasses and let it rip. He had the head of a professor, rather noble, balding, and the body of a genuine freak. He claimed that he was the only bodybuilder who could guest pose at over 300 lb and still keep his body fat so low that you could still see his six-pack of iron abs. He was certainly the only bodybuilder who spoke seven languages. He was bright and he read his body well. He made big gains quickly. He fast-tracked his career. He might have had what it took to put some heat on the Shadow, but he was coming from a long way back. When Yates became Mr O, El Sonbaty had only competed in six pro shows, never placing higher than seventh.

Ronnie Coleman was the other way. Everything came slow to big Ronnie. He was from Texas. He was a qualified accountant. He talked slow, he moved slow and his muscles grew slow. He even kept a day job, as a cop. He was just two years younger than Dorian Yates, but by 1990, he was only Mr Texas. His first time at the Big Show was in '92, the year the Shadow had ascended. Coleman finished sixteenth. By 1994, he'd moved up one place. In 1995, he finished joint tenth.

There was one exceptional thing about Ronnie though: he was freakishly strong. He could shift huge amounts of weight. And as he did so, he grew. And he'd never stop growing.

There were younger men, too, looking up at the King, murmuring about his crown. Lee Priest had arms that could blot out the sun. His guns could smoke anyone's. He had huge legs, too, and shoulders so broad it was said that he couldn't sleep on his side because the weight of his head hanging free might rupture something vital in his neck. Unfortunately for Lee, though, he was only 5′ 4″. He had a long body and short arms and legs. He got dwarfed up there. Jay Cutler was a better-looking boy, but he was too young. His muscle needed maturity. Gunter Schlierkamp was a huge German, but he was blocky as hell; he looked like a walking wardrobe.

This was Dorian's competition. The Shadow had them all; he knew it. And they knew he knew it. And he knew that they knew that he knew it. Chris Cormier even said he could feel it. Standing next to Dorian Yates onstage, he sensed 'radiation coming off him, like an aura'. The power of that muscle was tangible. It exerted a force all of its own. Cormier thought, 'I might as well forget about this guy and concentrate on being second'. There was something else, too, something strange. You had to witness him in the flesh. Such granite hardness had a property that could not be held on film or caught on paper. You had to see it live. You had to *feel* the latent power that Chris Cormier had felt. Peter McGough said that sitting next to Dorian and staring at his muscle was like looking at a stone wall. You could gaze at it for as long as you might examine a painting. It had depth. It had nuances. It had a crackling energy about it. One bodybuilder said that the first time he encountered Yates, he laughed. He couldn't stop himself. The Shadow was just so big and so bad, laughter seemed to be the only appropriate response.

Dorian understood better than anyone else the rarity of his condition. 'The Shadow', once a nickname conferred to convey his disappearing acts, took on a more subtle definition. His size darkened the minds of his rivals. It cast doubt and it blotted out hope. He worked on them, even when he wasn't there. He used his silence as a USP. His absence affirmed his myth. The Shadow was his brand: instantly recognisable, patently unique. And then once a year, he would visit.

Just like the rest of his life, his backstage routine was calculated to wreak maximum havoc. He would wear an old blue-and-white warm-up suit that Peter McGough named 'The Tardis'. There was something about the way it was cut that diminished him. It made him look small. But as its name suggested, everything was bigger on the inside. He would walk in and take the best dressing room without asking if it was his. He would remove the blue-and-white tracksuit. Just as they were about to be called to the stage, he would walk into the pump-up room and let them get an eyeful of him, let them see that it was over for another year.

McGough began to think of Dorian Yates as the Anti-Bodybuilder. In America, they all flapped their lips 24/7 in the bullshit breeze. Nineteen-inch arms grew to twenty-three inches. Everyone was in their best shape ever, all the time. No one was scared of Dorian Yates. His absence just proved he was losing it. The bodybuilding mags didn't get him either. They couldn't handle the lack of hyperbole. They shrank from his silence. A *Flex* hack told Peter McGough: 'I can't write about this guy. He doesn't say anything. He appears out of nowhere.' McGough had pointed out that this was a pretty good story.

The Americans took his reticence for weakness. They got their excuses in early. If he was to win again for a fourth time in 1995 it would be because Flex Wheeler had been badly injured in a car accident and could barely compete. If he was to win again it would be because he had a fat Weider contract, and everyone knew that Joe and Ben called the shots. If he won again it was because the incumbent Mr O always won. Dorian said nothing in his defence. Talk was cheap and there was plenty of it. Alone among his peers he understood that the sport was purely visual. He arrived in Atlanta, Georgia, on 9 September with an irreducible argument: a body that would really get them talking. Fifteen minutes before the prejudging began, as his friend Steve Weinberger oiled him up (and what a job that was – like painting the outside of a house), he said: 'In 1993, I showed up with a bazooka. Last year, I felt like I had one hand tied behind my back. Today, I'm ready to launch an intercontinental missile . . .'

One by one, he sliced and diced them: Levrone was a distant second; El Sonbaty was third; Shawn Ray was fourth;

Vince Taylor fifth; Chris Cormier sixth. Flex Wheeler was eighth. Ronnie Coleman was tenth. This was the natural order. He'd beaten them when he was bad and he'd beaten them when he was good. He was square with them and he was square with history. The Shadow had his era.

Peter McGough got an era, too. Joe Weider had given him a job, on *Flex* magazine. The Yanks didn't really like it, much as they didn't really like Dorian Yates. Joe Weider remained supportive. McGough recalled once not being able to get an interview with Kevin Levrone. Weider picked up the phone on Christmas Eve and rang Levrone at home. McGough didn't need much nursemaiding, though. Soon, he was editor-in-chief.

Flex occupied a unique position in the sport. It wasn't just a muscle mag or a training manual. Because Joe Weider owned it, and because he was called 'the father of modern bodybuilding' and because his brother ran the IFBB and because they and Arnold Schwarzenegger were the three who had turned the thing into a $300 million industry, *Flex* was sort of the official magazine of bodybuilding. It had all of the top athletes under contract to do exclusive photo shoots and interviews and to make appearances on behalf of the Weider organisation. The editor of *Flex* had clout. He chose the magazine covers. He decided who got contracts and who didn't. He recommended how big the contracts should be. He had the ear of the Weiders and of Wayne DeMilia. Behind the scenes, the editor of *Flex* could flex some muscle of his own.

Weider chose McGough because he was a tenacious journalist. But he also chose him because McGough instinctively understood his reader: a kid with dreams of muscle. The kids reading *Flex* already knew why bodybuilders wanted to be bodybuilders: they wanted to be bodybuilders themselves. It was not about the *Why* – it was about the *How*. How did Dorian Yates get to look like Dorian Yates? And if they could follow the training programme that made Dorian Yates into what he was, what might that programme make them into? Peter McGough's *Flex* began to reflect the new order of the sport. It started to report on the Era of the Freak.

Dorian Yates had in his head an image of what body-building was. It was about blood and guts in the gym, about the purity of hard training. When *Flex* shot Yates they shot him working out: eyes agoggle and great crevasses of effort carved in his face. You could practically smell him. *Flex* became as raw and as ripped as the men in its pages. It got freakier. So did other mags and websites. The Era of the Freak fed itself, and its public urged it forward with their patronage.

By the Big O climax to 1996, four years after Dorian Yates launched the Era of the Freak at the Civic Auditorium in Atlanta, six of the Mr Olympia entrants had followed him over the 250 lb in-competition weight. Yet Mohamed Benaziza was dead. Andreas Munzer was dead. Paul Dillett had frozen up. Mike Matarazzo had collapsed after the 1993 Arnold Classic. And Ben Weider's life ambition was to have bodybuilding included as an Olympic sport. Wayne DeMilia accepted that something had to be done. In-competition drug testing was introduced for IFBB pros at the 1996 Mr Olympia. Prohibited substances included diuretics – deadly tablets that produced the ripped-raw dry look but that depleted the body of salt and minerals vital to organ function in return. The event took place over two days at the Arie Crown Theatre in Chicago. The first evening's show was a massacre of the established order. Three defending Olympia champions – Ms Fitness and Figure Mia Finnegan, Ms Olympia Lenda Murray and the

Over-40 Masters Mr Olympia Sonny Schmidt – were beaten. The body of the Shadow, weighing in the following evening at 257 lb, was not so easily dismissed. He didn't care about the diuretics test. Diuretics were anathema to him. He was at his contest weight two weeks before showtime, having reduced himself by a pound or two a week over the preceding three months. He wasn't like some of the others, losing ten pounds of fluids in two days: they stepped onstage like ticking bombs.

The Shadow was a little flat though, a lick or two from his best. Nasser El Sonbaty got as close as anyone had to outmuscling him. Shawn Ray was cut like diamond. Flex Wheeler had recovered from his car accident and he'd sprouted a hefty harvest of bulging bulk. Levrone the Muscle Machine was on. Paul Dillett looked like a road map. Ronnie Coleman broke the top six for the first time. There was less between them than there had ever been. But Yates held firm and won every round. Shawn edged Nasser and Nasser edged Kevin and Kevin edged Flex and Flex edged Ronnie. And then Nasser El Sonbaty failed the diuretics test and got himself DQ-ed.

It was his body that surrendered in the end, smashed on the iron wheel of his will. His era had progressed in increments of two: years of greatness in 1993 and 1995, years of consolidation in 1994 and 1996. His best ever off-season was 1997. He felt he could add ten more pounds of muscle without losing his intense hardness (it didn't sound like much, until you picked up something that weighed ten pounds and held it for a while). Yet a curious physical entropy, ultimately fatal to his competitive career, was about to turn order towards chaos. For a year, his left elbow had been swelling up. The scar tissue caused by training was the problem. Then early in June, he got a chest infection. Later in the month, he tore his right thigh and couldn't work his legs for three weeks. On 1 August he collapsed after a light cardio session on the stationary bike. He began coughing up blood and was hospitalised. The aspirin he had taken to counter the inflammation in his elbow had worn through his stomach lining. He'd needed three blood transfusions in three days, almost ten pints in all. He was discharged on 4 August and told to rest. His haemoglobin count was down among the dead men's. He went back to the gym. Debbie convinced him to 'play the cards he was dealt' and not train flat out. Somehow, his physique remained in astonishing condition.

Three weeks before the show, his mind finally asked a question for which his body had no answer. Obsessively focused, unwilling to accept failure, he was completing a pull-down exercise with some absurd weight or other when his left elbow went bang. It was an Armageddon for his arm. He felt like someone had stabbed him hard with a hot sharp knife and left it in, and then he went numb and into shock. His triceps, which was the shape of a horseshoe and ran down the back of his upper arm, had become detached from the bone. The muscle weighed a couple of pounds but was now held in place by the few determined fibres that had survived the trauma. The bruise that announced the damage was so severe that 'bruise' didn't really cover it. It was a haematoma and it ran from his shoulder to his wrist and around his underarm to his lats. Surgery to reattach the flopping muscle was the only treatment. He refused it, of course – he'd have missed the Olympia.

Any sort of exercise was out. Lift weights? He couldn't even pull his trousers up. Debbie had to do it for him. For twenty-one days he kept his triceps still and tried to stop a year's worth of muscle from ebbing away, dead cell by dead cell. Until the first night of the show, he dared not even flex his arm.

It was the best-kept secret in bodybuilding, a sport in which nobody could keep anything secret. While the Shadow faced odds he wasn't sure he could beat, all the tittle-tattle about him went on: he changed his blood, he swigged human growth hormone down neat, he took Chinese herbs and ate Russian bear meat and did deals with the Devil and Joe Weider to let him keep his title. No one wanted to explain him in mortal terms. No one wanted to accept that such an excessive structure could be constructed in the mundanity of the Temple gym. It had to be magic. It had to be juju. It had to be juice. And all the while, the real story eluded them; the Shadow's great secret – his ruined left arm.

Onstage, the pain almost made him pass out. Posing hurt anyway; you had to tense and grind all that muscle, keep it bloody and full, while you were tired, stressed, dehydrated. For whatever reason – no one knew why, they hadn't done it for nine years – the IFBB had split the 1997 Mr O over two nights, prejudging on Friday, the free-posing round and the posedown on Saturday. Dorian feared the prejudging most. Over two rounds, he must hit a series of four and then seven compulsory poses. In each round the judges would then make a series of call-outs so that three or four competitors could be compared to one another while they hit all of the compulsory poses again. There were twelve judges, and each could request any combination from the line-up. Even between call-outs he had to stand in line semitensing his muscle. During some of the compulsory poses he would not be able to hide his left arm away.

He'd been in California for seven days and he'd hardly slept. All he'd thought about was his triceps. On the Friday before the show, he was drying himself after a shower when the arm locked up again. He'd iced it and the swelling subsided, but it had given him six days of hell; he was afraid to use the muscle in any way. Now up onstage, he was forced to. But while he was working himself up over a small muscle on the rear of one arm, the crowd were rocking and rolling to the rest of him: 270 lb he weighed, his biggest ever. His thighs swept outwards as broad and as hard as curving freeway ramps. His shoulders balanced them: he'd have to edge through doorways side-on. His neck started somewhere up behind his ears. He had fourteen years of heavy training packed on to him: such density and muscle maturity wasn't going anywhere, even if he hadn't been using it for a week or two. He stepped from the stage after the prejudging in his usual Mr O state of mind: he had them all again. He knew it and so did they.

The following evening he posed for three minutes to a version of Carl Orff's *Carmina Burana*, stopped anyone else knocking into his triceps during the posedown and picked up the outsized medal and the Sandow trophy from Joe Weider. Three weeks beforehand, he hadn't been able to dress himself. Two months beforehand, he'd been in hospital. Seven years beforehand he'd never won a body-building contest in America. Twelve years beforehand he was broke and living in a council flat in Birmingham. All of this went through his mind. The one thing that didn't occur to him was that it was over: not the Era of the Freak, but his part in it.

The triceps got sewn back on in New York on 28 October, four weeks after the contest. Eight months later, it still wasn't right. He couldn't train to his usual intensity. He pulled out of the Mr O with the intention of coming back, dramatically, in 1999, but the notion was a transitional one.

His mind needed a soft landing. By September, he had faced the reality of his situation and he flew first class to Los Angeles to tell Joe Weider that he was retiring. He flew back again two weeks later to read his abdication speech – carefully hand-printed on some hotel stationery – to the crowd at the 1998 Mr O. He took the piece of paper home with him. He had it laminated and he hung it up at the Temple gym, on a wall facing a board holding his six Olympia medals. He looked at both of them, the medal board and the speech, and they both said the same thing: it was over. His afterlife had begun.

*

It was the day of the British Grand Prix at the Wembley Conference Centre. It was a big moment for Kerry Kayes and for British bodybuilding. Everyone was keyed up. Even the bad weather was in top shape. The storm that blew in was in contest condition. The wind brought down half a building out by the shells of the Twin Towers. It took out an old lady while I was parking my car. It just blew her to the ground and pinned her there while it worked her over. The muscled-up clouds bullied their way through the skies. Only muscle could offer a response, and much of London's muscle was en route. Cars gridlocked by the building collapse had big men squashed comically in their small seats. The tube trains brought a cargo of human beef. Two huge crews piled out of minicabs. The doormen at the Wembley Conference Centre were unsettled. Coming towards them were hundreds of people who looked just like doormen. In the high winds and squalling rain, many of them were wearing sleeveless T-shirts. A couple were wearing *shorts*. You could rank them by the speed they moved. The bigger they were, the slower they got, great

74

hisses of breath leaking effortfully out of them. Moving slowest of all were the competitors themselves, who were distinguishable by their faces – all shades of rich brown from the tinned tan – and by the baggy workout suits they wore.

This big squad had its leader, too. His face hung on banners and appeared on leaflets. His name was on everyone's mind. His iconic image informed their style, from dress to walk to talk. Here, today, Dorian Yates was King.

I passed him as I was walking towards the dressing rooms. He was wearing a tailored grey suit, single-breasted, and a matching tie. It was the first time I had seen Dorian in anything resembling normal clothing. For him, it was abnormal clothing. Suits were designed for mortals. Dorian looked ten feet wide. We shook hands. I felt his soft handshake. The King walked on. Slowly.

Backstage, the pros sat around, doing nothing, still in their warm-up suits. No one was saying much. They were in the usual state of the competing bodybuilder: low on carbs, stressed, frazzled from all the travelling, dehydrated, hungry, unable to think straight, wanting to get out there and get it over with. This was the circuit; this was the grind of their professional lives. They could only get in contest shape once or twice a year. Anything more was too hard, too unhealthy. The sport was set up to reflect the fact. There were contests every spring, climaxing in Ohio at the Arnold Classic. The Mr Olympia came in October, and immediately afterwards, the European shows began. The Mr O was the most prestigious, obviously, followed by the Arnold Classic. If a pro was competing twice in a year, these were the events they would choose to peak for, and they'd look to pick up extra dollars in the surrounding contests if they could hold their condition and stick to the diet. The other best-known contest, Wayne DeMilia's Night of Champions, came in May and was more of a one-off. It always had a large entry of mid-level pros and up-and-comers who may not qualify for the Mr O or the Arnold.

The bodybuilding mags would commission their year's worth of pictures around these events, flying the athletes into LA and shooting hundreds of rolls of workout pics at the local gyms immediately before or after the big shows while all the beef was still bulging.

The European tour was a good earner, if you could handle the travel. There were usually three or four shows within a week or two of one another. Five or six of the top ten or twelve bodybuilders would show up for each. They'd compete against the best of the locals. The prize money was pretty good: $10,000 or so for first place. Everyone in the top six got a couple of thousand at least. The crowds were rowdy and enthusiastic. The pros could sell signed photos and slip in a few gym appearances and fly back home thousands of dollars richer for the trip.

It wasn't enough for everyone. Ronnie Coleman had just won $110,000 and a Cadillac Esplanade at the Mr O, and told Kerry he wasn't coming to England unless he was flown in first class. Kerry declined to do so. 'Me and Dorian fly at the back of the plane,' he'd said, 'so why can't he?' Kerry had paid for Flex Wheeler's economy flight, but hadn't heard a word from him since, and no one knew where he was. Kevin Levrone had lost his passport. Gunter Schlierkamp, who had become an overnight sensation after finishing in fifth place at the Mr O, had appearances booked in America. Markus Ruhl, a monstrous freak from Germany, flew in and then immediately succumbed to food poisoning and flew out again.

Kerry had a marketable entry, nonetheless. Of the men

76

who'd competed at the 2002 Mr O seven days before were: Chris Cormier, who'd finished third; Dexter Jackson, fourth; Dennis James, tenth; and Ernie Taylor, fourteenth; plus Claude Groulx, Tommy Thorvildsen, Jaroslav Horvath and Paco Bautista who'd placed lower down. They sat around, moving more slowly than everyone else, bad beasts at the top of their food chain. Below them, less sure, more tense, were some up-and-comers: Art Atwood, a big American who was trying to chisel his rampant beef into a more pleasing shape; Giovanni Thompson, a handsome Dutch guy who looked like he should be modelling for *GQ*; Pete Brown, a heavy-set, taciturn Sheffielder whose real name was Elvis. 'Pete' matched his character much better.

Least cocksure were the rookies. Ricky Welling wouldn't be put off by anyone else's body – he was blind. Despite his handicap, he'd won a pro card. It was a remarkable achievement in a sport that relied entirely on visual presentation. Harold Marillier had won the afternoon's amateur contest and got a direct entry into the evening show as the world's newest pro.

They started to strip and get oiled. The black guys had an advantage here. They didn't need to slather up in tan. The white guys, although they were actually far from white, had just their base coats on. They added more to get the wet look that allowed their bodies to come alive under the stage lights. They pumped up with light weights and thick rubber bands to get the blood flowing into their muscle. The effort was enough to make them sweat and breathe heavily. They didn't spend much time looking at each other. The Olympia had taken away the mystique of their physiques – they had all seen more than enough of one another in Las Vegas. Everyone had tried to hit their best form there. Now they were in various stages of decline. The main problem was in 'smoothing over' or 'going flat'. To the inexpert eye, such deterioration would be impossible to spot. What was gargantuan a week ago would be merely immense now and just plain vast in another week's time.

The big boys got their game faces on. Apart from the money, they had plenty riding on the show. Cormier was looking to affirm himself as a potential Mr Olympia next time, and as the best of the rest right now. Dexter 'The Blade' Jackson was the new Shawn Ray, no mass monster yet perfectly proportioned. He'd never taken a pro title, despite finishing second six times – he needed a win. Ernie Taylor hadn't finished high enough at the O to qualify again for next year, only the top ten were invited back, but he could do it with a top-six place at the Grand Prix. Dennis James, an American who'd moved to Thailand, wanted a high finish to keep his name in front of the mag editors and the IFBB; he had come in just off in Las Vegas and had disappointed.

None of them wanted to appear as if they were slipping, ceding ground.

Claude Groulx was almost forty years old and still in great condition. He'd always been underrated. Tommy Thorvildsen had taken a big gamble and relocated from Norway to California. Pete Brown wanted to take Ernie Taylor and be Britain's number one. Everyone had a reason to compete hard. They padded around in flip-flops and posing trunks and checked themselves in the mirror. They got their pals and girlfriends and partners to give them the once-over. Dexter Jackson glared balefully at his reflection, daring it to cheat him. In one corner, Wayne DeMilia was putting Chris Cormier straight about the judging at the Mr Olympia. Wayne spent quite a lot of his time putting bodybuilders straight about various things. He was very good at it, mainly because he got lots of practice.

Chris: 'C'mon, man, they're just judging names. Don't matter what you look like . . .'

Wayne: 'Chris, in the end, it's a bodybuilding contest. The biggest guy's gonna win . . . The guy with the most muscle's gonna win.'

Wayne walked off. Chris shook his head, slowly, and began checking himself in the mirror again.

'Who do you like?' I asked Kerry, who was standing with his back against a wall, looking wall-eyed.

'Dexter . . . Chris . . . Maybe Dennis. Dennis looks big. Chris needs to keep his hair on . . .'

He nodded over at Cormier. 'They have people in their ear all the time, "Ooh, you should have won, Chris. You looked great. You looked ten times better than he did," and all that. Then they believe it.' Kerry looked up at the ceiling. 'That's bodybuilding, my mate.'

Wayne came back and told Kerry that the judges were ready to begin. 'C'mon, guys,' Wayne shouted. 'Five minutes now. Five minutes please. Let's get ready to go now . . .'

Ernie Taylor touched his toes a few times. Dennis James grabbed a bar and pumped his arms up some more. Dexter Jackson was brushing something invisible from his ribcage. They assembled, slowly, into some kind of line. No one looked at anyone else.

The Mr Olympia show informed the rest of the body-building year. It hung around like smoke in the minds of the competitors, it provided a world order for the judges, it set an agenda for the magazines and websites. It dictated guest posing fees, it made new stars, it broke some men.

Seven days after it, the competitors were still stumbling clear of the wreckage, dodging the fallout. Ronnie Coleman had won, for a fifth time. It hadn't been a popular choice with anyone, except for Ronnie. Big Ron was certainly big, but mostly in the wrong places. He had a distended belly hanging over his posing trunks; it had been stretched by years of eating six meals a day. *Flex* magazine had described it, memorably, as looking like 'a pot of overcooked ravioli'. He was huge from the back and small from the front. His ludicrously large lats had thrown almost every other body part out of whack. Ronnie had been Mr O for five years, he was almost forty, he wasn't improving any and the pros and the fans were getting itchy for change. But he wasn't ready to move over (God was telling him to keep going, he said), and no one had got close enough to strike down a winter king. Kevin Levrone had been second, bringing his body back from the dead once more, Cormier third and Jackson fourth, but the real star had been Gunter Schlierkamp. No one knew what the hell Gunter had been doing all year, but whatever it was, it had worked. He was 6'2" and weighed almost 300 lb. The earth shook when he moved. He was about the biggest thing anyone could remember seeing, and he had a movie-star smile, a humble manner and he posed to the music of Journey. The Americans loved it. The booing when he was announced in fifth place had only finished once he had mounted the dais and spoken to the crowd, an accolade usually bestowed only on the winner.

Cormier was still pissed about it all. He'd got no change out of Wayne DeMilia, but he wasn't in the mood to let it go. In fact, he'd carried on for anyone who wanted to listen. 'Ronnie aged overnight on that stage . . . It should have been Kevin or myself . . . Ronnie didn't deserve it . . . I don't think his stomach is ever going to be flat again, and that's not what it's about . . .'

I'd spoken to Ernie Taylor about the O, too. He was still suffering. He'd been drawn out last, which put him right on the end of the line-up at the edge of the stage. He had almost been hidden by a TV camera crane. He got some bad call-outs. He'd placed fourteenth, but he'd seen one judge's scorecard that had him fifth and then later seventh, and another which put him sixth. He was suspicious.

'Backstage, no joke, when we were pumping up, everyone except for Dexter, Gunter, me, Art Atwood and Ronnie were out of shape,' he said. 'Ronnie's back was great but he was way off from the front. Kevin gets through on his name.'

He was also aggrieved at getting called out with an also-ran named Craig Titus. 'I'm telling you,' he said, 'his gut was out here . . .' He made a gesture over his own flat stomach. 'He fooking looked like he was having triplets, man . . .'

They walked onstage and spread out along the line marked at the front. Wayne told them to keep further apart from one another. 'OK, gentlemen,' he said, when he was happy. 'A quarter-turn to the right, please . . .' All twenty-two of the bodybuilders spun round and the show began.

Chris Cormier, Dexter Jackson and Dennis James got the first call-out from Wayne DeMilia. Ernie got the second and it seemed to cheer him up. He flashed his big-time grin. The judges worked slowly through the comparisons. If drugs were bodybuilding's zugzwang, its losing move, then the judging was its sore point, its grassy knoll, its Area 51. It was in arguments – in furious rows – over judging that people fought, screamed, yelled, wept, flounced out and quit competing for ever. Valuable friendships were forfeited in disputes over the thin lines of numbers passed down from those tables. The only consensus to be found about the judges and their judging was that they got everything wrong. In the Era of the Freak, with the crowds screaming for super-size and men becoming inexorably, unstoppably larger, no one really understood what it was the judges were actually looking for whilst judging. The response from the judges was that they could only judge what was put in front of them.

I'd dug through fifty-one pages of the IFBB Professional Rules. They came down from the mountain in the kind of language you heard in the television addresses of despotic leaders from doomed regimes. They laid down the law about many things. They told the male judges what colour socks they should put on for judging ('*dark, with black shoes*'); they described, lavishly, what little the competitors should wear ('*posing trunks of a solid, non-distracting color, made from cloth fabric, which are clean and decent. Metallic material, such as gold or silver lamé, or shiny rubberized material may not be used to make up the trunks. The use of padding anywhere in the trunks is prohibited*'); they even adjudicated upon the kind of tinned tan the bodybuilders could legitimately apply ('*Products which produce an unnaturally colored tone, with an orange, yellow, red, green or gold hue, are strictly prohibited. Bronzing agents that produce a metallic look are also strictly prohibited*').

Attached to the pro rules document were the IFBB Technical Professional Rules, Appendix A of which contained the most direct instructions to judges:

When assessing a competitor's physique a judge should follow a routine procedure which will allow a comprehensive assessment of the physique as a whole. In the compulsory poses, he or she should look first at the primary muscle group being displayed. The judge should survey the whole of the physique, starting from the head and looking at every part in a downward sequence, beginning with general impressions, looking for muscular bulk, balanced development, muscular density and definition. The downward survey should take in the head, neck, shoulders, chest, all of the arm muscles, front of the trunk for pectorals, pec-delt tie-in, abdominals, waist, thighs, legs, calves and feet. The same procedure for back poses will also take in upper and lower trapezius, teres and infraspinatus, erector spina, the gluteus group, leg biceps group at the back of the thighs, calves and feet. A detailed assessment of the various muscle groups can be made during the comparisons when it helps the judge to compare muscle shape, density and definition while still bearing in mind overall balanced development.

You could ask each of the judges what the rules meant to them, and get twelve different answers. No one knew. I'd rung Wayne DeMilia to ask him. I'd said I thought Appendix A was confusing for the bodybuilders because it didn't state definitively what sort of physique the judges were looking for.

Wayne disagreed at two hundred words a minute. 'It's confusing to the athlete if they look at it in that way,' he said. 'Every contest is a different story. It depends on who's there and what condition they're in. Then you go to the judges. Every judge has their own opinion. You don't want all judges to judge the same. Some judges like guys who are small and ripped, some judges like athletes who are more symmetrical. Some judges like big, massive guys. You get a cross-section.

'You can't say "we want cuts this year". You gotta judge on what you see in front of you. You're judging the same thing in a different form every round. Round one, the judge is dictating to the athletes, "I want to judge your muscularity, your definition, your symmetry, your separation, your proportion in a semi-relaxed state from all four sides. In round two I wanna judge those five things in the seven compulsory poses." In round three the athlete is saying to the judge, "OK, you're gonna judge me in those five things, but as I present them to you." And if the athlete has a weak point, and wants to hide it he has that option. Of course, they're all so stupid, they don't hide it. Even the guy with that weak back will turn round and do a rear double-bicep.'

Perhaps not surprisingly, bodybuilding had loads of controversial decisions on the books. Arnold Schwarzenegger's seventh Mr Olympia title, which came in 1980 in Sydney, was the most famous. Schwarzenegger, who had been retired from pro competition for five years, told all the other competitors that he'd just come to town to commentate on the O for the CBS TV broadcast. They only found out two hours before the show that he was planning to compete. He'd trained for just eight weeks, but nonetheless he got the decision over men like Frank Zane, Mike Mentzer and Boyer Coe. A film of the event, *The Comeback*, was edited to exclude the sound of the audience, who were chanting 'rigged, rigged, rigged' and who'd yelled 'bullshit, bullshit' at an enraged Arnold.

Ronnie Coleman had barely won an Olympia that wasn't the subject of fierce scrutiny. In 1998, he'd been behind Flex Wheeler until the fourth round and beat him by just three points; in 1999, Wheeler, second again, had removed his medals in disgust and walked around with one finger in the air to convey his own judgement; in 2000, Kevin Levrone was widely accepted as having done enough to edge Big Ron; in 2001, Jay Cutler was ahead after two rounds and lost by just four points.

A 255 lb Nasser El Sonbaty was astonished to be beaten by the 225 lb Flex Wheeler at the 1997 Arnold Classic. Even Dorian Yates had been stiffed, by Chris Oskys way back in 1986.

These were just a few. Almost every show provoked outbreaks of booing at one point or another. The minor placings were nearly always the subject of harrowing argument from somebody.

Wayne DeMilia relished every one of them, and thought that they added greatly to the interest in his promotions.

'In any sport that is judged by humans there's gonna be controversy,' he'd jabbed down the phone. 'Look at boxing. Especially on the pay-per-view thing. Costs fifty, sixty bucks. I say, "Man, I'm never buying it again," then the next fight comes and they're giving me all the hype and I'm there. I'm calling up saying, "Hey, I want the fight tonight." In boxing there's three judges. A guys asks each of them, "Why'd I lose?" One judge says, "You weren't aggressive enough." Another says, "Your defence wasn't so good." The third says, "You didn't show ring generalship and use your left jab enough." Well, you're going back and saying, "I dunno why the heck I lost."'

Wayne was a sharp operator, a cute cookie. He wore dark socks – I checked. Joe and Ben owned the sport, but Wayne ran it: he was their representative on earth. The athletes were always falling in and out with him. He made sure that they all understood one very important point: he was boss.

The judges whirred through the prejudging, as it said in the rules, from head to toe, from top to bottom. The first sets of call-outs established the day's order: Cormier, Jackson, James and Taylor were clearly ahead, the prime beef.

Claude Groulx, Tommy Thorvildsen, Art Atwood and Jaroslav Horvath were contending for the remaining places in the top six, the elite positions at any show. Behind them, Paco Bautista, Pete Brown and Mike Sheridan pushed for the top ten. It was easy enough to tell; the comparisons began with the best men, and then gradually became diluted by the inclusion of the lower-ranked competitors. After six or seven call-outs, the top four were done: they would not be compared to the lesser competitors. There was no need. It was worst of all for the five or six pros who were out of contention. They had to stand in line for an hour or so looking eager with no call-outs at all, until they got a token one or two at the end. They were happy to get offstage and hang about in the pump-up room as the second half of the pro show began.

Each competitor got three minutes onstage alone, with music that they provided themselves. Most popular was some kind of power ballad to open, to which they'd strike some slow, classical poses, immediately followed by gangsta rap or heavy metal. The black guys favoured rap. The Europeans loved their metal. Jackson and Cormier had been drawn numbers four and six. Dexter flashed his Eddie Murphy grin and posed to something called 'I've Come to Party'. He wasn't a big bodybuilder, but he had earned his nickname of 'The Blade'; his lines were sharp, his muscles were deeply separated and cut, he was idyllically proportioned. Cormier had a smoky charisma to him. He played to his ladies' man rep. He used 'It's Getting Hot in Here' as his music. Everyone had their own little party trick or signature pose. Tommy Thorvildsen performed a back flip from the standing position. Ernie Taylor incorporated martial arts kicks and did the splits. Claude Groulx knelt down with his head bowed and stretched out his arms to

PUMPING UP SOME PRIME BEEF:
GUNTER SCHLIERKAMP GRINS
AND BEARS IT BEFORE THE
BRITISH GRAND PRIX 2003

PREPARING ARMS:
JAY CUTLER READIES HIMSELF
FOR THE STAGE AT WEMBLEY
CONFERENCE CENTRE

RONNIE COLEMAN
UNVEILS HIS GALACTIC BACK

… AND FIRES UP
HIS FREAKY FRONT

GIVING IT SOME: JAY CUTLER OUTMUSCLES
MARKUS RUHL DURING PREJUDGING AT
THE ARNOLD CLASSIC 2003

RONNIE COLEMAN
AND KEVIN LEVRONE
GO TRICEP TO TRICEP

THE LINE-UP FOR THE FIRST COMPULSORY POSES,
MR OLYMPIA 2003

Posedown for the Mr Olympia 2003:
(*left to right*) Dexter, Ronnie, Jay, Gunter, Kevin and Dennis James flex it out

Don't try this at home:
Ernie Taylor at the British Grand Prix 2002

RONNIE AND JAY ARE CALLED OUT TOGETHER AT THE MR O 2003 –
DENNIS JAMES AND LEE PRIEST LOOK ON

POSEDOWN FOR THE BRITISH GRAND PRIX 2003: *(RIGHT TO LEFT)* GUNTER, JAY AND
ERNIE FIGHT IT OUT WITH TROY ALVES, MUSTAFA MOHAMMAD AND JOHNNY JACKSON

RONNIE COLEMAN SAYS A PRAYER AS HE HEARS THE RESULT OF MR OLYMPIA 2003

either side; he looked like Dali's *Christ of St John on the Cross*.

Jackson, James, Cormier and Taylor all performed powerfully. Jackson won the round, James was second while Cormier held off Ernie by just one point.

The judges simply ranked the competitors on a sheet of paper, awarding the best man one point, the second two and so on. It was a simple method in which the lowest score won. DeMilia had devised a system where the computer randomly selected one judge per round as an 'alternate', thus eliminating their score. It then removed the three highest and three lowest scoring judges. From the twelve judges, then, just five papers counted in any one round, and the judges were unaware of which they were. 'To fix a contest, definitely beyond a shadow of a doubt,' Wayne had told me, somewhat gleefully, 'you gotta buy off nine judges. I figured this out mathematically. You gotta buy off nine judges. In our sport, with all the big mouths and gossips and everything else, you think nine judges could keep their mouth shut? And let's face it, you go to nine judges and one says, "I don't wanna do it," you gotta go to number ten . . . You think that one other guy ain't gonna talk? "Hey, he tried to buy me off, I didn't take it. He didn't offer me enough money . . ." How much money is it gonna take?'

Backstage, another bodybuilder was pumping up. I'd seen him earlier and hadn't thought anything of it. He looked pretty much the same as all the others – big guy, warm-up suit, moving slowly (perhaps even more slowly than the rest) – but he wasn't. He was there to guest pose. Kerry introduced him to the crowd during the break between the free-posing round and the announcement of the top six finalists.

'When I first knew Simon Robinson, he was a lad trying to get a pro card,' Kerry said. 'He used to drive all the way from Mansfield to my gym in Manchester so I could check him over. Late one night I had a call from Simon's brother asking what time Simon had left the gym. He hadn't come home. Turns out there'd been a very bad car accident, and Simon was in a coma. Doctors had to amputate his right leg below the knee. A few days later, he had problems and it was amputated above the knee. His other leg was broken in nine places, and when it healed, it healed crooked so it had to be rebroken. He had broken ribs and internal injuries. When he came out of the coma, I had to tell him that he'd lost his leg. I said to him, "Be strong. Your family is outside and they need you to be a man." Simon looked up at me and nodded.

'When we first started running this Grand Prix in Manchester three years ago, Simon came to the show in a wheelchair. Two years ago, he came in on crutches. Last year, he walked in unassisted. Tonight, he's guest posing . . . Simon Robinson . . .'

It was an astonishing sight. He appeared from the back of the stage, swinging his hip to lift his artificial leg up the steps. As he neared the stage front and began his routine, everyone in the room stood up and acclaimed him. There were tears on his cheeks as he struck the poses. What a moment it was. His body was a marvel, even in a hall full of them. The circumference of his left thigh visibly exceeded that of the artificial one. His waist was tight and his shoulders and chest broad and thick. His arms were smoking. He was dry and hard and vascular. He was in contest shape, but he'd already won all of his contests. This was his valediction. The ovation went on long after the music stopped. Plenty of people in the audience were in tears along with him. They understood enough about training to know one thing: that they could never really understand what it was to be Simon Robinson.

That understanding was important – without it, it would have been just another made-for-TV moment. Every time bodybuilding challenged me to call it small-time, and irrelevant, and worse, it threw up something funny, or mad, or touching, or even redemptive, and this was one such thing. Unprompted and without prior arrangement, Dexter Jackson, Chris Cormier, Dennis James and Ernie Taylor walked out onstage and stood in line with Simon in the middle, the highest position. Kerry called them through the seven compulsory poses, and that night, Simon Robinson's circle was squared.

The twenty-two-man line-up was called back to the stage for the final time. They were each given a big medal. Then Wayne DeMilia read out the competitor numbers of the top six, in ascending order.

'Number four, step forward please . . .' Number four was Dexter Jackson.

'Number six, please . . .' Chris Cormier.

'Competitor eleven, please . . .' Claude Groulx.

'Number twelve, step forward please . . .' Dennis James.

'Competitor fifteen, please . . .' Tommy Thorvildsen. There was one place left. Ernie stared straight ahead and wondered if he was going to be stiffed again.

'And competitor seventeen . . .' A roar went up and Ernie smiled and stepped forward.

The unlucky sixteen trudged off. The top six stood on the line and ran through the compulsory poses once again, and then Wayne DeMilia called for the posedown. The music began and the six of them jumped from the stage and started to walk through down the aisles between the seats. People took pictures furiously. The bodybuilders dipped beneath this sea, but there were six distinct and random spots in the hall where flashbulbs popped. Men hurled themselves into the frame to get a snap of themselves with a pro. Women copped a feel where they could. At that moment it must have felt great to be a bodybuilder, some seconds of pure narcissism as people they had never met worshipped their bodies, objectified them in the purest sense. It was chaotic, but fun. Wayne eventually ordered them back to the stage. He called the results in reverse order. Tommy Thorvildsen was sixth. Claude Groulx was fifth. Ernie was fourth. It was the controversial decision for the evening. There was lots of booing, and Ernie looked rueful as he got his prize. Chris Cormier got third and Dennis James and Dexter Jackson joined hands for the announcement of second. James it was, and Dexter Jackson had his first pro win. A few more tears were spilled, but Jackson's body brooked no real argument. The Blade was a good champion to have.

Ernie had had a rough week. Fourteenth at the O, and now fourth behind a soft Chris Cormier. He was low. 'I thought Dexter won it fair enough, and me or Dennis should have got second,' he said quietly, once he was back in his warm-up suit. 'Chris Cormier was way out of it. At the moment, I don't want to do any more shows. What's the point if I'm getting marked down all the time? I'm not good friends with the judges and I don't live in the States. Things like that shouldn't matter.'

Dexter Jackson sympathised with Ernie. He told him his condition was 'awesome'. He said that Ernie had to hang in and he'd soon start placing better.

Ernie knew it was true. The evening hadn't been a write-off. He'd qualified for the next year's Mr O, and he'd proved he was a class above any of the other British athletes. All of his contracts would be safe.

I took a brief inventory of who was happy and who wasn't. Dexter was very happy. Dennis James was pretty happy, too: he'd beaten Chris Cormier, who'd finished seven places above him at the O. Claude Groulx was happy. He said he thought he'd looked the best he'd looked in six years as a pro. Tommy Thorvildsen was happy. He'd underperformed in Las Vegas, but now he had a top-six finish to build upon. Art Atwood said he'd learned a lot about competing from one week to the next. He'd also got his wife to ask Dorian what he felt he should do next. Dorian had told him to bring up his back and shoulders to balance himself out more, so Art had a blueprint from the very top.

Another man was going to the Mr Olympia, too. Wayne DeMilia, his pragmatism somehow both pricked and stirred, had invited Simon Robinson over to pose at the biggest show of all, as his personal guest.

Chris Cormier was most likely unhappy, but he'd performed well at the O and had probably peaked there. In addition, he was chasing Kerry around trying to make sure that his prize money was distributed to the wide variety of people who had claim on it. It was another chaotic night for Chris. Ernie could at least depart for a feast. He hadn't entered Dorian's Dutch Grand Prix, so that was his year done. The off-season beckoned him, with all of its food and its work.

I went to see Kerry to find out if he was happy, but he'd been overworked to the point of actual brain death. He was utterly drained. But he could see that the crowd were pleased. They'd come for muscle and they'd got it. Now all of that muscle was planning to pack up and leave for

Amsterdam, and elsewhere there was even more muscle on the move. In Arlington, Texas, Big Ron Coleman was preparing to board a flight to Holland, too – first class and paid for by Dorian Yates.

Mr O was on his way.

4

Big Ron Eats Breakfast

Dorian's girlfriend's hotel was towards the end of a thin street near Centraal station. The cab couldn't get all the way down there, so I walked the last bit. The hotel was called the Luxer and it was easy to find: it had a great throng of people standing around outside it, looking in through the windows. It was a beautiful old building, tall and slim and dark, with full-length glass doors. It was too narrow for a lobby as such; instead, the doors opened directly on to a bar. The check-in was at a small till on one end.

Dorian was standing near the entrance, and he beckoned me in. Lily, who was very beautiful, was allocating rooms to everyone. Chris Cormier was sitting at a table just inside the doors. He was with his girlfriend, and also Dexter Jackson and Dennis James. The crowd of people outside were staring in at them, and also at Dorian. Wayne DeMilia was there, too, and Kerry Kayes was at the other end of the bar with his wife, Jan. He told me that he was here 'on holiday', and he seemed to be enjoying sitting back and watching someone else do the work. I asked him if Ronnie Coleman had arrived yet, and he said, 'I dunno. I'm on holiday,' and he smiled a blissful smile to indicate that Big Ron wasn't his problem this time around.

It was late in the afternoon, two days before the show, and everything seemed slightly chaotic, which I was coming to realise was quite normal. Dorian had acquired the services of a man called Papa Mike, who was handling logistical stuff for the Grand Prix and dealing with people who couldn't speak English. He was a squat Dutch guy with a boxer's nose and he hugged everyone that he was introduced to. Papa Mike seemed to know most of the people who were standing outside the hotel trying to get in, as well as everyone who was inside.

Ronnie Coleman had indeed been seen at the Luxer. This was something of a coup for Dorian, and given the usual uncertainties that surrounded bodybuilding and bodybuilders, a great relief, too. Dorian had pulled out all the stops, he'd said to me before everyone went to Amsterdam. He'd begun negotiations with Coleman some months before. Big Ron had given a commitment to appear. Dorian had included him in all of the promotional literature; his face was on all of the flyers and posters. Big Ron gave the show some clout, and it needed some. There had been no Dutch Grand Prix for some years; Dorian and Lily had decided on a resurrection. Tempting Mr O overseas was a good start. But then they'd run into snags. Ronnie had suddenly said he wanted a first-class return flight from America, a ticket that cost several thousand dollars. Grand Prix promotions didn't run on margins of thousands of dollars. Dorian had got Ronnie on the phone and he'd done some straight-talking and now his successor as Mr Olympia was in Holland.

The next morning, things were quieter in the thin lounge at the Luxer. The barman was a middle-aged guy who had his hair in mini-dreadlocks, one of the thousands of strays who washed up in Amsterdam and then never went home. He was an evangelist for the city, letting everyone know which the best cafés were and where the prettiest girls sat in their windows in the red-light district.

At the far end of the bar was a small dining room into which the food arrived via a small hatch in one wall. Periodically, the barman would dive in and out of a door by the hatch and the bing of a microwave could be heard. There were no big fry-ups, though. These were bodybuilder breakfasts, great bowls of porridge mostly, and other heavy fuel. Most of them had begun carbing up for the show, a process that would make their armadas of muscle fill like galleons in sail.

And there he was, at the front table by the little steps that divided bar from dining room: Big Ron, five-time Mr O, fresh from the first-class lounge. He was sitting at a table for one on a low chair, which made him look even bigger, like a grown-up at a kids' tea party. On the table was an enormous plate and on the plate was Big Ron's breakfast of champions. It was a giant baked potato which he'd cut a cross in and then pushed together. Steam was rising out of it. He looked at it for a while and then poured a couple of sachets of ketchup into the middle of it. Next to it he had a bowl of steamed veg and some thin strips of dried meat. Big Ron began, dolefully, to fork dry potato into his mouth. He chewed it very slowly.

Bodybuilding reminded me a bit of heavyweight boxing before it got silly, with all the different world titles and belts and cable TV companies and fighters dodging each other. There was one champion and everyone recognised him, even if they moaned about the way he'd won his title. It was a truth universally acknowledged that Mr Olympia was the best bodybuilder in the world, even if he competed just once a year and didn't enter the other big tournaments like the Arnold Classic or the Night of Champions.

If Mr Olympia did venture out to a Grand Prix or two, it was a given that he would win: if he was going to get beaten, it would be onstage at the Olympia. Since 1984, only Lee Haney, Dorian Yates and Ronnie Coleman had held the title, and both Haney and Yates had vacated it safe in the knowledge that they had been the defining competitor of their age. Ronnie Coleman, though, had not enjoyed such security of tenure. He'd competed in nineteen shows as a pro before he won one, the 1997 Russian Grand Prix. After that win, he'd been sixth in the Hungarian Grand Prix, fifth in Germany, third in Finland, fifth at the British and fourth in the Czech Republic. It hardly made him favourite to take over from Dorian Yates as Mr Olympia.

His results in the big ones had been getting worse, rather than better. In the 1996 Mr O – his fourth – he broke into the top ten for the first time, finishing sixth. A year later, he was down to ninth. He'd got a second and a third at the Night of Champions in '95 and '96, losing to Nasser El Sonbaty and then Flex Wheeler. At the 1997 Arnold Classic, he was a distant fourth behind Wheeler, El Sonbaty and Michael François. When the 1998 season started without Dorian Yates, it was likely that the next Big O would perm any one of Kevin Levrone, Flex Wheeler or Shawn Ray, with Coleman in the next group down, a group that included Paul Dillett, Vince Taylor and Lee Priest.

Wheeler and El Sonbaty duked it out again at the Arnold in March '98, with the monstrous El Sonbaty edged out by Flex's orbs and ellipses for the second year in succession. In May, Coleman made his mark, outmuscling Kevin Levrone in an upset at the Night of Champions. Suddenly, Big Ron was the dark horse for the O itself.

He won it by three points from Flex Wheeler. Flex had been ahead after two rounds, but the big crowd favourite had been Nasser El Sonbaty, who gave them a feast of muscle – twenty stone of it. Nasser ended up third, Levrone fourth and Chris Cormier fifth.

It was not a definitive win. In '99, Big Ron was lucky to beat Flex Wheeler again. Levrone thought he'd beaten him twice, in 2000 and 2002. At the 2002 show, Levrone had won both of the evening rounds (a year on, at the Olympia press conference before the 2003 show, Coleman would chide Levrone, asking him, 'When was the last time you beat me?' Levrone replied, 'Last year.'). In 2001, Jay Cutler beat Ronnie in both the first two rounds and lost by four points.

Coleman had not replicated the dominance of Haney and Yates. He always seemed slightly vulnerable, protected as much by protocol as his physique. His best year was perhaps 2001, when he had become the first man to win the Arnold Classic and the Mr O in the same year.

One thing kept Big Ron out in front, and that was his size, pure and simple. He wasn't well proportioned. He wasn't symmetrical. But he was undoubtedly, indisputably enormous. And he was old – nearing forty now. In body-building, age – or at least muscle maturity – was an advantage. Deep, full muscle bellies came after year upon year of training laid thick fibres down like cable. Ronnie Coleman had been training for twenty-six years. None of his opponents could match that. When he stood next to them, there was something *extra* about him. He just seemed somehow larger, almost indefinably so. It appeared to come from the inside out, a subtle yet unmissable depth.

I saw it for myself, after he'd finished his breakfast. I jumped into the hotel's small lift, just as the doors were closing. Big Ron was already inside, with Chris Cormier and Dexter Jackson. The lift took eight people but we only just fitted. Chris and Dexter were big men, but Ronnie, he was something else. His arms were like legs. His back started somewhere out near his elbows and stretched like a field for several acres. His legs kept this super-structure upright, great bowed pylons. There was a powerful inward gravity about him. He was breathing effortfully. Chris and Dexter didn't bother looking at him, but I couldn't help it. He didn't seem to mind, or even notice. It must have happened to him all day, every day.

The funny thing was, Ronnie was a cop, or at least he had been until he became a three-time Mr O in 2000. He had stayed on the force in Texas as a reserve officer, working unpaid two days per month. There were lots of pictures of him grinning and bursting out of his uniform. He looked like two cops.

Having been a cop brought a problem for Big Ron, though, and it was an obvious one, *the* obvious one, the oldest one, the zugzwang. Anabolic steroids were controlled substances in America. Ronnie Coleman therefore maintained that he was natural. He'd been on the Jay Leno show and said so. This had of course provoked much mirth in bodybuilding circles. They had seen lots of natural bodybuilders. Natural bodybuilders had their own federations and competitions. They didn't look anything like pro bodybuilders. What they looked like were pro bodybuilders before they took any steroids and turned pro. Ronnie Coleman, though, was the king of the jungle, the biggest beast, the Baron of Beef. It was his USP, it's what had kept him, precariously, at the top of the heap. Down in Arlington, Texas, away from view, he walked around at a galactic 325 lb off-season.

The mass monsters who had grown up during the Era of the Freak were finding that 300 lb physiques came at a price. One of them was that when you took growth-promoting hormones, it was impossible to dictate exactly what grew. It wasn't just muscle. Doses of human growth hormone, for example, were known to cause bones to elongate and intestines and stomachs to grow.

The consumption of the sheer amount of food required to support such a body also increased the size of the stomach. As a result, the great new plague of modern bodybuilding was the 'gut', a gross distension of the belly that was very visible when the athletes were in contest shape. It was nothing to do with body fat. The abdominal muscles, the steely six-packs, were still in full view. It was to do with what was deeper inside, a growth of the stomach and intestines. Wayne DeMilia and Peter McGough had both acknowledged the problem. Some of the guys just couldn't hold it in. And poor old Ronnie Coleman often looked like he'd swallowed an armadillo.

There was another new phenomenon in bodybuilding, too, to go with the guts. There had been a rise of the guru. There weren't many gurus, but they were becoming the thing to have as a pro bodybuilder. What exactly they did was opaque, filed under the general heading of contest preparation. Really, they were there to deliver their man to the stage ripped and dry and huge.

All of the gurus had their own methods and theories and voodoos on how it was done. Coleman had been working with a guru, a man named Chad Nicholls. Nicholls kept his technical secrets under wraps, too, but he was a vociferous online presence, running a popular Internet site called Muscle Mayhem. He also often became involved in message board scraps, bulletin board bust-ups that aired lots of dirty secrets. During one, a vicious row with a bodybuilder called Milos Sarcev about the use of drugs called plasma expanders, he let something slip about Ronnie Coleman. He wrote: 'The '98 NOC [Night of Champions] was the first year I worked with Ronnie – we didn't use ANY PE [plasma expanders] – Manitol – special blends – Albumin – NOTHING. We used the diuretic that I use today – except back then it was a little different version than now – a little stronger and faster, which is something that has been changed over the years.'

Coleman was actually incidental to the argument, but it was a revealing aside. Nicholls also laid into Shawn Ray, who had named him publicly as a 'drug guru'. Nicholls had replied: 'To be real honest with you – I don't really have a problem with it because I am an adviser in a sport that revolves around drugs. So, yes, I advise athletes on nutrition, training and, yes, supplementation. So, I guess there are drug gurus and drug users – I guess that makes me the drug guru and you the drug user.'

Ultimately, the spat had become so violent and damaging that Peter McGough had made a very rare public intervention and called them to order. Within a few days, it was forgotten. Allegiances shifted, as they always seemed to, and everyone carried on.

There was one other drug myth, though, and it was that every pro took lots of gear. Kerry Kayes had explained it best to me the very first time we'd met, at the Wembley Plaza hotel. It was all to do with genetics. 'Imagine,' he said, 'that you were born with two little bricklayers inside you, to build your muscles.' Then he gestured at Dorian. 'Now, Dorian was born with seven little bricklayers inside him. So you could take a lot of gear, and now you've got five little bricklayers inside you. But Dorian's still got seven . . .'

For obvious reasons, very few pros were open about their usage, but those who were laughed at the amounts they were said to take. Lee Priest, a man who probably packed more muscle on his frame per square inch than anyone, used a very light cycle of anabolics.

It wasn't the men at the top who had to; they were the genetically blessed, touched by the gods of muscle. It was the strugglers underneath who dabbled with dosages.

Ronnie Coleman might not have been natural, but he was *a* natural, blessed, gifted, touched. By the age of thirteen, people were asking him if he worked out; he didn't and he had to keep saying no, but it got him thinking, 'Damn, how big would I get if I *did* work out?' He was a savant for the weights, he was born with rare strength. He got big. He went to college, and qualified in accountancy. He got bigger. He joined the police force. He got bigger still. Brian Dobson, from the MetroFlex gym in Arlington, encouraged him to enter bodybuilding shows. MetroFlex was a hardcore place, a lifters' gym. Their claim was that 'year in, year out we produce more champions than all the fitness centres combined'. Dobson had a great physique himself: he pumped what he preached. He opened up the gym 365 days a year.

Ronnie won his first ever show in 1990. He became Mr Texas. Thus began his slow ascendancy. He cried the day he quit the police force, but there was no way he could stay. Being Mr O was a full-time job, and it paid more than $500,000 a year. The Texas Police Force paid $46,000. He cried every time he won the Olympia, too. He was known

101

for throwing himself on the ground and sobbing, and then making long and rambling speeches to the crowd in praise of God and his mom, who had raised him alone and remained his staunchest fan.

He'd made a famous training video at MetroFlex, called 'The Unbelievable', which showed him working out with extreme weight. 'The Unbelievable' and a tape of one of Dorian's workouts at the Temple gym called 'Blood and Guts' were the two bodybuilders' videos that the fans loved best. Followers of Ronnie were hardcore guys. They revelled in his strength and size, and didn't concern themselves with aesthetics.

Now Holland was waiting for Big Ron and all of that muscle he brought with him. It was the morning of the show. I'd been out for a walk around Dam Square and when I got back to the Luxer, the crowd at the doorway had returned. Inside, at the bar, things were happening. Lily was covering two huge trays of sandwiches. She and Chris Cormier's girlfriend had got changed into halter tops and tight bolero trousers. Dorian's face was screen-printed on to the clothes, right over their breasts and backsides. I looked at Dorian and he had a thin smile on his face. His sense of humour was as dust dry as he used to be on Mr Olympia day.

As the coach couldn't get up the narrow street outside the Luxer, it had parked up in a bus stop outside Centraal station. Slowly, a stately group of the world's best bodybuilders, former bodybuilders, officials and girls in uniforms with Dorian Yates's face covering their secondary sexual characteristics walked out of the Luxer and towards Centraal. Slowest of all, right at the back and on his own, with a big holdall over his shoulder came Ronnie

Coleman. He was wearing a blue sweatshirt with 'SFPD' written on it. He moved at the pace of man who knew that the world wasn't going anywhere without him. It was a late-autumn day with a cold, high sun. The light in Amsterdam was celestial; it poured down. It was remarkably beautiful. Each time a bodybuilder went up the steps of the coach, it rocked on its suspension. I got a seat at the front, and Ronnie Coleman sat down right behind me. The coach was going to Haarlem for the Dutch Grand Prix. Haarlem was a town about a forty-minute ride from central Amsterdam. Dorian had said he hadn't been able to fix up a suitable hall in Amsterdam itself, but that was OK, the show was self-contained. The show was arriving by bus. I leaned over the back of my seat and said to Ronnie Coleman, 'There'd be a few pro bodybuilders pretty happy if this coach ran off the road and went up in flames . . .'

He smiled. He knew it. Two weeks ago, he'd won his fifth Olympia and he seemed to be at the head of a new world order. He had taken care of the Flex Wheelers and the Shawn Rays and the Kevin Levrones. The new usurpers were young and huge, new Freaks for the Era of the Freak. There was Jay Cutler, a blond behemoth not even out of his twenties and already pushing 270 lb sliced and diced. And Gunter Schlierkamp, who was probably going to be the first man over 300 lb in contest shape. Gunter had been the star of the Olympia, only placing as low as fifth, Wayne DeMilia had said 'because the judges just lost him in the first round'. By the time they'd found him again, he was a long way back. They wouldn't be losing Gunter next time, though. Dexter 'The Blade' Jackson, sitting at the back of the bus, had just picked up his first win. Dennis James, sitting right next to him, was figuring out the best way to get all his beef in shape for show day, and once he did, he would become a match for anyone. This was the new shape of things, the new mass, the gathering momentum.

Ronnie's voice was wide and southern-fried. His cadences were heavy. He was all long vowels and mushy consonants. He put his hands up on the seat back in front of him. His palms were broad and square. He had big yellow-white calluses from gripping iron bars. His energy levels seemed low. He'd dieted a long time for the Olympia, he said, for more than three months. He was keeping the diet going because he'd entered a new contest that was debuting in a week's time in New Orleans. It was called the Show of Strength and the sponsors had put up a huge purse, almost as big as the O. The word was that they'd wanted to top the Olympia for prize money, but the IFBB wouldn't allow them to. The winner of the Show of Strength would get $100,000. Big Ron had his eyes on the prize. Dexter, Chris Cormier and Dennis James had entered, too, and so had Gunter Schlierkamp.

We began to talk about what Big Ron was going to eat when the New Orleans show was over. 'Cheesecake, man,' he said, looking out of the window of the bus and into the celestial light. 'Cheesecake's my number-one thing. Then any junk food, get as much of it as I can. 'Bout a month after the show, though, I have to slack it off again, get real.' He paused for a while. 'But pizza . . . hamburger . . . All that, I love that,' he said.

'What's it like having a potato for breakfast?'

'That potato was all right,' he said. 'Lots of sugar in a potato, you see. Carbs me up. We can't keep talkin' about food . . .'

We talked about his trips to Europe instead. Since he'd been Mr O, he'd come over and won the British Grand Prix twice. He closed his eyes and said, 'It's no big deal. We come over and show the people what we do, so they don't have to come on over to us. Y'know, it's the joy of my life, really. Winning Mr Olympia . . . being Mr Olympia . . . it's something I really, really enjoy. I can't put it into words, what it is, but I been workin' out for twenty-six years, and I never in a million years thought I'd be Mr Olympia. I didn't know I had what it takes for that. I got a big-time love for it. Making money at it don't hurt . . .'

He didn't care about his critics, either. 'I've won by two points, four points or whatever . . . You only gotta win by *one* point, man,' he said. 'An' if you wanna beat the Mr Olympia, you gotta knock him right out, you know? You gotta knock the champ out, like boxing.

'I wanna go as far as I can go. I just gotta wait, see how it pans out. Five is pretty tough. If I can get six, I'll be just as happy. I would cherish that if it came to me. Seven, eight, who knows, man? Who knows what's gonna come along. You're competing against the best in the world, fifteen, twenty-five of them and they're all good because they gotta qualify. Only God knows what's gonna happen . . .'

I was pretty sure that Ronnie knew he was going to win the Dutch Grand Prix, though. As we rolled into Haarlem, Dorian came and sat at the front of the coach. Ronnie had gone to sleep, with his arms folded over his chest and his shoulder against the window. He snored gently. The show was at a big leisure centre. The coach had to travel right round it to get to the car park by the stage entrance. Dorian stood up and got the driver to open the doors. There was a kid who was trying to direct him into a small lane in the car park. 'This right?' Dorian said to him. The kid began talking to him in Dutch. Dorian was peeved. 'No, no, speak English, man,' he said and he stepped down from the coach and stood in front of the kid. All of a sudden he looked huge again. It was amazing how he could do that. It was like he was back inside the Tardis warm-up suit. He seemed to be able to change the impression of his size whenever he wanted to. The kid got on the coach and steered the driver to the right spot. He did it in English, so that Dorian could understand him, too. Someone woke Ronnie Coleman, and everyone filed inside.

All of the bodybuilders had shuffled off somewhere to get ready for prejudging. There was a small expo in one of the ante-rooms of the sports centre. I found a copy of *A Warrior's Story: A Portrait Of Dorian Yates*, a book Dorian had written with Peter McGough. I'd been looking out for it, but it seemed quite hard to find. It had a sticker on it that said 'last one'. It cost 34.10 euros, which seemed a bit steep, but I bought it anyway. The crowd grew. Inside the arena, Dorian and Lily had laid on a terrific show. The stage was wide and deep and it had a big screen to one side which had a laser show on it. In front of the stage were large dining tables for the VIP guests, laden with fruit and wine.

The competitors came out into the pump-up room. It was small and they were big, so they were shoulder to shoulder in there. Claude Groulx was lying on the floor talking to his wife. Dexter Jackson ate a crisp. Chris Cormier and Dennis James were getting oiled up and checking each other over. Chris contracted his muscles a few times in the mirror and then shook himself loose. Ronnie Coleman hadn't yet arrived. The atmosphere was very relaxed, different to how it had been at Wembley. Perhaps Ronnie Coleman was the cause. The result was a given, at least in terms of first place.

The crowd didn't care. Plenty of them were staring through the fire doors near the pump-up room, trying to get an early look. They were talking excitedly in guttural Dutch. Some of them shouted the names of the competitors.

It was a pretty big field, eighteen entrants. There were two Dutch guys, Giovanni Thompson, who had been drawn right after Ronnie Coleman and would have to follow him onstage for the posing round, and Ed van Amsterdam, a big, blocky athlete with a bulldog jaw and little blond kiss-curl that made him look like Buzz Lightyear. Ed was always smiling. There was also Alison Maria, who competed under the Curaçao flag, but lived in Amsterdam. They got ready to walk to the stage. Ronnie Coleman had arrived quietly and joined the back of the little crush in the pump-up room. Wayne DeMilia told them 'two minutes' and wished everyone a good show.

The arena was full, and the crowd were raucous, ready for some muscle. They were the usual mix of big guys and their girls. Dorian came out and spoke to the crowd. They crowed at him, yelled his name and shouted 'Beef!' which came out like 'B-HOEEF!' It was a traditional cry. 'Where's Ronnie?' someone shouted. 'Don't worry,' Dorian said into the mike. 'Ronnie's here . . .' and everyone cheered and whooped. Wayne DeMilia called the line-up to the stage and the crowd went off again, standing up, craning, looking for Big Ron. The Americans came out in the middle of the line, like royalty: Dexter, Dennis, Chris and, between them, Mr O. Ronnie gave them his trademark wave, which involved raising both of his arms above his head, palms facing the ceiling, and pumping them up and down. He got the first call-out from Wayne, of course, with Chris and Dexter.

Ronnie stood in the middle, dwarfing Dexter, who was shorter as well as noticeably leaner. Dexter was crisp and dry, but the fans weren't that bothered by his thin waist and cubed abs, whatever the price he'd paid for them. Not when the biggest man in the world was labouring through the compulsory poses next to him. Ronnie was nowhere near Dexter's condition, but he had so much muscle it looked like it was hanging off him. His great lats seemed to droop round by his hips. Thick teardrops of molten beef dripped heavily from his thighs. His bottom lip poked out as he concentrated on contracting his body.

On the other side of him, Chris Cormier was less comprehensively outsized. His condition had come on since Wembley. When he turned to the rear, you could see the large Gothic cross tattooed on the back of his neck and down between his shoulder blades. It had someone's name underneath in script, and two dates. It was a memorium in flesh, etched into one of the world's greatest bodies. It was some testament. Chris was bold and confident, even next to Ronnie Coleman. Each time Ronnie hissed out air and hit a pose, Chris would smile at him.

Ronnie was back in line after a couple of call-outs. Big Ron stood semi-tense, breathing heavily. He kept towelling sweat from his shaven head with a white cloth. He drank water from a large bottle. He looked up at the ceiling several times. He appeared tired and unfit. His stomach was pretty big. Dorian had told me that it was permanently uncomfortable hauling all of that bulk about. The heart was working hard. So was the metabolism and the digestive system. It was all high maintenance in there. Dorian had taken Ronnie to a restaurant near the Luxer. He said that Ronnie had struggled with the walk there.

In the break between the prejudging and the posing round, everyone hung around the pump-up room. Ronnie seemed a little more comfortable. A guy had cornered him and was talking about a complicated workout system that involved attaching electrode pads to the muscles and passing a current through them to make them contract. The wearer didn't actually have to move at all while this was happening.

'You use that?' he asked Ronnie.

Ronnie glared at him in astonishment. He looked down at his vast body. 'Nope,' he said, and walked off.

There were a couple of female police officers there, too. They were talking to Giovanni Thompson, who was laughing and letting them feel his muscles. Chris, Dennis and Dexter stood about quietly, allowing everyone by the fire doors to stare at them and take pictures. Someone brought in the trays loaded with sandwiches. The season was almost over: within five minutes the sandwiches were gone. Lily came back with two boxes filled with the competitors' medals and trophies. Markus Ruhl, the huge and amiable German who'd had to withdraw from the British Grand Prix with food poisoning had arrived to say hello. He lay on the floor eating crisps and telling everyone he felt better.

The posing round began. Tommy Thorvildsen was first. He did his back flip and everyone cheered. Chris Cormier was third on, and he performed his 'Hot in Here' routine again. His girlfriend stood in the wings with her Dorian Yates uniform on.

Ronnie was number eight. He came out to James Brown's 'Payback'. He was an incredible sight. He didn't move particularly well – how could he? – but his poses contained great power and he held each one for a long time. When the music had finished, he just carried on. He got down from the stage and went into the crowd. There was a brief period of mayhem before he got back to the stage. Everyone shouted 'Beef! Beef!' and he walked off.

There was a terrific buzz in the hall. Mr O gave bang for his first-class buck. Giovanni Thompson had to follow him.

The show might have fallen flat, but inspiration had struck Gio Thompson: he came out handcuffed to the two women police officers he'd been flirting with backstage. He was wearing one of their caps. Everyone laughed and cheered. It was great. He broke free of the cuffs and everyone cheered again.

Ronnie won, of course. He got his prize from Lily and Chris Cormier's girlfriend, and he made one of his emotional speeches. He asked the crowd if they wanted him back next year, and they yelled and screamed, so he said that he would come. Chris was second, Dexter third and Dennis James fourth. Giovanni Thompson was fourteenth.

I walked back to the coach with Kerry. It was late. He was pleased for Dorian. The show had been a great success. Dorian had presented Kerry with a framed memento of the day, too. Their partnership was going well. When everyone had got on board, Dorian jumped up and did a headcount. There was no way back to Amsterdam for anyone who missed the bus and we were one person short. People were trying to work out who it was.

'Where's Ronnie?' Kerry asked eventually. No one knew. Kerry nudged me and said, 'See, bodybuilders, mate . . . What did I tell you?'

After about five minutes somebody found him, and everyone cheered and clapped when he came up the steps of the bus. He was smiling and still holding his trophy, and he seemed energised by the show. He had a gleam in his eye as we drove back to Amsterdam along dark streets, a big bus with all the muscle in the world inside it.

Next morning, there were no crowds outside the door of the Hotel Luxer. Dexter Jackson was sitting at the bar on his own. The barman with the mini-dreadlocks was back. There had been an early flight to America which lots of people had taken. Most were headed for New Orleans and the Show of Strength. So was Dexter, actually. He didn't sound like he was planning to come back to Amsterdam.

'You didn't like it?' the barman said, astonished. 'Man, you the first *man* I ever heard say that. Why didn't you like it?'

'Man, issa *smell*,' said Dexter. He was from the South, too, like Ronnie Coleman. Each word took him about a second to say. 'Smell from them cafés and bars, man. Everywhere I go, dope is all I can smell. Mind, I got some friends would like that . . . But I don't like it.'

He was right, too. Amsterdam stunk of skunk, just as advertised.

'But we free here,' said the barman, who was still evangelical for the place. 'It's a free society, man.'

'That ain't necessarily good,' said Dexter.

'At least we don't kill people here. No death penalty, man.'

'Shit, man,' Dexter said. 'Maybe some people *need* killing.'

The barman went into a long explanation of Dutch homicide law, which apparently distinguished between something called a 'Big Kill' and something else called a 'Little Kill'. Dexter looked sceptical.

'Well, big or little, you still dead,' he said, which was indisputably true. He went quiet for a moment. 'I ain't seen any place that's better to live than America, and I been everywhere,' he said, and got ready to fly home.

Six days later, Gunter Schlierkamp beat Ronnie Coleman at the Show of Strength in New Orleans. It was the biggest shock that anyone in bodybuilding could remember. It was the first time that a reigning Mr Olympia had ever been

111

defeated at a contest other than the Mr Olympia. Lots of people said that Ronnie should have won. Lots of other people said that he'd had it coming. But no one knew for sure, because there had been only a few hundred people at the show to see it happen. Ronnie had gone back to Texas muttering darkly about the result.

After his appearances at the Olympia and now the GNC Show of Strength, Gunter Schlierkamp had become the new sensation in pro bodybuilding. He had appeared onstage in New Orleans at 300 lb. He'd outmuscled the biggest man in the world and won himself $100,000. He had started something called 'Guntermania'.

No one seemed sure of the precise implications of the result yet. What was clear was that Mr Olympia was more vulnerable than ever before.

The GNC Show of Strength had made one man even happier than Gunter Schlierkamp. Wayne DeMilia was back in his office planning the biggest Mr Olympia show of all time. As the off-season came and everyone went home and ended their diets and ate and ate, you could almost hear him singing.

5

Arnie; Arnold; The Arnold

It's 1976. Dorian Yates is thirteen years old. Ronnie Coleman is eleven. Andreas Munzer is ten. Gunter Schlierkamp is seven. Jay Cutler is four. A young photographer called George Butler has hired the nearest screening room to Gold's gym at Venice Beach. He has taken all of the bodybuilders from Gold's to look at the first 35 mm print of *Pumping Iron*, the film he had just made about them. It's one of those perfect southern California evenings, when it doesn't seem right to live anywhere else in the world. The screening is over. The sun is dropping down towards the Pacific Ocean and it illuminates the bodybuilders in this beautiful amber light, this horizontal light. George Butler, who has a movie-maker's eye for a shot, appreciates the moment. And then, one by one, the bodybuilders come up to him and say:

'George, you've *fucked us* . . .'

Twenty-seven years on, George Butler laughed at the memory and said: 'They went, "This is the worst piece of *shit* we've ever seen." What they were really saying was, "this isn't the way we see ourselves at all. This is not the way

113

eider sees us. This is not the way the magazines ortray us." For about two weeks I lived in dread. And then *Time* magazine wrote a big article, and it was in the national press and suddenly they all realised that maybe I hadn't screwed them and they all loved it . . .'

I'd contacted George Butler because he and his friend Charles Gaines were kind of responsible for modern bodybuilding. Or, at least, they were responsible for making Arnold Schwarzenegger into a star, and Arnold and Joe Weider, who had also derived great benefit from the *Pumping Iron* book and movie, were responsible for modern bodybuilding.

And although it was twenty-three years since he had been Mr Olympia, and Lee Haney had managed to win the title more times than he had, and that now even the fifteenth-placed freak at the Mr O would make him look decidedly non-freaky, Arnold Schwarzenegger was still the best-known bodybuilder on earth. In fact, he was probably the only bodybuilder anyone outside of the sport had ever heard of, with the possible exception of his adversary Lou Ferrigno, the Incredible Hulk. And despite everything that had happened to him since, and despite the public's view of the sport as a weird little backwater, Schwarzenegger had remained involved with it. He fronted the Arnold Classic. He kept up a relationship with Joe Weider and he some-times gave interviews to *Flex* magazine when he wouldn't talk to the *New York Times*.

It was a golden time, as they all remembered it. Charles Gaines had an assignment to cover a small bodybuilding event in Holyoke, Massachusetts, for *Sports Illustrated* magazine. It was spring 1972. He'd just published a novel called *Stay Hungry*, which was about a small-town bodybuilding gym under threat from a property development syndicate. George Butler, who had grown up in East Africa and Jamaica, went along to shoot the pictures. What they found up in Holyoke was something strange and extraordinary. George Butler took a photograph that day that still hangs on his office wall. It was of a bodybuilder called Leon Brown, who was the reigning Mr East Coast and who worked in a Chinese laundry. 'It's a perfectly flexed back,' Butler said, 'and his arms are outstretched horizontally to the ground and all of his back muscles are flexed. It's like looking at a weird flying object. There's little motion or vibration in the picture and it has this wonderful kinetic energy to it.'

Butler took another zingy reportage shot a few months later, on 16 September, backstage at a bodybuilding contest in Brooklyn. There are four competitors in the frame, all looking at someone or something out of shot. Three of them are diminished by the fourth, Arnold Schwarzenegger, who appears to be floating as he pushes himself up on the backs of two wooden chairs. George told me that it was the first print of Schwarzenegger that he could remember developing in his darkroom. The *Village Voice* published it the following week, and it was the first time, as far as anyone could make out, that Arnold had appeared in the mainstream media.

Gaines and Butler had found their subject. From Arnold, human essence flowed. He had an awesome physicality, but he had more than that. He was lively, funny, clever, cruel, quick, brave, egotistical and, above all, he was rapaciously ambitious. The life force poured from him. He had been Mr Olympia for three years. Long before he was the Predator and Conan the Barbarian, a decade before he became the Terminator, he was the Austrian Oak, an indelible vision of

115

human perfection. George Butler saw it, and so did Charles Gaines, but they didn't see it as Joe Weider did, or as the bodybuilding fans did, or even as the bodybuilders themselves did.

'We discovered that, if you begin with Egyptians, go to the Greeks, go to the Romans, go to Michelangelo, right through the history of Western art, you'll discover that there's a tremendous interest in the musculature of the male body,' George Butler said. 'So we may have been far out, but we weren't that far off the main line of what interests people. We really thought we were on to something. We were watching, and saying, there's no one else in the world who's watching. No one else in the world.'

You kind of had to believe in destiny, or fate or history. Arnold almost uncannily paralleled the character of Joe Santo in Gaines's novel *Stay Hungry*. It was as if Charles had received advanced cosmic warning of him. Gaines and Butler liked Schwarzenegger not just because he was huge and fitted with some Platonic ideal of manhood. They liked him because he was unlike anyone else in all of bodybuilding, or in anything else at all. Arnold told them about a recurring dream that he had. In the dream, he was King of all of the Earth, and everyone looked up to him.

He was living in a small condominium in Santa Monica with his girlfriend Barbara Outland and he'd been in America for four years, hanging about at Venice Beach, working for Joe Weider and waiting to get noticed. George Butler recalled that Arnold was also attending night school and had drawn up something he called 'The Master Plan'.

'It was kind of a campy mix of Nietzsche and a Soviet five-year plan, only it was more of a fifty-year plan,' Butler recalled. 'He wanted to be very big. My own particular view is that he had it in his mind to be President of the United

116

States, King of the Universe. Probably if there are extraterrestrials out there, he'd like to rule them as well.'

Arnold had laid out the Master Plan for Butler and Gaines. 'I will come to America which is the country for me. Once here I will become the greatest bodybuilder' – with his accent he said it 'baddybuilder' and still does – 'in history. While I am doing this I will learn perfect English and educate myself, but only with those things I need to know. I will get a college degree and then a business degree. I will invest in real estate and make big money. I will go into the movies. By the time I am thirty I will have starred in my first movie and I will be a millionaire. I will marry a beautiful and successful wife. By the time I am thirty-two, I will have been invited to the White House.'

To Arnold, the Master Plan was as clear and as tangible as his recurring dream. To George Butler, it would have been absurd but for one thing: Schwarzenegger had already begun to accomplish the goals he had listed for himself. The idea that anyone might succeed in Hollywood via their muscles was an unlikely one, but then, everything about bodybuilding was unlikely.

'What he did do, clearly,' Butler said, 'was choose the hardest path to fame and fortune that any potential Hollywood star ever chose. *To become King of Hollywood through your muscles?* I mean, give me a break. He'd been in Los Angeles for four straight years trying to claw his way beyond the beach. No one would give him the time of day.'

Butler and Gaines went to Sandy Richards, who was the editor-in-chief of Doubleday, a New York publisher, and explained their idea for a book on bodybuilding. Gaines's novel was becoming quite successful. Butler had published a well-received book on Vietnam. They were on the up. Richards decided to give them a deal for the bodybuilding book, which he didn't get at all, with a view to them doing something 'more serious' for him afterwards.

Butler and Gaines were serious, though. They had drawn a straight line through time that connected the mighty body of Arnold Schwarzenegger with a long-established male ideal. They had felt the kinetic buzz of connecting with a story that no one else in the whole world could see. They had ideas and notions about the meaning of manhood and of muscle that didn't appear in Joe Weider's magazines. They had their Nietzschean anti-hero with the Master Plan, and he brought them his supporting cast.

Arnold had a sidekick and foil called Franco Columbu, a tough Italian who could never quite match his master on the show stage. There was Mike Katz, who had built a giant body in response to being bullied as a skinny kid; Ed Corney, a bouncer who'd first gone to a gym to become a bigger bouncer; Ken Waller, a pro football player; Frank Zane, a health freak who'd grown and grown into a real freak.

'It was an entirely unselfconscious, unformed sport,' said George Butler. 'What Gaines and I were able to do was define the sport with the book. And what we had was a wonderful collision of highly colourful characters who were willing to cooperate with us and we were sort of all in it together.'

Arnold didn't really care what Butler and Gaines's angle was. What he liked was the fact that they were able to place stories in *Sports Illustrated* and *Village Voice* and mainstream magazines like that. It couldn't hurt the Master Plan to appear there.

'I think he saw those early times – still sees them – as a period of innocence and fun before he became quite the huge star he's become, which as you know has its pressures

118

as well as its advantages. It would be a tremendously burdensome thing,' Charles Gaines said. 'All of us were young and relatively well off and it was sort of a golden time. And more importantly, we were all contributing to the outing of a phenomenon, which was really quite special and interesting and wonderful – that nobody knew about. We were in on a secret; this thing was going to be enjoyed by everybody if we could just get it out there, so there was a sense of collaboration and of working on something important together. A sense of energy and great fun and brio.'

Gaines was speaking from his home in Alabama. He had another, too, in Nova Scotia, a farmhouse that he'd built himself in the Canadian wilds and then written a great book about. He didn't write about bodybuilding any more, he said, although people had asked him to. He felt too divorced from it. He'd watched friends of his lose out in the steroid wars; livers had given way, testicular cancer had afflicted some, there had been lots of other horrors. They'd got too big, too. The straight line from Michelangelo to Mike Katz had fractured long before it reached Ronnie Coleman.

He no longer felt the hot buzz of connection to the story, and that seemed slightly sad because he'd been a bodybuilder since he was a kid, thirteen or fourteen years old, when he had a friend called Johnny Gunn and another called Fred Crab who had a load of weights in the basement of his parents' house.

Johnny Gunn would say to him, 'Gaines, let's go pump iron' – 'Only he said it "A-R-O-N", that was his accent . . . so Johnny Gunn and I started pumping iron. We'd say, "We're pumping iron on Friday," that was our phrase for it. As far as I know, Johnny Gunn entirely invented it.'

Gaines ended up with what he described as 'a huge upper body', but could never quite get ripped and he had skinny

119

calves and insufficient genes. Also, he said, 'becoming a bodybuilder would have been a wildly incongruous thing to do given the social circumstances I grew up in here in Alabama. Though I was no stranger to being rebellious, it's not something I would have done.'

In October 1972, Butler and Gaines went to Iraq to cover the Mr Universe contest for *Life* magazine. The entire general staff of the Iraqi army turned up at Baghdad airport at two thirty in the morning to welcome Mike Katz, who was Mr America.

'It looked like a sight out of *The Arabian Nights*,' said George Butler. 'When Mike got off the plane – and he was a very big man – each general and colonel and field marshal, and I'm sure to this day that Saddam Hussein was there, would come up with their British military swagger stick and they'd sort of tap Mike Katz on his pectoral muscle and then burst into the biggest smile you've ever seen. Mike was Jewish and this was quite the confrontation of cultures.'

Butler and Gaines and Katz and the other bodybuilders had the most extraordinary time in Iraq. In America, body-building happened in places like Holyoke, Massachusetts, and no one knew about it. In Iraq, 15,000 people tried to gain entry to the movie theatre where the Mr Universe contest was held. George Butler took pictures of guys trying to tear off the doors and climb in through the windows, and of rows of men two-hundred-deep in the hot streets outside. Iraq was at war with Syria at the time, but the war stopped for the Mr Universe contest because it was shown live on television across the Middle East. A few days after the show, Butler took the bodybuilders to the Hanging Gardens of Babylon and photographed them there, and they all wondered at the world as they stood on the time line that connected them to history.

When George Butler got off the plane in Thurrock on the way back to New York, he stopped at the news-stand and the headline on the *Herald Tribune* said: LIFE MAGAZINE FOLDS. The pictures he took in Iraq were never published. But Butler wasn't easily discouraged. 'We'd had a fantastic time in Baghdad, and no one has ever been treated better than we were there. And all over the Middle East we discovered that bodybuilding was a national sport – Egypt, Israel, Lebanon, Persia . . . So we were sort of zeroing in on the popularity of bodybuilding abroad as well as the hidden popularity of bodybuilding in America.'

Then George Butler mortgaged his house and spent $30,000 of his own money making a test film of Arnold Schwarzenegger because he thought that Arnold should be in the movies. He shot some terrific footage and convened a hundred or so potential investors at a screening in the Townsend studios in Manhattan. Most of the audience had never heard of Schwarzenegger and they laughed when he came on camera. When he stripped and oiled himself up, someone groaned loudly. Butler had given everyone a photocopied sheet of information and he was about to deliver a pitch that he'd rehearsed endlessly when someone in the crowd ('a prize-winning writer') stood up and said: 'George, don't go any further. We're all your friends and if you ever put this oaf on the screen you'll be laughed off 42nd Street.'

Butler and Gaines submitted their manuscript for *Pumping Iron* to Sandy Richards at Doubleday shortly after Butler's humiliation at the Townsend studios.

'There was a breathtaking silence,' Butler remembered, 'and then he wrote us a letter saying, "You guys cheated me, I want my money back, the book is ridiculous and no one's ever going to pay any attention to Arnold Schwarzenegger, ever. My salesmen can't sell it, no one will buy this book, give me my money back," and he was very rude about it.'

The letter, in part, read: *No one in America will buy a book of pictures of these half-unclothed men of dubious sexual pursuits.*

*

Columbus, Ohio, in February wasn't the America of Arnold Schwarzenegger's dreams. It was flat and minerally cold. It had bare winter trees along its straight, plain roads. It had cabs that had run around their clocks three times. They coughed along and sloughed the snow into grey piles at the kerbsides. The light was low and grey, too. Under a permanent soft dusk, Columbus prepared for the Arnold Classic 2003. Kerry had given me the name of a hotel to check into but I couldn't afford it, so I was staying at a Holiday Inn by a freeway ramp halfway between the airport and the city. Outside, the snow had become sleet. I read the little brochure in the hotel room about Columbus. The town had one famous son, the golfer Jack Nicklaus, who hosted a tournament there each year. The reason that the Arnold Classic was in Columbus was because of Jim Lorimer. He had been the promoter of a show called Mr Pro World and in 1970 he persuaded Arnold Schwarzenegger to enter the contest. Arnold had just competed in London and so Lorimer laid on a private jet to pick him up from his commercial flight to New York and bring him to Ohio. Schwarzenegger won Mr Pro World. He received a $500 cheque, an electric watch and he was interviewed by ABC Television. Expanding his Master Plan on the spot, Schwarzenegger took Jim Lorimer aside and told him: 'Some day I am going to stop competing and I'm going into promoting. I'm going to raise cash prizes to over $100,000.

122

And when I retire from competing I am going to come back to Columbus and ask you to be my partner.'

By 1976, they were promoting Mr Olympia together. The Arnold Classic began in 1989. First prize in the men's bodybuilding in 2003 was $100,000. But the Classic was no longer just a bodybuilding show. It had a strongman contest, female bodybuilding and fitness and figure shows, arm-wrestling and bench-press and other strength competitions, a five-kilometre 'pump and run' and a fitness expo that took up a huge hall in the Columbus Greater Convention Center. The Arnold Classic lasted for three days and about 100,000 people came each year. Columbus liked Arnold Schwarzenegger very much indeed. He had repaid his gratitude to Lorimer and Columbus many millions of times over in green.

Kerry had told me that Arnold was pretty easy to spot in Columbus. Every time he went anywhere, they closed roads and gave him a police escort. You would often see his big black town car heading to the Greater Convention Center or the Veterans' Memorial Hall driving slowly down the street topped and tailed by lots of other cars. Kerry had met Arnold on several occasions, he said.

Kerry and Dorian came to the Classic every year. Dorian Yates Approved took a stand at the fitness expo and some of the people who worked for the American side of the company came too. One year, Kerry's wife Jan had won the top prize in the annual Arnold Classic draw, which was a role as an extra in one of Arnold's films, but she didn't really want to do it. She hadn't even realised that she was in the draw in the first place. Arnold had pulled her up onstage during the bodybuilding contest and asked her if she'd ever been to a show like this one before. Everyone in the crowd was shouting 'It's Kerry's wife . . .' and Kerry was laughing

123

his head off. Arnold's office had rung Jan three times to set up the filming, and she'd had to come up with ever more unlikely excuses.

The expo hall at the Greater Convention Center was the size of two or three football fields and there were thousands of freaks inside. This was an alternative America, one in which everyone was big, but no one was fat. The exhibitors came from everywhere and sold everything: protein bars, protein shakes and every kind of supplement; training equipment; bodybuilding videos and photographs; workout clothes; multi-gyms; weights. Hummer had driven a giant car into the middle of the floor. Weider publications had the biggest stand, an octagonal booth right in the centre of the hall. Some guys called Animal Protein had set up a wired cage with bench-press gear in and lots of big men milled about wearing lifting belts and fingerless leather gloves. One company were selling bobble-head dolls of Ronnie Coleman. There were some Russians who did demon- strations with what they called a kettle ball which was practically impossible to lift. There was a stand selling George Butler's prints of Arnold. Almost everyone had employed fitness models and expo girls to stand around in workout gear and hand things out. Down the aisles the freaks moved on. This was their arena. Everyone was as pumped up as they could get and wearing their muscle gear. Everyone who had any kind of biceps had them out for display. The biggest guys wore singlets and shorts and swaggered slowly. Their girlfriends wore less than they did. The female freaks were the freakiest of all, ripped and vascular with cracked baritone voices deepened by testosterone. Huge fake breasts were everywhere. We were in the Land of the Freak, Home of the Weird.

The Dorian Yates Approved stand was easy enough to

spot – it had a tall pole with a cut-out of Dorian's head on it that spun around. Behind its counters, everyone lolled around. Dorian hadn't shown up yet, but Kerry and Jan were there, and Brian Bacheldor, who helped to devise all of the formulas for the Dorian Yates Approved supplements, and a powerlifter called Andy Boulton, who Brian trained and who'd just dead-lifted a world record of 915 lb. There were lots of people who worked for Dorian Yates Approved in America, too. The business was becoming increasingly successful. They were launching a protein supplement specifically for women which came in a big hot-pink tin and seemed to be selling out very quickly. At the Arnold, you didn't really have to spruke for trade. The expo was rammed. People flowed past the stands all day, every day for ten hours, shoulder to shoulder. The aisles were so full it sometimes took ten minutes to get out of the hall. Almost everyone stopped at the Dorian Yates Approved stand. The Shadow's name was arresting.

Kerry was wearing what he called his 'American watch'. It was an ostentatious gold Rolex inlaid with diamonds which someone had given him as a gift for saving their life, he said. 'I can't even see the time on it. I only wear it when I'm in America,' he explained. 'They love all that over here.'

He was right. Bodybuilding was a bit like rap music. The muscle shirts and the parachute pants didn't seem complete without a great gold chain or bracelet or a giant watch. It was something to do with physical scale too. Everything was bigger, so the jewellery had to be bigger to keep in proportion. And if the jewellery was meant to be big anyway, well, then it had to be huge to stand out. Some people looked like they'd just robbed banks or carjacked pimps.

Kerry seemed to know everybody. He'd give them all a hug and they'd invariably need to tell him something pressing. 'They all have to come here,' he said, 'to pay homage . . .' and he winked.

I had a walk around the expo. At the big supplement company stands, the bodybuilders that they sponsored showed up to sign photos and have their pictures taken. Long lines had formed around them. Gunter Schlierkamp was there and you could tell that he'd climbed the ladder; that he had ascended. Everyone knew about the win over Ronnie Coleman in New Orleans. All of a sudden Gunter looked like a star. He'd had his hair highlighted and styled. He was tanned and kept flashing his high-voltage smile. Most of the bodybuilders would sign photos grimly and not say much, but Gunter was different. He talked to everyone and smiled for the pictures and even rolled up his T-shirt sleeve and did biceps poses with anyone who wanted to compare size. He kissed girls and picked up babies and made everyone laugh. He'd had some T-shirts made which were grey and had the words 'It's On' printed on the front and then 'Guntermania' printed on the back. He was right, too. Lots of people bought one, even though they only came in one size, which was the size that fitted Gunter. He was skipping the Arnold and preparing directly for the Olympia, which he was convinced he could win.

Ronnie Coleman wasn't competing in Columbus either but he showed up too, and before long he had a line in front of him that was just as long as Gunter's. Ronnie signed each photograph incredibly slowly and effortfully. Even writing the words 'Ronnie Coleman' required muscle. When he'd finished he'd look up and hand the picture over silently while people gazed at him. As they walked away, their awe came bubbling out: 'Jesus . . . did you SEE Ronnie? Man, how *big* is he? He must weigh three hundred twenty pounds . . .'

126

The pros charged ten dollars per photo, whoever they were. Ronnie's rate was the same as everyone else's. Indication of rank came only through the size of the queue and the choice of 10x8s they had on the desk in front of them. Ronnie and Gunter and Jay Cutler or even Dennis and Dexter would have five or six choices available, in colour and black and white. Some of the lower rankers only had two. A couple of very new pros had *one*, and they remained on the desks before them, in unyielding stacks.

Dorian arrived at the Dorian Yates Approved stand. He had on a Sean Jean T-shirt with the word 'Peace' written on the back. He'd told me that he liked buying designer clothes now that he no longer weighed twenty-one stone. He had a calfskin document case worth half a year's salary. From it, he took a stack of 10x8s, seven selections, and put them on the table in front of him. He opened up a box and pulled out a number of copies of *A Warrior's Story*, the book I'd bought for 34.10 euros when I'd been convinced that I was purchasing the last one on earth.

'You should have said,' Kerry said when I told him. 'I've got about 20,000 in the warehouse . . .' and Dorian laughed.

It took Dorian half an hour to move a hundred yards at the Arnold Classic. People grabbed at him, stared, took pictures, asked questions, told him about their lives, handed him their children. None of them did anything that others had not done hundreds of times before. Dorian understood that what they wanted was to be close to Dorian Yates, six times Mr Olympia. He had developed a persona that enabled them to do this and nothing more. They got a nod, a smile, a handshake, an answer to take away and keep. Hunter Thompson wrote about Muhammad Ali that he had at least nine layers to him, and 90 per cent of people never got beyond layer three or four. Dorian didn't need nine layers, but he needed some and he kept them for himself.

'Dorian is a very deep man,' Kerry had told me, before we'd left England to come to Columbus.

Soon there was a long queue in front of Dorian, too. As well as buying the ten-dollar 10x8s, almost everyone wanted to have their picture taken with him.

Later, when Dorian had been for a pee, which took him a good twenty minutes what with people stopping him every few steps as he made his way to the restrooms, I asked him how many times he thought he'd had his picture taken since he'd first become Mr O.

'Two hundred thousand, at least,' he said. 'Maybe quarter of a million.'

His doctor prescribed him eyedrops to use before he went to events like the Arnold Classic, because looking into flashbulbs the number of times that he had to might damage his retinas.

Every now and again, someone had to take all of the ten-dollar bills he'd got for signing the 10x8s and put them in a box. The box was becoming quite full. When he went for something to eat, the queue shortened, but didn't go entirely.

Even though he lived in one of the grandest houses in Los Angeles, John Ernster loved to come to the Arnold Classic and the Mr O and sit in the Dorian Yates Approved booth delivering one-liners. John Ernster had made his money from cheese. Kerry told me that he'd supplied all of the Taco Bells in America. Then Ernster had learned that whey, a by-product of cheese processing, was worth something too. Whey was almost pure protein. And as the bodybuilding freaks got freakier, they needed more and more protein to sustain their super-size. If they consumed all of the protein they required by eating, they'd be eating all day. Whey protein, which could be powdered and then hydrated in fluids and made into shakes, delivered two or three chickens' worth in one drink. For a while, whey became gold dust, and Ernster was a prospector, panning his cheese. Pure whey protein had been superseded by science, but John was now in partnership with Kerry and Dorian in the American side of Dorian Yates Approved. He'd always been a frontiersman. He'd flown fighter planes in the war, he'd lived an epic American life. He was eighty-two years old, had two rows of million-dollar teeth and he was still full of the force.

'Hey, skinny,' he said to me, grinning. 'You gonna put me in this book?'

'I don't know.'

'Well, if you do, make sure you call me "Long Dick".' His eyes shone.

Kerry said: 'This man is the unknown Joe Weider.'

At last Dorian strolled back from his lunch, took his place behind the 10x8s again and waited for the queue.

'Enjoy your food, Doz?' Kerry asked. 'Good, cos it's just cost you three grand . . .'

Standing in line at the sandwich counter, Kerry and I ran into Chris Cormier. Chris was competing at the Arnold. He was the second favourite for the title, behind Jay Cutler. He lifted up his T-shirt. We admired the rows of chromed abs.

'Not bad, huh,' he said. 'Check this out.' He twitched. His obliques kicked in. He was so ripped, you could see the feathers, the fibrous divisions on the surface of his muscles, through his skin.

'Better than the British, huh?' He wasn't kidding.

Kerry bought a chicken sandwich with mayo and all the trimmings.

'Hey, Chris . . .' He bit it.

Cormier flipped him the bird and smiled his woozy smile.

Later, Dorian asked Kerry how Chris was looking. He and Chris were friends.

'Good,' Kerry said. 'Feathers on his obliques.'

'That's Chris,' Dorian said. 'He always shows you his stomach or his legs.'

Peter McGough dropped by the Dorian Yates Approved stand. Joe Weider had just sold all of his magazines, including *Flex*, which Peter still edited, to a man called David Pecker for $350 million. 'Joe still thinks he can run it,' Peter said drily, 'and so far, no one has contradicted him . . .'

The deal looked like it was a good one. Pecker was a live wire. He wanted to revamp the Olympia, get the European tour going a little harder. Peter McGough seemed confident that he could do it.

He and Dorian greeted each other warmly. I remembered a story that Peter had told me. Every year before the Olympia, he had got into the habit of writing Dorian a letter of encouragement, just a few sheets that ran through some areas that McGough thought Dorian might need to pay particular attention to. 'And every year,' he'd said, 'the letters got shorter and shorter. By the end, I sent him two pages. The first one said, "Things you need to do at the Olympia", and the second was blank except for one line which said, "Don't forget your posing trunks".'

And then after the 1998 Mr O, when Dorian had announced his retirement from the stage, McGough received a letter back that began, 'I thought it was time that one came the other way . . .'

*

130

When Sandy Richards refused to publish *Pumping Iron* George Butler and Charles Gaines took the manuscript to Dan Green at Simon & Schuster. At the time, it wasn't called *Pumping Iron*. It wasn't called anything at all. 'We were tossing ideas around in Dan Green's office,' Gaines said, 'and Dan said, "You got any ideas what you wanna call it?" and I said, "As far as I'm concerned there's only one title. It's gotta be called *Pumping Iron*." And I can very distinctly remember Dan Green saying – and I'm sure George can – "Oh my God, you can't call it that. What does that mean? It's an awful title" . . .'

Simon & Schuster offered to publish the book, but with no advance for Gaines and Butler. Perhaps they'd already got sight of Gaines's wry introduction, which observed that while subcultures 'as esoteric as midget wrestling and pimping and the Roller Derby have been thoroughly documented' bodybuilding hadn't, and that was in part because 'since its beginnings . . . it has advertised itself with consummate tackiness, confining itself to the back pages of pulp magazines and, in the national consciousness, to the same shadowy corners occupied by dildos and raincoat exhibitionists'.

Something extraordinary began as soon as *Pumping Iron* was issued. It was as if the iron will of Schwarzenegger was radiating from it. It had four print runs immediately on publication, and was soon into its *fifteenth*. Its 'dark and hidden' subculture was on the national agenda. Although the cover was a picture of Ed Corney winning the Mr Universe show in Iraq, Arnold was the book's central character. It was here that his famous quote that getting a pump in his muscle felt as good as coming got its first run.

The media were the last to see it. The *New York Times* refused to review *Pumping Iron*. Someone there told George

Butler it was 'fag bait', which wasn't really the considered response you'd expect from the *New York Times*. A few weeks later, the book was on their bestseller list.

Barbara Walters, who was then probably the most famous TV journalist in America, agreed to have Butler, Gaines and Schwarzenegger on the *Today* show in November 1974. The first thing she said to George when they arrived was, 'I'm delighted to have you guys on my show, because you seem to be literate and well dressed and proportioned, but . . .' and here she looked at Schwarzenegger, 'I wish you hadn't brought that *big turkey* to the studio . . .'

When the segment began, the first thing she asked Arnold was, 'Do you take drugs?'

'Yes,' he'd said immediately. 'I take steroids because they help me an extra five per cent. Women take the pill. They are somewhat similar. I do it under a doctor's supervision . . .' He told her that bodybuilders weren't, on the whole, mad, gay or dumb. He explained, patiently, the basics of nutrition and why muscle could never turn to fat. By the end of the piece Walters was touching Schwarzenegger's arm and expressing her delight at how soft it was when it was unflexed.

Soon, his momentum had become irresistible. Bob Rafelson, a movie director who'd made *Five Easy Pieces*, read *Pumping Iron* and became enthused. He bought the film rights to Gaines's novel *Stay Hungry*. Rafelson cast Jeff Bridges and Sally Field but could not find anyone to play Joe Santo. Gaines suggested Schwarzenegger. Rafelson said something along the lines of 'No way am I having some know-nothing Austrian bodybuilder as a main character in a major motion picture'. Nonetheless, Gaines persisted. Arnold charmed Rafelson. After a few weeks' tuition, the acting coach Rafelson had appointed for him, Eric Morris, said Schwarzenegger was 'one of the smartest people I've ever met'.

When *Stay Hungry* rolled in April 1975, George Butler was trying to find support for the movie version of *Pumping Iron*. 'At one point I did sort of a circuit of Hollywood to see if I could get conventional financing for my film,' he said, 'and I went to see a man, Ned Eannen, who was then production chief at Universal. I went into his office first at his secretary's behest, sat down. He came in, he made a couple of phone calls, he ignored me completely. Then he looked up from behind his desk with a stare that I will never forget and said, "Young man, I am appalled by your behaviour." I said, "*What?*" He said, "I want you to leave this office. The idea that Arnold Schwarzenegger could be the star of a movie is the most appalling thought I've ever encountered. You're insulting my intelligence. Get up and leave."'

Butler got money here and money there and all the while things like this kept happening. People got one look at Schwarzenegger, with all of his muscle (he was just a few years away from being described by Clive James as 'a brown condom filled with walnuts') and his dense accent and bridled at the sheer unlikeliness of him.

For Arnold, belief begat belief; strength became more strength. Unlikeliness was no obstacle at all. He came from Thal, a Styrian village in the Austrian mountains. His father Gustav was a town policeman who had joined the Nazi Party – with great irony considering the course of his second son's life – on 4 July 1938. He married Aurelia Jadrny in 1945. Meinhard was born in July 1946, Arnold on 30 July 1947 at 4.10 a.m. Gustav was said to be vain and cruel, an authoritarian who made his sons write him essays and compete for his affection. Aurelia was dutiful and compliant. Meinhard was a golden child, the family star set for a shimmering future. Arnold was often ill and often scared, cowed by Gustav, a misfit. Gustav fostered the rivalry between the brothers. Arnold developed the classic response to a domineering parent: he both loathed Gustav and wished to emulate him.

These kinds of details of Schwarzenegger's life were eked out over years by the media. Arnold volunteered little personal information to anyone, even Butler and Gaines. By the time he was established in America, he appeared to regard his childhood as malleable, material to fuel his legend.

'We interviewed him at length for the movie and the book,' Charles Gaines said. 'We got the Arnold version of his childhood very early on, the fact that his father was a policeman . . . his brother and his friends. Arnold has never been totally forthcoming with anybody as far as I know. George may know more than I do. I never felt I had more than a cursory working knowledge of his childhood and his relationship with his parents, but it was enough for the purposes of what I was doing.'

Meinhard and Arnold, Arnold and Meinhard; this was the darkest subtext of his story. Like opposed twins, only one could prosper. At first it was Meinhard, athletic, good-looking, his father's son. But then it was Arnold, also athletic but more driven, a swimming champion, then a curling champion, then a bodybuilding champion. Meinhard loved women and women loved Meinhard. He had many girlfriends, and one of them, Erika Knapp, had his son Patrick in 1968. Arnold's success with women grew only with his extraordinary body. Neither stayed in Thal. Meinhard went to Germany, Arnold to Germany then England and then America. Arnold's success earned him

Gustav's love. Caught on the other side of equation Meinhard started to drink. He began working for a publisher in Kitzbühel. Arnold got a job with Joe Weider in California. By 1970, he was Mr Olympia. Meinhard rented one room of someone else's house. Arnold began to invest in real estate. Meinhard drank heavily. Arnold was one of the fittest men on earth. Meinhard assaulted a woman and went to prison. Arnold lived in the Land of the Free.

On the evening of 20 May 1971, Meinhard Schwarzenegger, depressed and drunk, was killed in a car accident. Somehow, Meinhard the golden child and Arnold had exchanged destinies.

Late in 1974, George Butler, who was by now the producer and director of a movie of the *Pumping Iron* book, had enough money to begin shooting. He and Charles Gaines had been with Arnold and Franco Columbu, and Mike Katz and Ed Corney, Ken Waller and Bill Pearl and the rest for a couple of years. They were able to storyboard large sections of the film and to use the friendships and conflicts and rivalries between the bodybuilders to construct a genuine narrative. The film would climax at the 1975 Mr O which was to take place in Pretoria, South Africa.

Butler shot several celebrated sequences: Arnold apparently smoking a joint while wearing a T-shirt that says 'Arnold Is Numero Uno'; Arnold elaborating on his 'getting a pump is like having an orgasm' theory; Arnold demolishing Lou Ferrigno's fragile self-belief on the morning of the Mr O. But most famous of all is the scene in which Schwarzenegger claims to have missed Gustav's funeral because he was too busy training to go.

His precise words are: 'If you want to be a champion you cannot have any kind of outside negative force coming in to affect you. So I trained myself for that. To be totally cold and not have things going through my mind.

'And it was a sad story when my father died. Because my mother called me on the phone and she said, "You know your dad died." And this was exactly two months before a contest. "Are you coming home for the funeral?" she said.

'I said, "No, it's too late. He's dead and nothing can be done. I'm sorry, I can't come." And I didn't explain the reasons why, because how do you explain to a mother whose husband died, you just can't be bothered now because of a contest?'

This story above any other made the Schwarzenegger myth; the one about the unstoppable existential force, 'the King of all Kings', in George Butler's description. It played well with the footage of the machiavellian mind games he had used on Franco Columbu and Lou Ferrigno and the tales of his brutal practical jokes, and most of all it demonstrated his ruthless self-interest, his overarching ambition.

It wasn't true, or at least as far as anyone could make out it wasn't. George Butler remembered that he had told Schwarzenegger a story about a boxer who'd discovered that his father had died a few hours before he was to fight for the Olympic title. He'd fought and dedicated his win to his mother. The story had made some impression on Arnold, who said to George, 'That's what I would have done. Furthermore, my father would want me to do that and my mother would understand fully.'

When Schwarzenegger gave his interview to Butler's camera for *Pumping Iron*, bodybuilding's brutal timescales – the two months of contest prep – lent Arnold's version a harsh edge that the boxer's story never had.

When Butler watched the footage back in the editing room, he found Schwarzenegger so convincing, he began to wonder if his story was actually true, so he asked him. Arnold said that he had been guest posing at a contest in Mexico when Gustav had died, and he had gone on vacation immediately afterwards. No one could find him, and so he didn't discover that his father was dead until Franco Columbu met him at the airport and told him that Gustav had already been buried. Arnold said that he had taken the first available flight to Austria to be with his mother.

'To this day I don't know exactly what happened. There have been so many stories floated by Arnold,' George said. 'It's perfectly plausible that Arnold was training when his father died, and might not have been able to afford to go back, he may not have wanted to go back, only Arnold can answer that question, and I don't know that he ever has.'

Charles Gaines had heard both versions from Arnold, too, and he and Butler decided to leave the original one in the final edit of *Pumping Iron*. In the end, the story said something about Arnold Schwarzenegger either way. He understood the value of myth, he knew how to manufacture the persona that fitted his Master Plan.

'That's absolutely true,' Charles said. 'He was public-relations conscious and he's conscious all the time of what it is he's selling. As all movie stars are. They go on these TV shows to make people go see their latest movie, not talk about their personality. Arnold is a consummate salesman and he's always conscious of what he is doing professionally. He's not there to share his life with that person or to try and make the general public understand him better. He couldn't give a shit about that. He's there to sell the latest book or the latest movie or whatever.'

Everything about *Pumping Iron* happened slowly. The final sequences of the film, when Arnold defeated Franco once

137

more to become Mr Olympia for the sixth consecutive time and then announced his immediate retirement from pro bodybuilding, also served as his transition into movies – in a movie. It was the perfect postmodern moment for him. Arnold expected that *Pumping Iron* would be the vehicle that made him a star. Butler and Gaines knew only that he gave their film a vivid focus, a terrifically quirky twist. In fact, although Butler had completed filming after the trip to Pretoria, he didn't have the cash to finish editing the movie. *Stay Hungry*, which was to be released in the summer of 1976, did not satisfy Arnold's ambition. He felt that his role would not attract much attention given the status of his co-stars, who were as charismatic as he was and far more nuanced in the art of screen acting. No, *Pumping Iron*, in which he trounced Ed and Franco and Lou on camera as remorselessly as he had done on the stage at the Mr O, was the one that showed him off to best effect.

George was showing the raw *Pumping Iron* footage to lots of people who might give him the money to get it finished. They were agreed that it was interesting and compelling but they kept asking whether people would actually go to a cinema to watch it. Butler reasoned that the best thing to do would be to put on a bodybuilding show and invite the investors down to see how big the crowd was. He had no money, so he couldn't afford to hire a theatre. He tried the Manhattan YMCA but they were booked up. It occurred to him that a museum might let him have the space for nothing and he quickly became excited by the idea. It somehow fitted with all of the connections he and Gaines had made between art and muscle. The Museum of Modern Art turned him down; they'd been keen initially until they realised that they were confusing George with a conceptual body sculptor from Berlin. The Whitney agreed though, and so George Butler staged one of the strangest events that anyone in New York could remember.

He called it 'Articulate Muscle: The Body As Art', and made some beautiful posters that echoed the cover of the *Pumping Iron* book, with Ed Corney posing at the Mr Universe show in Iraq. Corney, Frank Zane and Arnold agreed to appear. A panel of art historians was convened. George invited his investors and put tickets on sale. Palmer Wald, the curator of the Whitney, asked how many people George thought might come. George said three hundred, although he was hoping for five.

By 5 p.m. on 26 February 1976, two hours before the show, he'd sold fifty tickets. Even Butler's zeal was dented. Two hours later, his doubts were at last assuaged. Three thousand people had wedged themselves into the fourth-floor gallery where the show was to take place. Several hundred more, including most of the investors, were shut outside on the sidewalks looking through the glass doors, where they could see museum staff still picking money up from the floor where it had been thrown by people in the rush to get in.

The art historians began their discussion, but the crowd soon started to shout them down, yelling for Arnold to come onstage. It became the biggest single event in the history of the museum. The *New York Times*, which had dismissed the *Pumping Iron* book as 'fag bait', wrote about the show. There were pictures of Arnold and Candice Bergen in *People* magazine. Andy Warhol pronounced his interest. Joe Weider was baffled. George got the money to keep editing.

Butler's final cut of *Pumping Iron* did not end with Schwarzenegger's victory in Pretoria, or with his retirement speech. Instead, it finished with a scene from the following day, shot on a bus on the way to the airport. In it, Arnold is telling Lou Ferrigno that now the show is over he is going to come to Lou's house for dinner, after which Lou's mother is going to fix Arnold up with Lou's sister. He does it all with such terrific charm that the subtext – the reinforcement of Schwarzenegger's utter mastery over his broken opponent – does not resonate until later. It was a master stroke from Butler. The sequence echoed thematically the one he had shot at Ferrigno's breakfast table on the morning of the Mr Olympia contest. With Lou surrounded by his family, Arnold shows up and begins sympathising with Ferrigno, saying that the contest has come a month too early for him. He allows this to sink in and then tells Big Lou that he'll never be Mr Olympia, and that he might as well retire.

Schwarzenegger is utterly irresistible as he humiliates Ferrigno. Somehow his scheming makes him even more appealing. It became impossible to watch *Pumping Iron* and not love Arnold Schwarzenegger. He was King of his World, as he said he would be. And Lou Ferrigno never would become Mr Olympia.

In the end, Schwarzenegger and *Pumping Iron* drove one another. The movie was a slow-burning hit. Tom Wolfe, Carly Simon and James Taylor showed up at the 1977 New York premiere. The film critic Alexander Walker, who was also there, wrote: 'This week, all New York really cares about is Arnold Schwarzenegger. He's everywhere, in all the papers and magazines and gossip columns. No dinner is complete without a new, mouth-watering detail about Arnold. In fact, if Robert Redford were to walk into the same room as Schwarzenegger, he would probably be in analysis for years, recovering from the shock to his ego.'

The momentum dissipated for a while, but when Arnold made first *Conan The Barbarian* and then *Terminator*, he pulled it along with him.

'It really kind of took place over a six-year period from about 1977 to '83, something like that,' George said. 'When *Terminator* came out Arnold really began to become a star and *Pumping Iron* achieved its full strength. But before then, people were not quite sure . . . it had an initial burst of interest and then it faded, and then it came back, and came back and came back and came back . . .'

*

Included in the price of a VIP ticket to the Arnold Classic was the chance to have your photograph taken with Arnold. This was to take place at the Veterans' Memorial Arena, before the prejudging for the bodybuilding show. A long line of people began at the doors to the pump-up room and circled around the first floor of the auditorium. The photographer had set up in one of the ante-rooms that sat to the side of the pump-up area. Arnold arrived from nowhere wearing a jacket and tie and stood in front of the photographer's backdrop. It was a slick operation. It had to be. There were several hundred people waiting in the line outside. They began to come in, escorted in small groups. Arnold had a man standing either side of him, as well as all of the other security people milling around. Whoever was at the front of the line came forward. The first man by Arnold took the photographee by the shoulders and positioned them next to Schwarzenegger. The photographer hit the button and a Polaroid popped out of the bottom of the camera. The guy on the other side of Arnold took the Polaroid, put it in a cardboard mount and handed it to the photographee as he simultaneously moved them away. Each picture took about thirty seconds, start to finish. Every person was next to Arnold for approximately ten of them. Even so, they had been shooting for about an hour and the line didn't look much shorter. I stuck my head in the room to see how things were progressing just as Arnold called for a break. Suddenly, the doors behind us were shut, and there were eight or ten of us left inside: the photographer and his assistants, the men positioning people either side of Arnold, Arnold himself and me.

How did Arnie look? He looked like a movie star. He looked like the Terminator. His face bore his only faults: the lantern jaw, the heavy brow shading tiny eyes. He had a kind of superannuated youth about him: his skin was ripped and peeled and pampered, his hair was lustrous. It *gleamed*. What secrets he had. He appeared unknowable. His life was fiction. It was mediated through his roles. He was Conan, he was the Terminator, he was the Last Action Hero. Arnold Schwarzenegger was Arnie. From unpronounceable dolt to cultural shorthand in half a lifetime.

Arnold dabbed his face with a white towel and blinked several times. He drank from a bottle of water. No one said anything, so I asked him what he thought the bodybuilding show was going to be like.

'Tonight,' he said quite dramatically, 'will not be for girlie men . . .' and we all laughed. 'Tonight,' he said, 'will not be for men who eat quiche . . .' Everyone laughed again. It was a good line. Arnold grinned and said he was ready to begin having his photo taken again, and the doors were opened and the great queue began to file through once more.

I admired the book *Pumping Iron* very much. Aside from its other qualities, which were many, Charles Gaines's writing had great moral force. He'd subtitled the book 'The

Art and Sport of Bodybuilding' and his words and Butler's pictures drew the line through history; they humanised muscle and the men that had it, they removed bodybuilding from that shadowy corner with the dildos and raincoat exhibitionists. More than that, *Pumping Iron* had moved the sport forward, it had placed it on the national agenda. Arnold had the platform for which he had hungered, too; one that offered him his American dream, the fulfilment of the Master Plan.

It made me think that I was somehow passive within the story, unable to affect its course. The Era of the Freak set an agenda of its own: to keep on getting freakier. Everyone, the bodybuilders, the judges, the magazines, the supplement companies, the fans, was forced to comply.

I looked at bodybuilders as if they were racing-car drivers or jump jockeys or boxers: they were engaged in an endeavour with inherent risks. As the power of competition diminished the natural margins between them they were faced with the choice of going on or pulling back. They had free will. They chose to go on. It made the momentum unstoppable. The judges and the crowd and the competitors themselves would not accept a backward step. The freaks must go on getting freakier. Muscle demanded it.

The bodybuilders came into the pump-up room to get ready to go to the stage for the prejudging of the Arnold Classic. A warm-up area in the centre of the room was set aside for them. It contained light weights and bands. Dexter and Chris were among the first. They were stripped and oiled already. Kevin Levrone was next, bigger still. Then Jay Cutler, who was 5' 9" and weighed about 270 lb. He was extravagantly wide and he moved extravagantly slowly. Then Markus Ruhl, the German who had been ill with food poisoning during the British and Dutch Grand Prix. He was simply inhuman. He was undoubtedly over 300 lb, but the beef was slapped randomly on his frame. There was no pretence of aesthetics about Markus Ruhl. His shoulders were, quite literally, square. His stomach was oval and armour-plated, a body part that belonged to a dinosaur. He called himself 'The Beast' and he was one. He looked like something en route to the slaughterhouse. Charles Gaines had seen Arnold Schwarzenegger and then turned his gaze backwards through centuries and looked at Glycon's *Hercules*, at Michelangelo's *David* and *Adam*, at Leonardo da Vinci's sketchbooks and found them all perfected in the body of the Austrian Oak. I could, at that moment, watch Arnold Schwarzenegger having his photo taken and then turn round to look at Markus Ruhl. They weren't more than forty feet or thirty years apart and yet they didn't look like members of the same species. But there was something thrilling about seeing Ruhl too, there was no denying that. He was on a mission to push back the frontiers of freaky size. And he wasn't the only one. Gunter Schlierkamp was too, and so were Ronnie Coleman and Jay Cutler. So would be the men who came after them, and the men who came after them.

When Arnold won the 1975 Mr Olympia, the event was divided into two: competitors who weighed under 200 lb and those who weighed more. The winners of each division would then compete against one another for the title. In Pretoria, Franco Columbu was the under 200 lb champion, and Arnold the over. When Arnold defeated Franco in the overall, Franco, who was 5′ 5″, weighed 185 lb. Markus Ruhl's *legs* must have weighed almost 185 lb.

Franco won the Mr O contest twice, in 1976 and 1981 (succeeding, but not beating, Schwarzenegger on both occasions). The closest competitor to him in terms of height in 2003 was Lee Priest. Lee was 5′ 4″. In contest shape he was 205 lb. Off-season, he could weigh *275 lb*. Wayne DeMilia said that he'd once seen Lee at *282 lb*, and Lee was so bloated DeMilia hadn't recognised him. The thought that Lee Priest could even contemplate stepping on a pro stage weighing 185 lb was laughable. The idea that anyone would pay to watch a pro bodybuilding contest in which competitors weighed under 200 lb was absurd, too. It would be like selling tickets to see someone run the hundred metres in fifteen seconds.

Somewhere between the evening at the Whitney and the Arnold Classic 2003, somewhere between Arnold and Markus, Franco and Lee, bodybuilding had become heightened, supercharged, post-human.

The bodybuilders got pumped up. They shone and glowed. They were the colours of cars – sunburst orange, metallic bronze, burnt sienna – and as hard as chrome. There were lots more of them preparing now: Tommy Thorvildsen, Melvin Anthony, Stan McReary, Darrem Charles, Troy Alves, Amir Hadir, J.D. Dawadu, Eddie Abbew, a 6′ 4″ giant called Quincy Taylor, plus Chris and Dexter, Kevin, Markus and Jay. Together they were an astonishing sight. It seemed to double them, to square them, to cube them. They said nothing to each other. They searched for focus. Some guy from the IFBB, a military type in a blazer and tie and black socks, came in and yelled at them. I'd seen him before. He treated the bodybuilders with no respect at all. He told them to line up in numerical order and when a few couldn't find the man who should have been in front or behind them he began shouting. The athletes remained docile. They knew what they were about to face. They were low on carbs and water, dehydrated and drained. They could think of only one thing, and it wasn't who should be in front of them in the line. They went to the stage, where pain awaited them.

Posing hurt. It wasn't like the good deep hurt of the gym, or the whack of injury but more of a steadily ratcheted burn. In the deprivation of their condition, the constant squeezing and contracting and twisting provoked a steady ache. When they woke up on the day after a show they felt like they'd been mugged; stiff, sore and rueful.

The Veterans' Memorial Hall was almost full when they came on. They lined up and did the quarter-turns. Jay Cutler was called out first and to the centre, with Chris Cormier second on one side of him and Kevin Levrone third on the other. In the second call-out, Dexter Jackson replaced Kevin and in the third, to raucous cheers and shouts of 'BEEF . . . BEEF!', Markus Ruhl replaced Dexter.

Jay Cutler was clearly in front. He had been sore since the 2001 Mr Olympia, when he'd been ahead of Ronnie Coleman for two rounds before Ronnie passed him at the evening show. It was common knowledge that Jay had failed the diuretics test after the contest, but kept his place after Wayne DeMilia discovered that the lab he'd used for the testing at the Mr O, Quest Diagnostic, had lost their IOC accreditation. Cutler had skipped the 2002 Mr O and rested his body and now he was a real threat to Ronnie Coleman. He'd won the West Coast sweep of the Ironman and the San Francisco Pro in the last few weeks and here he was, ahead at the Arnold, stomping all over Chris Cormier and Kevin Levrone with his broad back and ludicrously cut thighs. He was filled with power and hubris.

After round one, Gunter Schlierkamp showed up and sat down right behind the judges. For round two, the competitors went through the seven compulsory poses alone onstage, appearing one by one. Then the judges prepared for the second-round call-outs. The first of these was always the most exciting, because it demonstrated who was contending for the title.

From his place in the middle of the judges' table, Wayne DeMilia said into the microphone: 'Jay Cutler in the centre please.' There were whoops and cheers and more shouts of 'BEEF!' Once again, Jay was leading a major contest after two rounds.

'Chris Cormier on one side please . . .' Chris waved at the crowd.

'And . . . *Markus Ruhl* on the other side please,' Wayne said dramatically. Bedlam descended. If anyone still doubted that the Era of the Freak had begun, those doubts had just been dispelled. Size ruled bodybuilding. Markus Ruhl-ed.

The second call-out featured Cormier again, with Dexter Jackson and Kevin Levrone. It meant that Jay Cutler had it nailed; the judges didn't need to see him with anyone else. Chris was probably second. Markus was high in their thoughts. Dexter and Kevin were top six going into the evening show.

I slogged back through the snowbound streets to the expo at the Columbus Greater Convention Center. Dorian was still signing and smiling. I told him about the call-outs at the prejudging.

'It is absolutely inconceivable,' he said, 'that Markus Ruhl can win this contest.'

*

'Arnold was kind of like the Matterhorn,' Charles Gaines had said to me. 'We didn't discover him. We just sort of came round the corner and saw him first. There he was. He already knew he was going to be famous . . .'

147

Before Charles and George had laid eyes on him, Arnold had gone from Austria to Germany – where he had met Albert Busek – and then to England. He went in search of a man called Reg Park, who was his first hero. He had put pictures of Reg Park up on his bedroom wall, which had made Gustav wonder if his son was a queer. Park was English although he had emigrated to South Africa after a glorious career in bodybuilding.

Arnold had first seen him in a cinema in Graz when he was thirteen years old. Park starred in a film called *Hercules* with Steve Reeves, and Arnold began to revere him for his size and toughness.

All of this was why I was walking up a street near the seafront in Portsmouth sometime before the Arnold Classic to meet a woman called Dianne Bennett, who was something of a legend in bodybuilding herself. She was sitting in the winter sun outside her rather grand old townhouse, the bottom floor of which was a working gym and had been for many years. She was born into what she called 'the iron game', in 1936, when her father, Bob Woolgar, had christened her Dianne 'because it was the closest he could get to the goddess of physical culture'. She couldn't remember ever living in a house that didn't have a gym attached to it. She grew up in the days when gyms were used almost exclusively for strength training and weightlifting and the bodybuilders were allowed a small area at one end away from the lifting platforms and got called 'cream puffs' by the weightlifters. At the time, there wasn't even a bodybuilding organisation, everything was run through BAWLA, the British Amateur Weight Lifters Association, so Bob Woolgar and some friends had started NABBA, the National Amateur Bodybuilding Association, in the early 1950s. 'And eventually,' Dianne said, 'you never had anybody lifting in a gym, it was all bodybuilding. Weight-lifting went off on its own and bodybuilding took off as NABBA.'

The acronym had shaped her life. She remembered the austerity of the post-war 1950s giving way to a new time when people wanted to look good and fit, and rationing ended and they began to learn more about nutrition. 'They were eating what we would now consider crazy diets,' she said. 'Eight pints of milk, getting the calories in. Nobody even knew about abdominals or obliques or those sort of things. If you look at people from the fifties, even Steve Reeves, you couldn't see an abdominal.'

Dianne, who had been a Tiller Girl and had won various fitness contests and who was quite a looker, had married Wag Bennett and moved to London. Wag was a training partner of Reg Park's, a big, strong man who could bench-press 500 lb. He and Dianne owned gyms and ran maga-zines and supplement companies and organised and judged bodybuilding contests. They had six children. Wag first saw Arnold Schwarzenegger in Germany in 1965, on 30 October, in the Wulle Rooms in Stuttgart. It was also the day that Arnold met Franco Columbu. Arnold was voted Junior Mr Europe, and Wag was struck by the sheer scale of him, already almost 6′ 2″ and fully formed at just eighteen. He'd gone AWOL from his national service to compete.

He came to London for the NABBA Mr Universe show in September 1966, a baby-faced giant. In the front row of the Victoria Palace sat one of the world's richest men, J. Paul Getty, a bodybuilding aficionado, and also Jimmy Savile, a former wrestler who was becoming a famous DJ. Chet Yorton was placed first by seven of the nine judges. The other two, including Wag, gave first place to Arnold, who had electrified the crowd.

'And afterwards,' said Dianne, 'he looked so forlorn, so we went up to him and he could see by the score sheets that Wag had put him first. And he looked very lost, so we invited him back to our home. And of course we had gyms and we had six kids so he knew we were a family who trained. He came back and stayed with us and trained with us, and I fed him. He was only a lad working at a gym in Munich and he didn't have any money or anything, so we would arrange a few times a year for him to come over and do a series of shows and earn some money.

'He'd start in London and he'd have to do a couple of shows for Wag and me, for which he got paid ten quid and for which he'd help get the hall ready, put chairs out. Then the first stop would be down here in Portsmouth for my mum and dad, on the pier or at the Wedgwood Rooms, and then he'd go on to Plymouth where another friend, Bill Jackson, had a gym. Then Wag would take him on a tour to earn money for food, and that's how it started.

'When he stayed with us, not only did he learn quite a lot from me about food, I also taught him English. When he first came into the house, I can remember I was at the sink like this, and looming in the doorway was this man, and it was "Hel-lo, Mrs Ben-nett", very slowly. I used to help him with his clothes. He came from a village in Austria, Thal, and he was a bit of a hick dresser. I can see him now in these sort of corduroy trousers . . . and they were very short. He always used to remind me a bit of a cartoon character called Li'l Abner. I said, "Arnold, you can't walk about like that with all your socks showing." We couldn't get any trousers that fitted, so I got him some boots as the bootleg came up higher. We got him some outsized shirts and things, cos we got them for Wag.

'And then he trained. He used to say he could only get a

150

decent pump when he was in Wag's gym. Until the time he came to us, Arnold had never used music to pose to onstage. We said to him, "You've got to use music and you've got to learn to pose to music." "No no," he said. But we won him over. We had to decide what music to use. It had to be something powerful, obviously. And you know of course that Reg Park was his idol, and he happened to be Wag's best friend. Reg is Jewish, and Reg always posed to the music from *Exodus*. So Arnold decided, yes, he'd use the music. In fact, we've still got the record. We'd put it on in the front room, and Arnold would stand there and Wag would say, "No, turn this way," and whatever. He learned to pose in our front room.

'Then when he was going to go to the States, he came and discussed it with us, "Should I go, should I not?" Wag told him that Joe Weider was the only person in this world who could afford to pay him to train.'

Dianne gave me a tour of the gym, where she kept some of the equipment that Arnold had trained with. There was a set of old scales that he'd used, and he'd sometimes say to Wag or Dianne, 'I'm not going to bed tonight until I weigh 230 lb,' and he might be two or three pounds off so he'd eat and eat until he weighed what he thought he should. Dianne showed me the machine that he'd used for thousand-pound calf raises. His calves had been the body part that gave him the most trouble. Wag had told him to cut the bottoms out of his training pants so that he could see them at all times, to remind him he must work harder on them. Dianne said that she'd never seen anyone train as hard as Arnold did.

Dianne lived above the gym, and she and Wag also had a similar place in London. We toured the house, which was decorated with striking murals of bodybuilders. She gave me some copies of *Body Power*, the magazine she had

151

published and edited, and we talked about her work as a judge. She was very guarded and defensive about bodybuilding, she explained, because it had been her life.

'I'm an old lady,' she said, 'but hopefully I keep up with what's happening and I'm aware that you cannot stop people doing what they want with their own bodies. If there's money involved, and ironically there's less in bodybuilding than almost any other sport, then it will happen. Can you see any other way, other than making it open, and monitoring it? Education, information, availability equals, to my mind, safety and honesty.

'Having a life involved in bodybuilding, my ideals and thinking have changed in the last ten years. More testing is not the way to go. I've been to national and international contests when at weigh-ins we've been told to officially mark down people who we could see were on steroids. That way they didn't get to the competition. It used to be very evident. Of course, there are signs now, too.

'Open up is my answer to it. Let's be honest. What's wrong with that? Because people will always do things to improve if it's available. If they can't get it legally, they'll get it illegally. We'd eliminate a lot of the damage. It's not like *Chariots of Fire* any more.'

It was an argument Dianne found difficult to make: her daughter Leigh had died when she was twenty-two from complications relating to asthma. She had been treated with steroids for five years, and Dianne felt that if Leigh had never started with them she might still have been alive.

I asked her who had the best physique she had ever seen, and I expected her to say Arnold, but she told me that it was Flex Wheeler. She felt that Arnold would have defeated him in competition, because Arnold was Arnold and he always found a way, but, she said, 'I remember seeing Flex six years

152

ago, and I'm not easily impressed, and I thought, "This is my ideal physique." It may sound corny to you, but I always think, if we were going to shoot somebody up into space to represent the male physique, you'd be proud to say, "Here is the best that the human race can produce."'

Arnold had gone to America in 1968, but he'd never lost touch with Dianne and Wag, or with the people who'd helped him in Germany and Austria. Dianne said that they would all meet every year at the Arnold Classic, where she often judged. Arnold would stop in when he came to Europe, too, and he'd call and chat about his life. She and Wag had watched his inexorable ascent, and it had come as no surprise. He'd even had the Master Plan at nineteen years old when he could barely articulate it in English.

'He used to sit at the table and say, "I'm gonna be the biggest. I'm gonna be the best. I'm gonna be a film star . . ." Yeah, yeah, yeah. This is why I'm so pleased to have known him then, and seen how he was. When we met last time, he said, 'Do you realise it's thirty-six years since we first met?' He knew where he was going and nothing was going to stop him.'

She remembered seeing him give a press conference for the first *Conan* movie, and thinking how much his English had improved as he charmed the forty or so hacks who had expected to be able to take potshots at him. She'd watched him years later take on the White House press corps as George Bush Sr's fitness adviser, and he made them all laugh and soon they were charmed by him, too. Now she thought he would certainly become President. He was Austrian and anyone born outside America was barred from the presidency by the US Constitution. For Arnold, the solution was *obvious*: he would change the Constitution.

*

The history of the *Pumping Iron* movie became convoluted and raw. Arnold was the control freak's control freak and he wanted to control the film. George Butler, who had believed in the project more than anyone, and given more to it, found it hard to let go. Charles Gaines was more ambivalent.

A new edition of the book, printed after Arnold's controversial comeback to claim a seventh Mr O in 1980, had him gloating about his win: 'I did it to have a good time,' he said. 'I did it to see them [his rivals] freak out and have diarrhoea, you know. And to be confused and be upset about it, and to have a career that they planned for themselves go down the tubes in two seconds.'

The 1980s became an avaricious decade; it was about self-improvement and self-absorption. Its stars were Schwarzenegger and Stallone; Americans on Wall Street and Main Street worked out. Jane Fonda had read *Pumping Iron* and she told Charles that she'd like to do a book of her own; he'd put her on to Dan Green, who'd published *Jane Fonda's Workout* and the fitness boom in America began. George and Charles made a second *Pumping Iron* film, this time on female bodybuilders, about which Gloria Steinem wrote: 'this is the next mind-blower in feminism'. It starred Bev Francis, the self-styled 'Strongest Woman in the World'. She and her husband Steve Weinberger would later become close friends and mentors to Dorian Yates.

As Arnold Schwarzenegger's achievements began to match his ambition, his past, with its curious mix of fierce loyalties and ruthless self-interest, with its artful blending of truth and myth, with its translucent screen of twentieth-century fame and money, became something else he would have to master.

Arnold bought the rights to *Pumping Iron* and he reissued it in 2002 for the twenty-fifth anniversary, along with a documentary about the making of the film. Ronnie Coleman and Gunter Schlierkamp posed at the opening party. George Butler was there and Charles Gaines wasn't. I could understand both. George had mortgaged his house to make the film, and he had brought artistry to it. He no longer owned it physically, but he had a claim on it. Charles felt that it was all a long time ago, and he had other things to do. 'I see it as not ancient history, but history,' he said. 'We had a great time doing it in the seventies and wouldn't take anything from having done it, but it's not a part of my ongoing life. *Pumping Iron* is not something that I think about much or wish I'd done something different with. It's not something that I have much connection to. Whenever I think about it I think about it in the warm amber light of the time when we did it, which pleases me. But I don't want to go to any more openings. I've done that.'

Arnold was going to run for the governorship of California, everyone knew that. He was just deciding when. The reissue of *Pumping Iron* was a smart move. It was public acknowledgement of his past. The same too with his admission that he had used steroids, which were not controlled substances in America in the 1970s. He could not be badly beaten up by these things. His other early attempts at selling himself would prove more problematic. In a 1977 interview with a girlie mag called *Oui*, for example, he had quite obviously exaggerated aspects of his life to give the audience exactly what it wanted to hear (he'd said that he and some other bodybuilders had taken a willing girl upstairs at Gold's and that 'the guys who can fuck in front

155

of other guys' had done so; he also added, generously, 'I have absolutely no hang-ups about the fag business.').

George Butler had just made four films about the explorer Ernest Shackleton. He said that he hadn't really looked at Ronnie Coleman or Gunter Schlierkamp at the *Pumping Iron* party, and he was at best ambivalent to the Era of the Freak.

'I'm probably just someone willing to take big risks,' he said. 'I'm not a gambler in Las Vegas, but I'm a gambler in my film-making. You've gotta put your money where your mouth is. I took a bet on the book and I was right. If you're betting on a horse race, you really don't know much. But if you're betting on logic, then you know a lot about potential, and I just felt that there was a big audience for this subject, and I was right. We were very determined to do it and that's what bodybuilding needed. And what bodybuilding lacks now is any imagination. We were putting Arnold in a ballet studio, we had him painted by Jamie Wyeth. Everything we did with bodybuilding was to make it original and put it in a new light and mostly to bring outsiders in to see it. And we were in competition with Joe and Ben Weider who only wanted bodybuilders to do bodybuilding. They probably lacked the confidence to go to the outside world. They had tunnel vision. They'd been very successful at what they did. Their object was to make money. My object was to have fun. We took bodybuilding out of the castle and put it in the fresh air and it's gone right back in.'

Arnold Schwarzenegger did not attend his brother's funeral, just as he would be absent from his father's a year and a half later. Meinhard does not appear in Arnold's autobiography, *The Education of a Bodybuilder*, although Gustav and Aurelia do. In one of his rare public remarks on the subject, he has said, 'Deep down I always expected something to happen . . . he lived more on the edge than I . . . Now, I wish he was here to enjoy all this with me. Back then, I just brushed it off.'

Meinhard had left Erika Knapp to bring up their son Patrick alone. Arnold did not discover that Meinhard had made him Patrick's godfather until after Meinhard's death. He paid for Patrick's schooling in Lisbon, and later made him a part of his family in America, telling Erika she had sent him 'half a Schwarzenegger' to look after. He has never publicised the story, even when under strong attack in his successful gubernatorial campaign. He has never used Meinhard's death to aggrandise himself, as he did with Gustav's. He has barely spoken of him at all.

Arnold and Meinhard, Meinhard and Arnold. This was Arnold, light and dark.

There's a much more inconsequential and funnier sign of Arnold's strange, divided character on the first few pages of *The Education of a Bodybuilder*. The dedication is to his mother, and also to Charles and George 'who I am honoured to count among my closest friends'. Just before this comes a page which says:

Also by Arnold Schwarzenegger

Arnold's Bodybuilding for Men (With Bill Dobbins)
Pumping Iron

*

'Tonight,' Arnold Schwarzenegger said into the microphone from the stage of the Veterans' Memorial Arena, 'is not for girlie men. It is not for girls who eat quiche . . .' Everyone roared and cheered. The line sounded off the cuff. He always spoke without notes. 'The Arnold Classic is not a contest for mini-men, which is why Franco Columbu is at home tonight . . .' No Arnold speech was complete without a Franco joke, either. The crowd were delighted. Arnold smiled. He was on home ground. He was before his people. He made some more jokes about the Kennedys and also Joe Weider. He presented some awards to the competitors in the Strongest Man contest that had taken place as a warm-up for the bodybuilding finals. He told everyone about *Terminator III*, which he'd just filmed, and advised us all to go and see it. He got Reg Park, who was now seventy-five, up onstage to help him draw the winner of this year's contest to spend a day with him on a film set. It was won by a kid from Hot Springs, Arkansas. The kid had a strong Southern accent. Arnold had some fun with that.

A singer named Daniel Rodriguez came onstage to perform the national anthem. He belted it out a cappella. When he got to the final line about the land of the free and the home of the brave, he hit some spectacular notes and began weeping with pride. As he did so, some of the military carried the Stars and Stripes onstage. It was not yet eighteen months since September 11. When we'd flown over Chicago's skyscrapers en route to Columbus, it had been impossible not to think of it. There was a sense of nationalistic fervour. Everyone in the hall was on their feet, on their chairs, cheering and hooting. Rodriguez sang another song which ended with him repeating the line 'America . . . America' several times, tumultuously. He was in tears again. Some of the audience were, too. They looked ready to jump up on the dais and bear Rodriguez off on their shoulders.

It would have been no surprise if Arnold had driven onstage in a tank and invited us to join in some kind of invasion, but instead it was the bodybuilders, almost as big, almost as wide.

They came out individually to give their posing routines. Kevin Levrone was fourth on, his size announced by Wayne as 5′11″ and 245 lb. Kevin sang in a band called Fullblown that sounded like Pearl Jam, and he posed to his own music. He seemed to take real pleasure in his body and he moved lithely from position to position, smiling each time he kicked in his muscle.

Chris Cormier followed him, also 5′11″ but a full ten pounds heavier and harder. He was ripped and stripped, too, glistening in his oil. He hadn't bothered resting up in between the prejudging and the finals. Instead, I'd seen him back at the expo hall, where he'd climbed on to the table of his supplement booth, removed his shirt and begun posing.

Chris was an enigma. There was one or two of him in every sport; a nearly man, a whirlwind, an unpredictable force capable of genius and horror. Today at the Arnold, it was almost genius, one of the most beautiful physiques on earth cast before a few thousand in Columbus. Chris turned his back to the audience and set one foot behind the other, like a man going up a step. He raised both arms into a double-biceps pose and the muscles in the top of his back performed for him. They raised up the tattoo of remembrance that dipped between his shoulder blades. He turned his head to the left and smiled.

The crowd looked at him. He meant something different to each of them: some saw the macho life of the gym in him; for others it was undoubtedly sexual; for me and lots more it was the opposite, something aesthetically beautiful but only that; for others still it was a crazy size thing, it was all about the beef.

For Chris – who knows how it felt up there; he seemed to like it, shifting about to Michael Jackson covered in oil and with his spangly trunks disappearing into his backside. He looked awesome and ludicrous, he was decadent and spectacular. We sat back and cheered him on, lapping it up.

Dexter came out and waged his one-man war against the mass freaks. He was 5′ 6″, 215 lb, full and balanced, proportioned, symmetrical, ripped; not quite a throwback to *Pumping Iron*, but almost. The future loomed over him. Quincy Taylor came on. He was 6′ 4″ and 295 lb. Tommy Thorvildsen was 5′ 9″ and 250 lb.

The last two were Markus Ruhl and Jay Cutler. Ruhl ripped the house down. Even before he appeared from the steps at the back of the stage, as Wayne DeMilia said, 'From Germany . . . five feet and eleven inches tall . . . at two hundred and eighty-nine pounds . . .' beef freaks were on their feet. Markus had a soft, friendly mug with a chrome-finned flat-top, but his head was a small ball perched on a hill of mutant DNA. He had the face of Bambi on the body of a rhinoceros. Markus had no real neck to speak of, although there must have been one somewhere. His lats were so big his arms had nowhere to go but outwards. His thighs moved past one another like two men in a narrow corridor. I looked for Dorian, but couldn't see him near me.

I thought about what he'd said: 'It is inconceivable . . .'

Markus finished off with his best shot, the most muscular. Maddened blood surged through him. His head and his body seemed engaged in a race to see which would explode first. Markus Ruhl didn't look like he was going to live very long at all. The Veterans' Memorial Arena went crazy for some time.

Jay was last on – 5′ 9″ and 276 lb. Even the beastly Ruhl would not outmuscle him, and Jay had by far the more pleasing shape and condition. He was the only one who had made a special tape to pose to. It started with a narration that called him 'the ultimate beef'. He moved to the centre of the stage and turned to face the rear. 'His back's just as big as a barn door,' the tape said, and as it made a noise like a creaky gate swinging open, Jay unfurled his wingspan as it did and sent the crowd to freak heaven.

I had a seat two rows from the front, immediately behind the judges' table. Arnold was a few seats to my right. He'd had his young son on his lap through most of the show. The boy kept grabbing Arnold's nose and tweaking it, and every time he did, Arnold would pull a face and make him laugh.

I could see the fourth-round scores going into the computer at the end of the judges' line. The program calculated the top six and displayed them. It went:

Number	Name	Placing	Points
2	Darrem Charles	6	126
4	Kevin Levrone	5	85
6	Chris Cormier	2	38
9	Dexter Jackson	3	72
14	Markus Ruhl	4	75
15	Jay Cutler	1	20

Wayne called the competitors out and announced the top six. The rest got a big medal from Arnold and walked off. Wayne called for the posedown. The bodybuilders jostled each other for a while and then got down from the stage and walked into the stalls. Chris stood in front of Arnold's wife Maria Shriver, who was beautiful in a very American way. Maria now had the small boy on her lap. Chris posed for them and they both laughed and clapped delightedly. The judges messed around with the computer some more. Arnold came back out onstage with various different sponsors. Darrem Charles got sixth. Levrone was fifth and then Dexter fourth, dropping a place with the very last scorecard added. Markus was called third and people booed then cheered, booed then cheered. Ruhl had arrived. Chris didn't look too surprised with second and he smiled his woozy smile at the $50,000 cheque. Jay got several trophies, a Hummer car and $100,000. He would now contend seriously for the Olympia.

Jay was exhausted, depleted. His efforts had been phenomenal, his self-denial apparent in his thin, dry skin, his dead eyes. Arnold took the mike and made some remarks about how great bodybuilding was, how it had allowed him to come to America with nothing and become Arnold. He was eloquent and witty and smart in his second language. He looked manicured and processed and produced. He looked like the king of all kings. With a flourish he handed the microphone to Jay Cutler. Jay's face slackened. He held the mike. 'I'd, uh . . .' he said. 'Duh . . . I'd, uh . . .' Jay said, fumbling over his speech, and Arnold smiled and took the mike back from him.

The crowd slowly dispersed. Wayne DeMilia, who had been ducking between the judges' table and backstage, stood in front of me, talking to another judge. Wayne said to him: 'Levrone's already saying he's retiring. Who else did we upset? Let's look at the list. I mean, who needs it?'

'*Jesus*,' the other judge said. 'I mean, there's a mirror back there. Look in it . . .'

Wayne was laughing. He relished all the drama. Backstage in the dressing rooms and the pump-up room there was more for him. The world order had shifted. Chris Cormier had pulled Dorian into one of the dressing-room cubicles. He was crying. 'Man,' he said, 'my sports psychologist says I've got to get rid of these negative influences . . .'

162

'Chris,' Dorian said, 'I've been telling you that for *six years*. You don't need a sports psychologist to tell you that. I *am* a fucking sports psychologist . . .'

Jay was being photographed with his trophies. His head was clearing. Markus Ruhl was changed already, and glowing. Dexter chatted to his friends. No one had to worry about the drug testers. Their plane had been held at Chicago because of the snow. One of the security guards was walking around holding a screenplay called *Lethal Dose*. Presumably, he was looking for Arnold. What did he imagine was going to happen? Probably exactly what Arnold had told him could happen: this was the Arnold, this was America. Bodybuilding gave Arnold his chance. It might give anyone a chance at anything.

The last day of the expo at the Arnold Classic was alive with the buzz. Lots of the bodybuilders were on the stands of the supplement companies that they were contracted to, smiling and signing. Gunter and Ronnie were there: Gunter big and charming, Ronnie huge and monolithic. Later, Jay came too, still stained the extraordinary colour of his tan. He looked like a machine. He'd eaten and drunk and the haze had left him. His eyes were sharp. He signed pictures with the slight, natural frown he'd developed. It seemed to keep people at their distance, just like Dorian's half-smile did. Jay may have sounded dumb onstage at the Arnold, but he wasn't. He wasn't the normal bodybuilder, living day to day, flashing his cash on cars and boats and women. His wife Kerry, who was always with him, was his college sweetheart. They had a slab of land in Las Vegas, where they'd built a house. Jay guest-posed a lot, his schedule was full of trips to Boulder and Bellevue, Pittsburgh and Kalamazoo. He ate ten times a day. He trained and rested. He had a stable life. He had a plan.

The layout of the expo kept Jay, Gunter and Ronnie apart, but their names were together on everyone's lips.

Kerry Kayes had the American watch on again. The Dorian Yates Approved stand did good business. They sold out of the new supplement aimed at women. Dorian had his photo taken another few hundred times. John Ernster showed up and sat looking at the passing fitness girls and joshing with Dorian. He told Dorian he should make a comeback. 'Never,' said Dorian, and smiled the half-smile to keep Ernster off.

The crowds thinned slowly and then the expo closed and the Arnold Classic was over. We packed up the Dorian Yates Approved stall. The great doors at the rear of the expo hall opened and forklifts started taking everything out. In just an hour or so, the floor was almost bare.

Kerry went outside for a cigarette. He motioned me to follow him. We stood by the shipping pallets and the forklifts and saw the Dorian Yates Approved stall in a big box. It would soon be carted off to the next expo and set up again.

'I wanted you to see this,' Kerry said. We looked at the end of the Arnold Classic 2003. 'Now you can understand the difference between the British Grand Prix and this. Hundred thousand people, millions of dollars. Imagine the money Arnold brings to this town . . .' He paused. 'I take a loss on the British, you know that, don't you . . . ?' He said. 'Thirty grand, I lost. They don't take a loss on this . . .'

Kerry stubbed out his cigarette with his foot and looked up into the rain.

'I fucking love America,' he said.

6

Andi Redux (ii)

The headline of *Der Spiegel*'s cover story on Andreas Munzer's death read: FAIR-HAIRED, STRONG AND DEAD. Days later, the following list was being reproduced in magazines, on the net, everywhere:

Daily cycle out of contest:
Ephedrine
AN 1
Captagon
Aspirin
Valium
Clenbuterol

Daily cycle 10–6 weeks before competition:
2 injects Testoviron at 250 mg
1 inject Parabolan
30 tablets Halotestin
30 tablets Metandienone
20 IE STH
20 IE Insulin

Daily cycle 5–3 weeks before competition:
2 injects Masteron
2 injects Parabolan
30 tablets Halotestin
50 tablets Stromba
2 injects Stromba
Insulin
24 IE STH

Daily cycle 2–1 weeks before competition:
2 injects Masteron
2 injects Stromba
40 tablets Halotestin
80 tablets Stromba
24 IE STH
Insulin
IGF-1

A few days before competition:
Aldactone
Lasix

No wonder Andi was dead. No surprise that his liver had melted. Consumption on such a scale represented an all-out war on the body; a do-or-die hit list dedicated to pure size, to awesome scale. Andi was not stupid. Andi was a student of growth, a specialist. Like all pro bodybuilders, his physiological and pharmacological knowledge exceeded that of the average quack. He would have understood that such a list was an agenda for the grave. I stuck a hand into Andi's bag of tricks and dug around: ephedrine, a steroid derivative, raises the metabolism and burns fat; AN1 is some kind of androgen receptor developed from rats, it helps steroids lock on to the muscle cells to stimulate growth; Captagon is a brand name oral stimulant that resembled methamphetamine; aspirin, the old reliable, thins the blood and kills pain; Valium is a proprietary diazepam that prevents seizures and muscle spasms; Clenbuterol is an oral beta-2-sympathomimetic that acts like a steroid, promoting muscle growth and increasing fat loss. It raises the body temperature, increasing the effectiveness of other steroids; it also has a strong anti-catabolic effect, decreasing the rate at which protein is reduced in the muscle cell and thus prolonging growth; Testoviron is a popular, long-lasting injectable steroid with strong anabolic effects, less harmful to the liver than an oral steroid; Metandienon is a variation of Dianabol, once called 'the world's biggest black-market drug', and noted for dramatic, instant muscle gain; Parabolan is a potent anabolic steroid, three times as effective per milligram as testosterone; Halotestin is an oral steroid that increases strength and muscle hardness and quality without large gains in bodyweight; Stromba is a 'cutting' steroid, sharpening muscle mass; Masteron, a fast-acting steroid, is a pre-contest favourite, reducing water retention and increasing aggression and power even as calorie intake is lowered; insulin is injected immediately before or after a workout to bring glycogen and other nutrients to the muscles; STH, also known as HGH or human growth hormone, increases the size and number of muscle cells, strengthens connective tissue and promotes fat-burning; IGF, or insulin-like growth factor, is exactly that, a synthetic chemical with anabolic properties; Aldactone is a brand name diuretic that flushes excess salt and water from the body; Lasix is another, causing the kidneys to produce more urine, reducing free water. Those were the desired effects. Those drugs fitted with the kind of body that Andi had: raw and ripped, dust-dry.

There were other effects, too. These fitted with the way Andi died: ephedrine can raise blood pressure and heart rate and cause gastrointestinal distress; malfunctioning androgen receptors have been linked to tumour growth, especially in prostate cancer; Captagon is used to treat attention deficit disorder and can be addictive; aspirin, as Dorian Yates discovered, can destroy the stomach lining if taken to excess; Valium can be addictive and depressive; Parabolan, anecdotally, causes 'roid rage' and kidney damage; Clenbuterol's muscle-gaining properties are repudiated by many bodybuilders, the evidence for its effectiveness coming from trials where it was used on livestock (it also caused a doping scandal when used to bulk up a champion bull) – used as a fat-burner, though it can be highly effective; Halotestin can place extreme stress on the liver, might cause acne, nasal bleeding, headaches, stomach pain, irritability and heightened aggression; Stromba is toxic to the liver, especially when taken orally; Metandienon increases water retention, causes high blood pressure, gynaecomastia, acne, liver damage and increased aggression; Masteron causes hair loss and heightens aggression; insulin, if misused, leads to hypoglycaemia, seizures, coma and death, and requires experience to administer; HGH is expensive and effects on muscle gain are sometimes disappointing; it can cause elongation of the feet, forehead and hands, overgrowth of the elbows, thickening of the skin and diabetes; Aldactone can disrupt kidney function and might cause gastrointestinal pain, dizziness and muscle spasms; the side effects of Lasix can include circulatory disturbances, dizziness, dehydration, muscle cramps, vomiting, circulatory collapse, diarrhoea and fainting; both Aldactone and Lasix, used to excess, might lead to severe organ strain through dehydration, low potassium and sodium levels and erratic heart function.

Andi's body had been brutally rendered. Force had been his guiding principle. He had forced his body into the shape demanded by his will; his body – his will – spoke for him, it demonstrated his creativity and desire, it represented his adventure and his sacrifice. Its grand scale and its dramatic collapse proved that Andi had strived to reach his limits, to define what was possible.

His death was a dark cloud falling. It dropped from the clear blue sky. For his family, it was awful and uncomprehended. Andi's sister, Maria Klement, said that the call from Munich came 'like an electric shock'. They had been close. Maria felt that she would have known if Andi was ill. 'Andi always paid so much attention to his health,' she said.

The landlady at the Kirchenwirt in Pack could not understand how Andi could be dead. She thought it must have been 'a doctor fault'. The regulars stapled a sign near the entrance to the lounge which, directly translated, read: TO ANDI – THE SPORT WAS HIS LIFE. THIS IS OUR WHOLE PRIDE.

Andi's father remembered that Andi 'was always a sensible boy. He never caused us problems.' Their despair was not hard to imagine.

Gunter Schlierkamp told me that he had been to dinner a couple of times with Andi while they were in LA in the week between the 1996 Arnold Classic and the San Jose Pro show. Gunter and Andi had always got along. They had many things in common. Both had been raised on farms. Both had seen Arnold Schwarzenegger and been galvanised by their vision of him; they had wanted to become him, or someone like him. Both had been sponsored by Albert Busek. Both were German speakers in an American game; they were outsiders wanting in. When he heard the news of Andi's death, Gunter did Andi a last favour. Andi had been booked to do two guest posings and Gunter Schlierkamp went in his place.

In a sport where no one could agree on anything, Andi had created consensus: everyone liked him. And everyone I asked used the same phrase about Andi, too. Kerry Kayes, Dorian Yates, Dianne Bennett, Peter McGough, Flex Wheeler, Gunter, all said, 'He was a nice man.' This, in bodybuilding, was the ultimate compliment.

Andi's death came down like a black cloud on bodybuilding, too. In Germany, Andi's death was big news. *Der Spiegel* ran a cover story. *Der Bild* reported on its implications. It was a sexy story, it had legs. It threw light on a darkened male subculture, and reinforced the prejudices with which it was held. Andi became a poster boy for drugs in sport, a bogeyman, a bad guy.

Erich Janner, the IFBB official who'd told Andi he was 'the best white guy behind five Negroes' at the Arnold Classic, flapped: 'It's so tragic it had to be Andi. He was our role model for a healthy diet.' *Der Spiegel* reported the words next to the list of juice and junk Andi was chucking down his throat and needling into his buttocks. Andi's death had thrown the sport into stark relief. Those within it had become inured to its excesses. They had developed complex defence mechanisms to deal with them. They had justifications and mitigations thought through and ready to go. The examination of Andreas Munzer's spectacular corpse became an autopsy for the sport. The court-appointed medical examiner gave the cause of death as 'multifunctional organ failure' caused by long-term poisoning by anabolic steroids. The liver was almost completely dissolved. More than twenty different illegal or prescription substances were found in the blood. There was also an 'acute poisoning' caused by an unnamed stimulant, a 'violent' problem with blood electrolytes and an abnormally high amount of potassium in the body. The senior physician, Randolf Penning, estimated that it would take weeks to detect the individual drugs in Andi's system and unravel them from one another to ascertain a precise cause of death. Manfred Wick, Munich's district attorney, began an investigation into potential violation of drug laws. Police raided several fitness studios and gyms in Munich.

Andi had not been the first to fall. In the autumn of 1992, Mohamed 'Momo' Benaziza, the 5′ 2″ shredded cube of muscle with cuts in his abs as deep as tyre treads and a back that had once shocked the Shadow himself, had taken off on the tour of European IFBB pro shows. He had with him a bag that contained – among other things – the diuretics Lasix and Aldactone. Momo competed in the Dutch Grand Prix on 3 October, even though someone there had said that 'touching his skin was like touching a dead person. It was so cold and clammy.' He began cramping during the show, but he continued and actually won. Afterwards, the cramps intensified to the point where he could no longer walk. Steve Brisbois, another pro, said: 'His face was hard and looked like a mask. His eyes were sunk back in his head. His jawbone was jutting out.' Seven hours later he had a heart attack and died. The diuretics had drained Momo of potassium and magnesium, minerals that were essential in maintaining proper heart function. He'd pissed himself to death.

After the Arnold Classic in 1993, Mike Matarazzo – who had finished sixth, one spot above Andreas Munzer – collapsed in a lift at his hotel. Wayne DeMilia took him to hospital where he told the doctor that he suspected Matarazzo had taken diuretics, hadn't drunk and had a body-fat level so low that he had begun to cannibalise vital tissues.

171

The doctor said: 'I've never heard of this stuff.'

'That's why I'm here,' Wayne replied.

Further back, a bodybuilder called Victor Faisowitz died with a temperature of 112 degrees, again after taking Aldactone. Tommy Sansone, Mr America in 1958 and then Mr Universe in 1963, died in 1974 from cancer after blowing out his immune system with Anadrol and Dianabol.

Sansone had been the first mentor of the most notorious bodybuilder of all time, the former Mr America and creator of the Intensity or Insanity training philosophy, Steve Michalik. After narrowly surviving his preparations for the 1986 Night of Champions, Michalik memorably said that his final ambition had been to drop dead onstage. 'I knew it was all over for me. Every system in my body was shot, my testicles had shrunk to the size of cocktail peanuts. It was only a question of which organ was going to explode on me first.' Michalik survived, after a drastic detox treatment in Australia somehow regenerated his radioactive liver.

Wayne DeMilia and the IFBB had first tried to do something about steroid abuse in 1985, after they began to see pronounced secondary sexual characteristics in female competitors who were taking testosterone ('We saw they were starting to, uh, *change*,' he told me). The problem was, the labs couldn't keep up with steroid technology. By the time they had developed a test, the athletes were on to something else. For whatever reason, Momo Benaziza's death hadn't taken bodybuilding to a tipping point. Andreas Munzer's did. DeMilia realised that something had to be done, especially about diuretics. They were devastating killers. There was no change in vital signs until the moment of cardiac arrest, because the body dehydrated from the extremities inwards. The heart was the last organ to constrict. And if DeMilia hadn't been ready to make a move, there was no shortage of media advice letting him know what was required. Kurt Marnul, an Austrian who had been associated with Schwarzenegger and Munzer told the magazine *Der Neue Grazer* that 'the athletes have lost all sense of proportion'. *Die Welt* laid into bodybuilding. They quoted Erich Janner as saying that some bodybuilders now hardly dare show their muscles in public. *Der Spiegel* just laid Andi bare. John Romano, an editor at *Muscular Development* magazine, said that Twin Labs, the supplement company that owned the publication, would no longer sponsor the Mr Olympia tournament unless drug testing was introduced. Some American magazines suggested that it was all Dorian Yates's fault for being too good. Only Peter McGough at *Flex* seemed to have a measured view. He wrote: 'It's through a realistic and practical understanding of the psyche that drives an athlete to be world class that we will be able to tame the monster. If all you can do is assume the moral high ground by pointing fingers every which way and bleating sanctimonious rubbish, then stop making your living from a sport that so obviously offends you.'

DeMilia acted. Testing was introduced for the 1996 Mr Olympia. (Wayne: 'Dorian's skinny, skinny . . . he still wins easy.') Judges were instructed to disqualify competitors who showed obvious signs of steroid use like excessive acne, water retention and gynaecomastia – the loathed 'bitch-tits'. Dianne Bennett remembered marking people down in the weigh-ins: 'That way they didn't get to the competition. It used to be very evident.'

Steroids were nothing new. Hitler was said to have fed them to his thugs in the 1930s, because he thought that they heightened aggression when used in small doses. They first came to international athletics in 1954, when Russian weightlifters used them in preparation for the world

173

championships. Soon they were everywhere. The East Germans had injected their Olympic squads up with so much gear that one of their female shot-putters had a sex change and became a man. Chinese swimmers looked like wrestlers. Sprinters, boxers and cyclists were getting jacked up; powerlifters lived in the same gyms as bodybuilders. By the close of the century, the only Olympic events never to have had a positive dope test were women's field hockey and figure skating. The reason was simple: steroids worked. And the people who knew most about how and why they worked were not doctors and drug companies, who had designed and used them for a different purpose, but athletes. And the athletes who knew most about them were the bodybuilders and the powerlifters. For ten years in the 1960s, the American Medical Association had maintained that steroids didn't build muscle. In the gyms, you could still hear them laughing at that one. Ten years after that, they pronounced them deadly (when he heard the news, Steve Michalik had said: 'Shit, that was like the FDA seal of approval for steroids. C'mon, everybody, they *must* be good for you – the AMA says they'll kill you.').

The basic premise of a steroid was simple. It was a synthetic version of the male hormone testosterone. They worked by attaching themselves to receptors in the muscle cells and sending a two-part message to them: endure and grow. Steroids reacted to ingested calories by converting them into first mass and then the energy required to build and sustain it. They provoked the synthesis of the molecule creatine phosphate, which allowed muscles to work for longer and thus grow more quickly. They also encouraged water retention in the muscle fibre, making it appear bigger.

It sounded simple, and it was. But the human body wasn't simple, it was complex and infinitely variable. What worked

174

for some failed for others. What gave one guy twenty-two-inch guns and legs like pylons gave another testicular cancer and bitch-tits. And the reasons they did so might be different every time. It could be down to diet, training, lifestyle, genetic susceptibility, quality of the drug supply or the skill of the person using them. It might be due to the minute variations in the human endocrine system, or the production of blood or blood sugar or amino acids or other naturally occurring chemicals. Cause and effect was everything. As the equations became more complex, users became more expert at mixing and matching steroids, at optimising their intake and performance in pyramid-shaped cycles. Many types of steroids entered the market, all doing subtly different things to muscles. First insulin and then human growth hormone became available to elite athletes. So did other drugs, like GHB, which had similar effects. Methods of delivering the high amounts of protein required by bodybuilders were refined, too. Three meals per day could arrive via power shakes that you might swallow in three mouthfuls. Something very simple had acquired its own rich biodiversity.

Dorian said that he equated the risk of taking steroids to smoking cigarettes. Some people could have sixty a day and still be lighting up on their ninetieth birthday. Others might need a lung cutting out at thirty-five. You didn't know till you tried it. Most people who did fell between those two extremes. There were no long-term controlled trials on their effects. A British medical board said such a trial would be 'unethical'.

The great thing about steroids for bodybuilding, as opposed to, say, track and field, was that it was not imperative to the user that they maximise athletic performance. Because sometimes they didn't. Bodybuilders were not

175

sprinters or swimmers, where infinitesimal blocks of time dictated success and failure. The fact that steroids enabled the user to train harder had an obvious benefit, but as long as they made the muscles bigger, it didn't matter if they made them slightly less efficient or less strong than the optimum.

There was a psychological payload, too. The United States Drug Enforcement Administration, and many other medical bodies, categorised steroids as addictive. Scientifically, this was unproven. They did not work, as recreational drugs did, by stimulating the 'reward' section of the brain. Yet they sometimes provoked compulsive use. What's more, they were used to excess by those with excessive personalities, by people whose self-worth and financial well-being were often bound up in their physical size. They were available through agreeable doctors and black markets, from far-off countries and on the Internet. They were a part of the currency of muscle, inextricably woven through the fabric of the lifestyle.

While all of this was going on, Ben Weider was trying to get bodybuilding into the Olympics. It was his long-held ambition. He spent a lot of his time glad-handing IOC delegations from distant places. A page or two at the back of every issue of *Flex* magazine was given over to grainy pictures of odd-looking men being handed various plaques and medals from the IFBB. Ben Weider donated a gym to Syria in 1991. He visited over a hundred countries, creating IFBB affiliations and spreading the word. He greased the wheels of the IOC on behalf of bodybuilding. He took a strong anti-doping stance. The IFBB signed up to the IOC drug-testing programme. He said: 'Cheating, by using steroids and other drugs, is not acceptable to the IFBB.'

But Ben Weider was caught in the sport's zugzwang, too. It wasn't as if bodybuilding was the only sport which had guys on the juice. It was just that in pro bodybuilding it was so *obvious*. It was this that kept Ben Weider's dream out of reach.

Wayne DeMilia implemented testing for the pro division after Andreas Munzer's death, and for a while the guys got smaller. But the sport was about big men getting ripped. That's what the crowds wanted. It's what Andi had wanted to give them. There could be no going backwards. The myth that such a body could exist without drugs, propagated by the denials of people like Albert Busek in his magazines, was exposed. The 'sensational journalism' was not in the papers. It was coming from Busek and the bodybuilding mags. Their stance was that these bodies existed without steroids. And they did not. Andi Munzer's body existed with steroids. And then it stopped existing altogether.

Yet Andi's death had mystery. Andi's death contained contradictions. I had shown the list of drugs Andi was said to have taken to Kerry Kayes and Dorian Yates the first time I met them, at the Wembley Plaza. Kerry said: 'Look at it this way. If you're a bodybuilder and you get caught with steroids on you, you're going to want to be able to prove that they're for personal use. If they think you're dealing, then you're going to do some time. Now, you might buy that much gear when you have the chance, but it might take you six months, a year to use it all. Who knows? But if there's a piece of paper or a list or whatever that gets found on you that makes out that's [the quantity] that you use . . .'

Kerry's explanation was plausible, I thought. It was a question of timescales, as he said. The condensed timescale of Andi's list offered him some protection against cheap thoughts that he might deal. Andi didn't deal. He had made a deal with himself not to. To avoid the accusation, he might have scribbled down a schedule that suggested consumption beyond anything that he might sensibly have considered.

I knew lots of pro bodybuilders. None of them was using the quantities claimed for Munzer, or even anything like it. Flex Wheeler had allowed himself to be injected with any amount of steroids when he was young and green and performing the role of lab rat in a Californian gym in the early 1980s, but he laughed at that kind of cycle now. The Pros were experts, self-taught chemical sorcerers with twenty-four/seven access to their labs. They had years of knowledge behind them. So did Andi. He would have understood that often less was more. He would probably have known, too, about Steve Michalik's drug use, about how excessive steroids had poisoned his system and finally stopped him growing, until, in rehab, as Paul Solotaroff wrote in *Village Voice*, 'it all started coming out of him: a viscous green paste that oozed out of his eyes and nostrils'. Michalik, who had been taking so much gear over such a protracted period that he had cysts in his liver the size of golf balls, had got clean and was now out there proselytising to high-school kids about the dangers of steroid abuse.

Andi would have seen some real muscle casualties, the gym junkie losers who'd bought the big steroid myth, that they can turn anyone into a Mr O, and who'd instead ended up bloated and squishy, with halitosis, bitch-tits and empty wallets. He would have known about Momo Benaziza in Holland in '92 and Mike Matarazzo in Ohio in '93. He might have been told about Heinz Salimayer, an Austrian bodybuilder who had died in the 1980s after using Lasix. Perhaps he had heard about the highest profile steroid casualty of all, the Gridiron star Lyle Alzado, a school friend of Steve Michalik, who died of brain cancer on

14 May 1992. Alzado, who had been hard and athletic enough in his prime to box an eight-round exhibition match against Muhammad Ali, blamed steroid use for the abject surrender of his body. 'I started taking anabolic steroids in 1969 and never stopped,' he admitted during the horror of his pain-filled final days. 'It was addicting, mentally addicting. Now I'm sick, and I'm scared. Ninety per cent of the athletes I know are on the stuff. We're not born to be three hundred pounds or jump thirty feet. But all the time I was taking steroids, I knew they were making me play better. I became very violent on the field and off it. I did things only crazy people do. Once a guy sideswiped my car and I beat the hell out of him. Now look at me. My hair's gone, I wobble when I walk and have to hold on to someone for support, and I have trouble remembering things. My last wish? That no one else ever dies this way.'

The more I came to know about bodybuilding, the more I came to enjoy the sport, the more I thought about Andreas Munzer and his strange end. I wanted to rebut the accepted notions on his death. I thought Andi's life's work should be acknowledged as more than just a list of drugs. I thought the weird magnificence of his body should be commemorated.

That, to me, was the least he was due.

7

An Interlude at the Temple

I wanted to understand the detachment that bodybuilders felt, that Dorian and Andreas and all of them understood. They were different, separate. When they walked in the street, that difference was apparent. They wore it. The pre-conceptions they met drove them further away. They grew sick of the stares and the pointing fingers. They covered up their bodies. They kept their culture for themselves. Obviously, I couldn't build a body like theirs, so I tried to build a mind like theirs instead. I went on a sixteen-week contest diet. It consisted of six meals per day: oatmeal for breakfast; turkey slices or suchlike mid-morning; tuna for lunch; some kind of fruit and maybe a power bar mid-afternoon; pasta or rice with chicken, turkey or tuna for dinner; fruit or turkey slices a couple of hours after that. Lots of water, no alcohol, no salt, no sugar, no fatty foods. I lasted five weeks. The cravings for anything with taste became overwhelming. I began to dream about food. I cracked. I fell eleven weeks short.

Dorian said that I could train with him at the Temple. I went on back day. When I walked in, Dorian and his training partner were setting up the gym. They decided on the weights they would use, and then they laid them out. They barely spoke as they did so. Dorian still trained heavy, that much was apparent. When the training stations were ready, he began stretching. He was supple and lithe. He prepared with focus and concentration. After a while, he went to the machines and the weights. He did a few warm-up sets while I rode the stationary bike. I watched him closely. He moved with the same precision as the machines in the gym. They looked like parts of a whole: Dorian's form was precise, and the machines responded in kind. He moved and then they did, and then he moved again and so did they. It was simple and perfect. When it was my turn, I flapped about underneath them amateurishly. I was just relieved I could lift something above the smallest weight. I'd been worrying for some time before that I wouldn't be able to. I tried as hard as I could. Dorian would say, 'Right. you're going to feel this *here* . . .' and he'd jab a fingertip into my back. He was always right. I went to failure. It didn't take too long. It was a strange sensation. There was no pain at all. I just couldn't lift the weight, no matter how hard I tried.

At least I was fit. I ran thirty miles a week. I had begun during a period of my life when I felt I had little control over anything. Things were happening and I could do nothing to stop them, so I looked for control elsewhere. I sought sovereignty over myself. I wanted change, some sort of escape or transformation. I ran every day back then, as far and as hard as I could. When I got back from a run, I'd pull my soaking training gear off and stand in front of the mirror. My gut disappeared. My chest filled out. My muscles got hard. My face got thin. I had my hair razored down. I shaped my body to the force of my will. I had control of some kind or another. Things began to change, slowly.

I still ran hard. I waited for the endorphin high, my chemical reward. It didn't come every night, but when it did, my mind reached. My imagination became fierce. I made decisions. I empowered myself. In uncertain times, the road became a given for me. It was an absolute. It could not be cheated or duped; I could only do that to myself. I never did, though. It was a pure thing. It liberated me.

I tried to equate it with bodybuilding. When I went out in the rain or the cold or late at night, and ran past houses with people sitting inside, I felt separate from them, I felt superior to them. I knew something that they didn't. Every now and again, I'd pass someone going to a gym in expensive gear, or out with a personal trainer, or I'd overhear people in canteens and restaurants talking about their diets and what they weighed and what they were going to do about it, and I'd laugh at them. These people didn't need personal trainers. They didn't need gym fees or Stairmasters. They didn't need Lycra gear or diet books. They needed determination. They needed ascetism. They needed to alleviate their weakness, their softness of mind. They needed to want *this* more than they wanted *that*. For a long time, I scorned them. And while I did, I thought, maybe this is almost how it feels.

THE SHADOW'S LAST STAND: DORIAN YATES WINS MR OLYMPIA 1997

WAYNE DEMILIA WORKS IT OUT

FLEX WHEELER

DENNIS JAMES

DYNASTY: BEN AND JOE WEIDER

KEVIN LEVRONE

CHRIS CORMIER

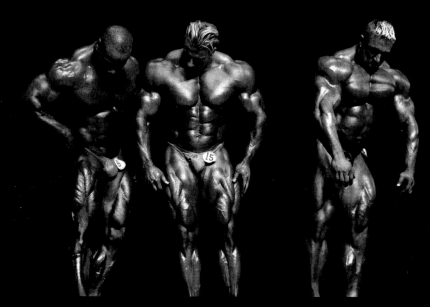

COMPARING CUTS: CORMIER AND CUTLER TRY TO OUT-SHRED EACH OTHER AS
MARKUS RUHL PUMPS HIS PECS AT PREJUDGING FOR THE ARNOLD CLASSIC 2003

BEAM AND SQUEEZE: TROY ALVES, 'MARVELLOUS' MELVIN ANTHONY, DARREM CHARLES
AND ERNIE TAYLOR GET CALLED OUT AT THE MR O 2003

NOT QUITE ELVIS IN VEGAS: GUNTER ADDRESSES THE CROWD AFTER HIS FIFTH-PLACE FINISH AT THE 2002 MR OLYMPIA

TERMINATED: ARNIE OUT-TALKS JAY CUTLER AT THE ARNOLD CLASSIC 2003 (*ABOVE RIGHT*), AND PRESENTS RONNIE COLEMAN WITH A TOP SIX FINISHER'S MEDAL AT THE MR O 2003 (*ABOVE LEFT*)

DORIAN YATES AND KERRY KAYES PRESENT DEXTER JACKSON WITH
THE TROPHY FOR WINNING THE BRITISH GRAND PRIX 2002

SIMON ROBINSON
SQUARES HIS
CIRCLE ON THE
MR OLYMPIA STAGE

(FACING PAGE)
CHRIS CORMIER AND
DARREM CHARLES
GIVE THE CROWD
AN EYEFUL DURING
THE POSEDOWN FOR
THE ARNOLD CLASSIC
2003

SHREDDED TO THE END: ANDREAS MUNZER ONSTAGE AT THE
ARNOLD CLASSIC 1996. TWELVE DAYS LATER, HE WAS DEAD.

8

Wayne DeMilia Works It Out

'Like I said,' Wayne DeMilia said, 'to me, I don't care. I work with what's there. Whatever circumstances I'm dealt with the contest, I make it into an event. If Jay isn't in, like he wasn't last year, my whole thing in my mailing and my advertising is "Who's gonna be the Jay Cutler of this year? Ronnie's one year older . . ." I do mailers on all different subjects: "Jay and Shawn aren't going to be competing, but they're going to be at the contest. Why don't you come to the expo and ask 'em why they aren't competing?" Y'know, ba ba ba ba ba ba ba . . .'

He paused, but only for a second. He was talking about the 2003 Mr Olympia show, which he was promoting at the Mandalay Bay resort in Las Vegas.

'Causing controversy is what makes people come. I look at what I'm dealt and play the cards accordingly. This year, I have something, it's gonna sell: Gunter versus Ronnie versus Jay. It'll probably be good for a couple of years. Because quite honestly, I don't believe someone is going to run away with it. Whoever wins, it's gonna be a narrow victory.

'Let's say Jay wins. Is Ronnie gonna retire? No. No way is Ronnie going to retire. Ronnie's making too much money to go back to being a cop full-time. Let's say it comes out Jay first, Gunter second, Ronnie third. Let's just say like that. Gunter's gonna say, "I'm fifth place in the Olympia, then I'm second . . . next year's gonna be mine." Ronnie's gonna say, "I'm coming back to reclaim the title." And if some other newcomer comes out of the woodwork and wins some other shows in the course of next year, that becomes a fourth player. And what if Levrone comes in, in the shape of his life, and beats them all? Anything could happen. Look at what you got *then* . . .'

Wayne DeMilia ran the IFBB Pro Division out of a house in New York. Often when you phoned him up you could hear his dogs barking in the background. Running the Pro Division divided up into promoting the shows, at which Wayne was masterly, and coralling the bodybuilders, which was more random and required more cunning. In bodybuilding, there were tigers and there were lambs, and Wayne was a tiger, like Joe and Ben Weider and Arnold, and most of the bodybuilders were lambs. In Wayne's words: 'They take life lightly.' Wayne didn't. He held on tightly. All of the official stuff to do with pro bodybuilding ran through Wayne, but so did all of the unofficial stuff: all of the buzz, all of the gossip, all of the news. It thrummed through him, and Wayne DeMilia worked it all out.

I met him for the first time at the British Grand Prix in 2002 at Wembley, when Dexter Jackson had won. Wayne was tall and stern. He'd travelled with his girlfriend, who was Japanese and very beautiful. He was washed out, smeared by all the time zones he had to fly through on the

European tour, which came right on the back of the Olympia. On the tour, he acted as head judge, and he did all of his other stuff too, all of the unofficial stuff, talking to the bodybuilders, keeping on top of the news.

Lots of people thought that Wayne DeMilia was a bad guy. On the Internet message boards he was cast as a Dickensian factory owner. He fed the bodybuilders his scraps while he rolled in the millions of the IFBB. The bodybuilders had their own gripes, too. In return, Wayne gave everything to them straight. He never sugared the pill. It was a shock, when all they ever heard at the gym was 'Oh, you look great . . . you're the man . . .'

The bodybuilders gave Wayne lots of shit because people were always telling them that he should be doing more for them. There would be no Mr O without them, they said, no European tour or high life in the IFBB.

There were always lots of rumours about how much money Wayne was making. It was the subject of dark mutterings, of side-of-mouth whisperings, of Internet postings. Dorian told me a story about Wayne and money. He'd just come offstage after one of his Olympias, still hot and sore and elated, and he was standing backstage with the Sandow statue at his feet. In his hand was a cheque for $100,000. Wayne had come and stood beside him and said, 'Hey, Dorian, I just made more money than you did out there . . .'

It was that kind of thing that enraged the bodybuilders. But, as Wayne maintained, they took life lightly. They didn't understand what it was to promote a show like the Olympia in Las Vegas. They had no conception of the scale or of the expense. They didn't really give him much to work with, either. One man would be champion for years and years. Everyone knew what the result would be before the show started. The 2003 Mr Olympia would be the first contest for half a decade that didn't feel like a lock. Ronnie versus Gunter versus Jay was manna from heaven for Wayne DeMilia, a gift from the gods of muscle. He wasn't about to miss out on it, after all of those barren years.

The bodybuilder's mentality seemed to appal and fascinate Wayne. In twenty years, he'd seen it all. He'd watched some of them blow their money; he'd been there for the fights and the scraps and the bust-ups; he'd seen Momo Benaziza and Andi Munzer die; he was there when Paul Dillett froze up and got carried offstage and he went to the hospital with Mike Matarazzo when he collapsed after the Arnold Classic in 1993. He'd seen athletes retire from the sport with nothing to fall back on, with no life except for the gym. He'd had them complaining about the judging and their placings and the prize money and the fact there was no union for the athletes. He'd seen it all and he'd heard it all.

Perhaps it was his manner that made you think he didn't have any respect for the bodybuilders. He always told them exactly what he thought, what he was doing and why he was doing it. They took everything lightly and they didn't understand how or why Wayne had things in hand, years ahead. Yet someone had to, or the whole sport would quickly cease to exist in any organised form.

Outwitting most bodybuilders wasn't a complex task. Wayne just liked to let them know every time he did it. Soon after the Arnold Classic, he'd done it again. A pro called Bob Cicherillo had tried to start up a union. Wayne had tried to explain to Bob what bodybuilders were like. He told him that he'd have to make letterheads and do mail-outs and charge a membership fee to cover it that they wouldn't want to pay.

'He said, "I gotta pay for envelopes and letterheads?"' Wayne said, going into the story. 'I said, "Yeah, Bob. And you gotta mail it out – postage, you gotta pay for that." So he got letterheads, he got envelopes, he mailed a letter out. We had about eighty pro bodybuilders at the time. He didn't get a response. Not one. Nobody wanted to pay a fee to be part of a union.

'You go back to 1981, they wanted to start a body-builders' association, run by Frank Zane, Boyer Coe and Mike Mentzer. Three big names at the time. They decided they were going to boycott the '81 Olympia. Because in 1980 Arnold won and they felt it was fixed. Now Arnold's running the show and Franco's coming back so it's going to be fixed for Franco. And they all sign a document saying they're boycotting the contest.

'I get a phone call from Boyer Coe, from a lobby phone, saying, "I just wanna tell you, Wayne, everybody's signed a form, we're boycotting the Olympia. I wanna be right up front with you."

'My other line's ringing. It's Samir Bannout. Samir says, "I'm in the hotel lobby, on a payphone."

'"Is Boyer Coe nearby?"

'"Yeah, he's two phones ahead of me. He's just hung up."

'"What do you want Samir?"

'"Even though I signed that thing that Boyer has, don't count it. I'm gonna do the Olympia. Because if everybody else is not in there, I'm gonna win."

'An hour later I get a call from Tom Platz.

'"Wayne, you know I signed that thing, but I'm going in the Olympia, because if no one's there, I'm gonna win."

'Well, in the next two days, every single person called me except the three guys that organised it. It's an individual sport. That's why there'll never be a union. And they will never be able to organise.

'I mean, Dorian Yates. When he was a bodybuilder and I wanted him to compete in the Grand Prix events, I had to raise the prize money. We were giving away $25,000.

'He goes, "What's gonna be first place?"

'"Ten, maybe twelve."

'"If you make these first three shows $15,000 first place, I'll compete."

'We had to raise the prize money to $30,000 a show and every other year he would do Spain on the Friday, Germany on Saturday, England on Sunday, so within a forty-eight-hour period he would make himself $45,000. Now that he's a promoter, he goes to me: "Wayne what's the prize money?"

'"It's $30,000."

'"Can't we lower it?"

[Later, I asked Dorian. He said he'd never asked for prize money to be lowered.]

'That's the way it is. I have Dorian calling me up: "How do we do this? Can you help me with that?" Shawn Ray now, doing all these seminars: "Wayne, can we do these seminars around the show?" Craig Titus with these after-show parties he's started organising: "Can you put it on there?" At the Olympia, Craig Titus is gonna do well because we're putting the party at House of Blues which is right at Mandalay Bay. Where are people gonna go? Even if they don't go to the banquet, they're gonna go to the party. I said to him, "Look, if it works, if I like it, we'll raise the price of the VIP ticket a little bit and include that in it." See, the difference between, say, me and the Weiders is, I'll help them make money in the sport. I understand how to make money from the sport and when his competitive days are over, what's a thirty-eight-year-old guy who's been a bodybuilder all his life gonna do? No college education, *what's he gonna do*? He's gotta make money within the sport.'

This was how Wayne spoke. He plunged you right into the middle of his thought processes. He showed you all of the connections he made. He pointed out why bodybuilding was like it was, and why it was never going to change.

Wayne DeMilia was tall and thin, but when he was thirteen years old, he had been short and fat. He was a short, fat kid from Queens, New York. His accent would never recover. One day, actually the last day of his freshman year at high school, Wayne went to the news-stand to buy a baseball magazine but there was nothing new, so he got *Muscular Development* instead. He pestered his father to get his old weights set out of the garage. With his usual thoroughness, Wayne painted each of the plate sizes a different colour before he began using them. That summer, he grew from 5' 5" to 5' 11". His voice broke. He went back to school with a beard and muscles. He had changed, outside and in. He had to write an essay on what he wanted to do in life. Wayne wrote: 'I want to run the Mr Universe contest and bring it to America.'

Instead, he went through college and became an engineer for AT&T. He was still doing that in 1973, when he started training at the Mid-City gym in Manhattan, which was owned by the guy who was putting on the Mr Olympia, Tom Minichiello. Wayne started gofering for him. He'd pick up the bodybuilders at the airport and ferry them into town for the shows. He started a little newsletter, written in pugnacious style. He got to know George Butler, who was making *Pumping Iron*, and through George he met Arnold

Schwarzenegger. By 1975, Minichiello had made Wayne the Metropolitan Area Director for the AFAB, an IFBB offshoot. He offered Wayne a shot at promoting a show, the East Coast Mr America, which took place each spring. Wayne didn't realise that he'd been sold a pup till he went round the gyms to drum up some interest. The big guys laughed at him. 'Tom has to have a spring show,' they told Wayne, 'or we'll all switch to the AAU [Amateur Athletic Union], and he won't have any competitors for his fall show, where he makes his money. He always loses money on the spring show. Now you're gonna lose your money.'

Wayne told the big guys not to worry. He had it all under control and he wasn't going to lose any money. He was going to get a sponsor. No one knew what that was. He found a small hotel reservations service at JFK and told them he'd put all of his competition bookings through them if they gave him $600. He took the $600 and rented a school auditorium in Manhattan. He hassled everyone at the Mid-City gym and sold out the show: 250 folding seats at $6.50 and $5 general admission. He made $1,000 and gave $500 to the guy who'd helped him out with the lights and sound. The winner of the contest got a trophy and a colour TV set. Tom Minichiello told him it was the worst show ever and that sponsorship for bodybuilding was a non-starter.

Wayne didn't care. He caught a plane to Los Angeles and waited in Joe Weider's office for three hours for a meeting with the great man. When he got in to see him, he told Joe that he wanted to run the IFBB the same way that they ran tennis or golf; with a series of qualifying events and a few major championships. Joe told him to write to his brother Ben. Wayne did, often. He helped out at shows to see where and how the money came in or leaked out. Joe used Wayne's ideas in his editorial column in one of his magazines.

Ben Weider sent Wayne a message: he'd give him fifteen minutes at the Mr America show in Montreal. Wayne went. He told Ben that Joe's ideas were really his ideas. Ben said the best Wayne could do was to see if he could get invited on to the pro committee that Joe had suggested the IFBB form. The pro committee had been Wayne's idea, too. Wayne asked who the chairman was. Ben told him it was Arnold Schwarzenegger. Wayne was thrilled: he knew Arnold through George Butler. He smiled to himself as he waited for the hotel lift outside Ben Weider's room. The lift door opened; Arnold Schwarzenegger was standing inside. Wayne smiled again. It was fate. It was meant to be.

At the pro committee meeting, Wayne got a show to promote. He booked a theatre, for the spring of 1978. Ben Weider said that the show was all Wayne's in return for a sanction fee of a dollar a seat. The theatre that Wayne had booked had 1,500 seats. Wayne had a friend called Charles Blake, who was pretty high up in advertising at NBC. He showed Wayne how to design and typeset a decent magazine ad for his show. He worked on a production design, too, something better than the usual black curtain and endless repetition of the 'Exodus' music. Wayne stole the name Night of Champions from one of Don King's boxing promotions. When Joe Weider saw the ads that Charles Blake had designed, he tried to hire him to work on the Weider magazines, only to find he couldn't match his salary at NBC.

Wayne slid a few more ideas into his first Night of Champions. He let the public watch the two prejudging rounds for the first time. They got to see the quarter-turns and the seven compulsory poses. Like George Butler, he saw a new way, but one based around showmanship and bigger sports rather than art history and Platonic idealism. He opened the evening with a choreographed slide show. He

191

told the competitors to bring their own music for the posing round. The theatre was oversold, people were standing in the aisles and at the back of the stalls. Wayne gave Ben Weider his sanction fee gladly. The agreement had been a dollar a seat; nothing about people standing. He was only an AT&T engineer, but he went home that night having changed bodybuilding.

The next day, the crash came. Wayne became depressed. He didn't want to work for AT&T any more. He had no agreement to promote more shows. Arnold was pissed off with him because he didn't agree with sanction fees. On 4 July, his phone rang and a kid asked him when he could get a ticket for Night of Champions II. Wayne told him there was no Night of Champions II, it had been a one-off show. The kid asked Wayne if he'd heard about *Rocky II*, the movie that Sylvester Stallone was making. If there could be two *Rockys* there could be another Night of Champions. Wayne sold the kid a $20 ticket there and then, and within three years he was head of the IFBB Pro Division.

The great thing Wayne did was to look at pro bodybuilding like it was a real sport. He was a sports fan. He could tell you anything you wanted to know about baseball, gridiron, boxing. He looked at how they treated their athletes and he copied that. He'd send limousines to pick up competitors at airports. He'd book them free flights and hotel rooms. He made them feel like sportsmen. In return, the bodybuilders wanted to appear at IFBB shows rather than NABBA shows. The problem was that bodybuilding wasn't a sport on the scale of the others that he admired. It interested only a few hundred people in each city in America. Wayne was promoting five shows a year and paying sanction fees hand over fist to Ben Weider to do so, and he and Charlie, who was still on board, were splitting a few hundred dollars at the end of a year. He still worked for AT&T.

He was hooked, though, helplessly hooked. Ben kept on at him to quit his job and go full-time. In 1986, he took seven weeks accrued leave from AT&T and never went back.

Wayne had been working things out ever since. He'd begun to structure the sport properly. He drew up contest rules and an IFBB constitution and he'd come up with a qualifying system for the pros. Amateur bodybuilders had to gain a professional card at an accredited tournament in order to compete in his shows. Wayne acted like the baseball commissioner or the PGA Tour commissioner. He ran the professional side of the sport. He grew it, found the sponsors, marketed the contests, upped the prize funds and ended up in Las Vegas at the Mandalay Bay hotel with the Mr O, a show that used to feature a black curtain and a repeating version of 'Exodus' for the music.

'Let's look at '92/'93. Helsinki in '92,' he was saying. 'We had $140,000 in sponsor and exhibitor money. In '93, we had about $175,000. In 2002, we had $912,000 in sponsorship money. More companies are evolving from within the sport. Now we're trying to get into pay-per-view. Whether it has the potential or not is up in the air. It's a risk. Two years ago at the Olympia press conference, Shawn Ray says, "I wanna know where the money from the Internet broadcast is gonna go. A hundred thousand people tuning in, ten dollars a person, that's a million dollars. Where's that million dollars?"

'I said, "Shawn, I'd love to have it . . . But there's no guarantee."

'You know how many people tuned into the Internet? We charged fifteen dollars for the video feed. Nine hundred and thirteen people tuned into the video streaming worldwide. It shows you how big the sport is, or how small the sport is. When you look at the subscription levels of *Flex* magazine, and each of those subscribers is a hard-core person, it's not that much. The total circulation of *Flex* on a good month is 200,000. *Two hundred thousand?* That's nothing. You know how many people live in America? Almost three hundred million. That's how small we are. You take baseball. The Tampa Bay Devil Rays. They're a terrible team. And they drew nine thousand people to the game the other day, and it's one of the smallest crowds they ever had. Nine thousand? If we had nine thousand paying people at Mr Olympia, I'd be running naked down Las Vegas Boulevard shouting, "This is the greatest ever."

'The most we've ever drawn paid was in New York in '98. Four thousand six hundred and forty-six paid. OK, remember that number: 4,646. We have a lot of comps in there. The Weider company takes a ton of tickets. The sponsors get comps, the athletes get comps and dah, dah, dah. There's five to six thousand people there, but that's the most we've ever had pay. I've never had five thousand pay. I might top that this year. This year is a very hot ticket. You got three guys that can win the title, the title's up for grabs, the champ may get dethroned onstage which hardly ever happens. Especially with a champ who has won, what, five times in a row? Almost unheard of, and there are two guys who could almost take him. And I see the amount of requests I have already and we haven't even advertised as yet.'

Wayne DeMilia was working it up and working it out. He had the figure 4,646 in his mind. Ronnie versus Gunter versus Jay was the key. He'd got 4,646 when the fans wanted to see who would replace Dorian on his retirement. What could Wayne work out when someone might replace

Ronnie, with Ronnie in the field?

The great thing was, everyone was doing all of the working out for him. Gunter Schlierkamp had worked out how to get his giant body in contest shape. He'd worked out how to work the crowds. He'd started Guntermania.

Jay Cutler had worked out how to win big shows after his narrow loss to Ronnie Coleman at the 2001 Mr O. He'd worked out and worked out and now the great swoop of his shoulders balanced the prodigious curves of his drumstick thighs. He was out to get even with Ronnie Coleman.

Ronnie Coleman was working out what went wrong in New Orleans. There were dark rumours coming out of Arlington. Ronnie felt humiliated. Ronnie thought he'd been stitched up at the GNC Show of Strength. Being Mr Olympia defined him, and as Wayne said, he was making too much money to go back to being a cop now. Big Ron was going to work, getting even bigger.

It wasn't just the bodybuilders getting excited either. The fans had started up right after the GNC show and carried on through the Arnold Classic, arguing, speculating, gossiping about Gunter versus Ronnie versus Jay. On the message boards at GetBig.com and Muscle Mayhem and Bodybuilding.com they fought it out with each other. They threw mud and waited to see what stuck. It got vicious and sometimes funny and occasionally out of control. Bodybuilding was exciting again. Wayne DeMilia had a show on his hands. He was pretty sure he could work out what to do next.

Wayne's figured Gunter versus Ronnie versus Jay could be a two, maybe even a three-year storyline, like a Don King fight with a rematch clause and then a rubber bout. He could spin it however he liked. He said that he could beat 4,646 at the Mandalay Bay, and put on the biggest promotion that bodybuilding had ever seen.

195

He understood that everything was getting bigger and that it probably couldn't be stopped. The Olympia promotion would be bigger; the crowds would be larger and the magazines and the supplement companies would sell more, and there would be more at stake, and so the bodybuilders would get bigger than ever before. Wayne was a pragmatist. He knew that the sport was hurtling towards an endgame of sorts, towards the outposts of the human frame. He was somehow pushing it to get there. After Momo Benaziza and then Andreas Munzer died, he'd acted over diuretics. Men were no longer freezing up or dropping dead. But he knew, as everyone knew, that professional bodybuilding was about excess. It was a drug sport, and most of the competitors used drugs, and there was nothing anyone could do to stop them unless they wanted to kill off the sport. There was no going back. It was catch-22. It was zugzwang.

Wayne said: 'We drug-test for diuretics because we were having so much trouble with athletes on diuretics. Between Benaziza's death and people passing out and stuff, we had to do it. Now, do I know that the guys take diuretics? Yes, I know that they do. There's diuretics they take that the lab doesn't even know about. There's nothing I can do. But you know what? No one has passed out onstage. No one is throwing up backstage. So we're not having those type of problems.

'Will the physiques continue to grow? Yes. But they gotta remember, if they outgrow their frames they're not gonna look good. Gunter's a big man. He can be bigger. You think about Arnold at his best at six foot two, he weighed 230. Gunter at six one and a half, a little bit shorter, weighed 301. And he was more ripped than Arnold. We're talking 1975, *Pumping Iron*, to 2002. We're talking twenty-seven years. Look at Dorian onstage at five foot ten and 270. Four inches shorter and forty pounds heavier than Arnold and more ripped. And now Gunter's taken it to over the 300 pounds level. We've had guys onstage at 300, but never in this kind of condition.

'When you stand next to Gunter, you realise how big he is. I'm an even six foot. When we were backstage, I said, "Gunter come here. Stand in the mirror with me."

'He said, "Is something wrong?"

'I said, "Nah, I just wanna see something. You're just a little bit taller than me but you're twice as wide."

'I'm a normal-sized man, 180, 185 pounds, I train. I been around this a long time. I'm impressed. I said, "Go ahead, get back in line . . ." It's amazing.'

Wayne paused, but only for a moment. He didn't need to think. He'd already worked this one out, hundreds of times probably.

'Are the physiques gonna continue to get larger? Yes. Can you take the drugs out of the sport? No. Can you take it out of any sport? No. You can't test for everything. Our society is a drug society. We got offensive linemen here in the NFL, if they're 310, they're small. You're talking about almost 400-pound offensive linemen. They'll tell you what they took when they retire. A great defensive player here was a guy called Lawrence Taylor, played for the Giants. Lawrence Taylor says, "I used to take cocaine, get hopped up this and that."

'Now, you kind of knew he was doing that, but you didn't care. You wanted him to sack the quarterback. You wanted him to take the cortisone because you wanted to get him out on the field cos you wanted to win and you wanted to be entertained. Then if there's a tragedy, you go, "Aw, that's terrible, I feel so bad . . ." Who causes the players to do that? We do. The fans. Because we pay the money and the best players are gonna make the most money, so the players are gonna take the risk. That's just the way it is in life.'

That's the way it was in life for Flex Wheeler, too. Flex had possessed the most beautiful physique on the planet, a body that Dianne Bennett wanted to send into space as an example of the very best we could do. Flex had rung Wayne DeMilia a few days before and told him that he needed a kidney transplant or he was going to die. Wayne had sighed. He had been telling Flex 'for a long time' that he should retire.

'I said to him many times,' Wayne said, 'I said, "Flex, you shouldn't compete no more." He'd come in with doctors' notes saying he's fine. How can I stop him legally from competing? He went the limit. Now, he's gone. Gotta have a kidney replacement. He took diuretics. They told him, don't take diuretics. He came off before the contests but it still did his kidney in. Now he needs a kidney transplant, he's on the list. The thing that's gonna kill Flex is – and for a lot of these guys who have medical problems – it's hard for them . . . it's hard for Flex Wheeler to be Flex Wheeler if he's normal size. Flex Wheeler, genetically, the size of his wrists, his bones, he is the same size as me. He should be a 180-pound man. But if Flex Wheeler was 180 pounds and trim, he wouldn't be Flex Wheeler. Flex Wheeler will probably do further harm to himself, even if he gets a transplant, trying to be bigger.'

It was a grim thought, grim because Wayne obviously considered it might be true. Flex had just finished writing a book about his life. It was called *Flex-Ability* and it was being marketed as a human-interest, against-all-odds-type book. I rang the publishers and arranged to speak to Flex.

When he came on the line, his voice was so soft and distant, I could barely hear him. Later, when I played the tape back, almost nothing he'd said had come out. It was morning in Los Angeles, he said, and he was still going to the gym and working out. He was trying to keep in shape for when the transplant came along. He was having dialysis while he waited. Flex said that he was a religious guy, devoted to his family, but that for a long time he hadn't been. He was a little lost soul from Fresno, with genetics so rare and refined, no one had really looked like he did before or since. It was precisely because he was small that he looked so good when he was big. His joints and junctions were tight and allowed the muscle to blossom outwards. He was rounded and full, all orbs and ellipses. Back in the 1980s, he said, when guys in gyms didn't really know much about steroids other than they made you big, he would take anything with no thought or method. He'd come in the next day, visibly larger, a living example of chemical force, and they'd all stand around and laugh and marvel at him.

Flex was great but he could never beat Dorian Yates. His life outside of bodybuilding, with girls and money and fighting and low self-esteem, left him at the mercy of the Shadow's ferocious focus. His best chance for the O had been in 1998, when Dorian had retired, but he'd lost out by three points to Ronnie Coleman. He was second again the year after, by twenty points. He'd won the Arnold Classic four times and the Night of Champions once. He'd probably earned a few million dollars, but most of it was gone, and now so was his body.

He said that he had a genetic kidney condition called focal segmental glomerulosclerosis, which he had inherited from his parents. The internal structure of his kidneys had become disturbed by scarring. Flex said that steroids hadn't given him the disease, he'd have got it anyway, but it usually came on later, in your forties. He'd had kidney problems for a while. He'd even competed drug-free at the 2002 Mr Olympia and finished seventh, which was amazing when you stopped to think about it, but all anyone said was, 'Man, did you see Flex? He's gone downhill . . .'

I'd once asked Dorian what Flex was like, and Dorian had sighed and raised his eyebrows. He told me that they'd had to share a hotel room in some kind of emergency, and that Flex had decided to order room service and then completely lost it. He'd screamed and pulled the phone out of the wall and thrown it across the room. 'He just went, like . . . *that*,' Dorian said, indicating an instantaneous eruption with his hand.

It all seemed a long time ago for Flex. I told him what Dianne Bennett had said about him, and he perked up. 'Yeah, I know Dianne,' he said. 'She said that? That's nice, man . . .' On my tape, the only time his voice became really clear was when he talked about God. He was a regular churchgoer now, and he was trying to live a good, clean life. He knew that he could never compete again. He said he thought there had always been two of him: there was Flex Wheeler, who was the big, arrogant bully, and there was Kenny Wheeler, who was just the boy from Fresno, trying to work it all out.

Wayne DeMilia was a pragmatist and Peter McGough was a romantic, but they both understood what the future of bodybuilding was. Wayne was putting the freaks onstage, and Peter was putting them in *Flex* magazine, and the freakier the bodybuilders got, the more often they were chosen to appear there.

I rang Peter. He said: 'That's the conundrum with *Flex*.

What am I going to do? Markus Ruhl got the biggest cheer at the Arnold – I'm going to put him on the frigging cover, because I want to sell magazines. But am I responsible for then encouraging all the young guys out there to get to 280 pounds, whatever it costs them? Can we go back? If we said, for instance, yeah, we're going to go back to the old physiques, can we go back once we've bred a monster. What would happen?

'I don't think that drugs are the reason Markus Ruhl is 280 pounds. They're obviously part of it. But the genetic pool is now so much bigger. In my day, nobody trained. Now, every high-school kid is gonna have a go at training. He's gonna fall into it either through football or something, and he might be good at it, he might respond to it quickly. So the genetic pool is much bigger, that's partly why you've got Markus Ruhl. And I do believe drug use is greater at the lower levels of guys who want to be Markus Ruhl, not Markus Ruhl himself.

'If we brought in drug testing, if we said, OK, it might make a difference, would the public then be interested in seeing a guy at 230 pounds, when they've seen a guy at 280 pounds? The genie's out the bottle. Everybody's raving about Gunter. He was 300 pounds at the Olympia. He's talking about coming in at 320 next year. And what am I going to do? We've got a lead story now, let's put Gunter on the cover – 320 pounds!'

Peter McGough was honest and decent. He said he'd turn half of the ads in *Flex* magazine away, if it was up to him. He wanted to bring back the vacuum pose, where the competitors sucked their stomachs up under their ribcages. Anyone with a big, druggy belly wouldn't be able to do it. He wanted to get rid of the drug 'gurus' who said they were dieticians and who prepared people for contests.

In the back of his mind was his biggest fear: if one of the guys dropped dead, how culpable was he?

'I've got that in the back of my head. The first time one of these guys drops, I'm out of here . . .' he said. 'I know what's going to happen. *Sports Illustrated* will be saying magazines like ours promote this, we glorify these guys, we're making these guys look better than they actually are.

'We don't pick a bad shot of anybody. This is why some of these guys think they're better than they are – if a guy's sort of doing a pose and for some reason he's blown his gut out, we take another picture. We don't touch them up, but we wouldn't show a guy with his gut hanging out. We've bred that look. We encourage it. I'm looking at Markus Ruhl and saying, "Wow, OK, he's going to come and be in the stable. Freak." That's what people want.'

It was catch-22 again. It was zugzwang. You could stay, or you could walk away, it wouldn't matter. In the *Flex* office, Peter McGough kept a boxful of about a thousand letters, all from readers who'd written to say that bodybuilding had changed their lives for the better: they'd been in prison, or going off the rails, or in abusive relationships, and they'd come through. Every time someone on the staff wanted to run something excessive, or over the top, Peter would tell them to pick a letter at random from the box. 'That's the reader,' he'd say. 'That's who the magazine is for . . .'

It was perhaps why he kept going. If Peter McGough wasn't running *Flex*, and thinking about this stuff, who would be? Probably a guy like John Romano, who wrote for a magazine called *Muscular Development*, a magazine that glorified steroid use.

'They say,' Peter said, '"I could look like Ronnie Coleman if I took as many drugs." Well, they couldn't. Why doesn't John Romano look like Ronnie Coleman? He's a guy who writes a column in the magazine saying, in one example, "There I was, lying on my back, shooting myself full of Dianabol." Dan Duchaine, the original drugs guru, once told me, "I tried everything I could, nobody thought more about drugs than me, and the biggest I got was 185." Now if he couldn't do it . . .

'The Ronnies of this world respond in a way that the rest of us don't to the muscular application of weight resistance, diet and the drugs. It's my solid belief that the guys at the lower level that you never hear about use more drugs than Dorian and Ronnie and all the rest. Maybe these magazines that push the drugs should think, "What are we doing? We are making people think it's all about drugs."

'A lot of people are making a lot of money from that on the drugs side. We're not the only sport, I'm sure it's rampant in every sport. It's the visual thing, it's easier to point the finger at bodybuilders. And because we're not a lobby – *Sports Illustrated* would think twice about taking on the NFL because they're a lobby who've got some power.'

Wayne DeMilia and Pete McGough had arrived at the same place by different routes. They both understood that they were in the Era of the Freak, and there was no stopping it. For their different reasons, they remained on the ride.

They were both excited about Ronnie versus Gunter versus Jay. So was I. So was everyone. Wayne asked me if I was coming to the show. I said there was no way I would miss it. Once you were in, you were in. The thought of Ronnie, Gunter and Jay standing next to each other onstage at the Mandalay Bay pushing 900 lb diced and sliced, gripped me. How could you not want to see it, even knowing how it was achieved?

This was it: Muscle. Catch-22. Zugzwang. It was almost here. It was almost worked out.

Wayne told me to drop him an email with a press request. A few months before the Mr O I did. He emailed back the same day. 'Absolutely no press credentials for people writing books,' he said.

I knew what he meant. He wanted to beat 4,646, and he wouldn't if he gave too many tickets away. I rang him and requested a VIP ticket, very close to the front. I asked him how much it would be.

'Six hundred dollars,' he said.

I faxed him my details. I got the feeling he was smiling as they arrived.

9

Gunter; Ronnie; Jay

(i) Jay Cutler Rides the Curve

Jay Cutler existed in the great sunbelt of West Coast America. He looked as if he belonged there. His muscle ripened on the edges of the Mojave Desert, in Las Vegas, Nevada, where he and his wife Kerry had built a house. Vegas was the fastest-growing town in America, and Jay was the fastest-growing man in town. He was riding the upward curve. He felt like his climb might never stop. 'I've basically won four contests in a row,' he said, 'and if you include the Olympia, the way it should have gone in 01, I should be five shows ahead. That's why I can sit here today and say that I'm sure that I can be Mr Olympia come October . . .'

He already considered himself the number-one body-builder in the world even though Big Ron was technically still Mr O, and Jay had never defeated him. Gunter Schlierkamp had though, and Jay had beaten Gunter Schlierkamp, so Jay figured that he was in the box seat. He had swept the 2003 early-season shows, making $140,000 in a few weeks with wins at the Ironman, the Arnold Classic and the San Francisco Pro. Two or three weeks before the Ironman, Peter McGough had signed him to a contract with *Flex* magazine that would probably pay him another $200,000 per year. He was entered in the Mr O, the Russian, British and Dutch Grands Prix and the GNC Show of Strength in the autumn. Wins in all of them would net him almost a quarter of a million dollars. There weren't many great livings to be made in bodybuilding, but Jay Cutler was making one of them.

It had really begun for him at the 2001 Mr O at the Mandalay Bay. He had come out of nowhere to beat Ronnie Coleman in the first two rounds of compulsory poses during afternoon prejudging. He took everyone by surprise. Wayne DeMilia had been backstage when the call came.

'Lisa Clark, one of the girls from the Weider magazines, comes backstage and goes, "You better come out, I think Jay just beat Ronnie,"' Wayne said. 'I said "What, *Jay*? Jay looks that good?"

'First round ends, Jay's up by three points. Prejudging ends, Jay's winning by *six*. I'm walking around the expo, I'm like . . . I'm in *shock*. I'm having people coming up going, "You got tickets tonight? I hear Ronnie's losing."'

At the evening show, with Wayne and everyone else watching, Coleman came back at Cutler. He got straight firsts from each scoring judge in the free-posing round and the final line-ups and comparisons. He beat Jay by twenty-eight points to thirty-two. The crowd lost it. Coleman got some boos. Jay Cutler, filled with a great sense of righteousness, felt that he had won the show. The result fed bodybuilding's many conspiracy theorists. The Internet message boards lit up. *Flex* magazine was besieged.

Jay's great righteousness was not particularly dampened

when he discovered that he had failed the diuretics test taken after the show. Jay's feelings were perhaps under-standable. It wasn't as if he was the only one using them; he was just the one who'd got caught. He sicced a lawyer on to Ben Weider, found a loophole and kept his second place. He decided not to enter the 2002 Mr Olympia contest. He won the Arnold Classic instead and then he stayed at home for a year, allowing his big muscles to blossom.

Wayne DeMilia heard someone say that Jay sat out the 2002 Mr O to make the 2003 Mr O even better. It was all a plan, you see. It was all a fix.

'Hey, I'm entertained by it . . .' Wayne said. 'People come up with these ingenious ideas. I mean, "*Jay stayed out of last year's Olympia to make this Olympia better . . .*" Excuse me? Jay stayed out of last year's Olympia because he was mad at me because he failed a drug test. And then he scared Ben Weider by getting a lawyer because Ben had left a loophole open.

'On the IFBB rules, it said all drug testing had to be done by an Olympic accredited lab. And Quest Diagnostics, the lab we were with, *was* an Olympic accredited lab because they used to have four or five of them in America. Then they made a change, and there was then only one accredited lab, at UCLA.'

The result stood.

'Jay was all over me, which he's admitted to now, now that he's my friend again. We sat and talked in Italy. He said, "I really hated you . . ."

'I said, "Yeah, you hated me because you failed a drug test."

'"Yeah but everyone else takes the same things . . ."

'"But you got caught. They know when to come off it. You didn't. But it's my fault, isn't it?"'

Wayne laughed.

'I said, "Jay, we weren't really mad at each other. It was all a *conspiracy* for this year's Olympia." You know, Jay's laughing. He said, "Yeah I heard that . . ."'

'It's all over the Internet,' Wayne said. 'The Internet has given credence to people who had nothing . . .'

Jay Cutler trained in Las Vegas every day, attempting to impose certainty upon his life. Like Dorian Yates, he had established something firm for himself to build upon. He'd grown up near Worcester, Massachusetts, working on the family farm (how many of them grew up on farms: Andreas, Gunter, Jay . . .) and helping out in his brother's concrete business. He'd met Kerry in college where he studied criminal justice and she studied nursing. He began training on his eighteenth birthday. He won the Teen Nationals in Raleigh, North Carolina, a year later. Back in Worcester, he moved in with Kerry. He met a local bodybuilder called Bruce Vartinian, who hooked him up with a diet coach named Chris Aceto. By 1996, he had a pro card. He made his professional debut at the 1998 Night of Champions and married Kerry a few months later. In 2000, he won the Night of Champions, came eighth in the Olympia and was runner-up to Big Ron at the British and Italian Grands Prix. By 2001, he was giving Coleman all kinds of trouble onstage at the Mandalay Bay. He and Kerry had moved to the West Coast, first to California and then Vegas.

He felt that his best years would come when he was 'thirty-one, thirty-two, thirty-three, thirty-four years old'. At the 2003 Mr O he would be just thirty, and ready to ascend into his era. He was sixteen weeks out from the show. He was planning to grow for the next four weeks and then he would begin to vary his calories and bring down his weight. He was talking to me on the phone at 295 lb. He thought he would step onstage at around 275. He said that he was 'there already mentally'.

He'd been out guest-posing at shows with Gunter and Ronnie, whipping up the interest in the Mr O. Jay didn't think that either of them could beat him.

'I feel Ronnie's thirty-nine,' Jay said. 'Gunter looked very, very good at the Olympia last year, but I feel he still has something to prove on the Olympia stage. He still hasn't broken the top five at a Mr Olympia contest ever. Ronnie is my main concern at this time because, one, he's one of the best Mr Olympias ever, two, he's very big, he gets in very good condition. But I think his physique is suffering the inevitable with age. I feel that I will prevail.'

Jay sounded very certain when he said this. He explained exactly the processes he would go through in order to 'prevail'. It was a nice word to use, 'prevail', not really a bodybuilder's word. It was the kind of word Mike Tyson used when he got into one of his communicative phases, when he'd speak with great lucidity and power.

He described his training routine as 'robotic', and what he was talking about was its relentlessness, its singularity of purpose and meaning. He stuck to a diet that involved eating ten times per day, sometimes getting up in the night to drink down a protein shake. Every moment of the day was shaped towards the furtherance of his Mr O mission.

Jay well understood how and why Wayne had worked up Gunter versus Ronnie versus Jay. He understood how events had made him complicit in it.

'People said that was a crazy decision for me to sit out the Olympia in 2002, but what did I do to help promote the sport of bodybuilding?' Jay asked. It was a rhetorical question. 'You're going to have the biggest Olympia probably ever this year. I'm coming back and the fans want to see that. You can think of many negative things when I decided to sit out, but I only helped the sport of body-building. It gained a little intrigue for the viewers and the readers of the book. A little more of a saga, I guess.'

Jay didn't see himself as an era man, going on and on like Haney or Yates or Coleman. He wanted to be out of competitive bodybuilding in five or so years. He wanted to move on up the curve. He wanted to exploit his all-American looks and his all-awesome physique. He was already negotiating some sponsorship deals and appearances that were unconnected to the sport. He wasn't suggesting that he might be Arnold, but he wanted out and he wanted up. He could make a few million dollars in the next five years and then take off.

'There's a lot of stuff I'm doing now, kinda off the record,' he said. 'But I'm looking into signing a deal with a car manufacturer which is kind of huge. This is an arena that none of the other athletes are in – it'll be in Wal-Mart and K-Mart, and I hope it might lead to other things. That's why being Mr Olympia could be an advantage to me, and also to our sport . . .'

(ii) Guntermania

Unlike most crazes or movements or trends it was easy to identify the precise moment that Guntermania had begun. Wayne DeMilia had just called Gunter Schlierkamp in fifth place at the 2002 Mr Olympia. Five thousand people booed and screamed and yelled 'Fucking fix!' and 'Bullshit!' at the judges. Gunter knew what to do next. He took the mike from Wayne and spoke to the fans. He said exactly the right things and they cheered and shouted for a while and then let Wayne get on with the show, and Guntermania had started.

Wayne told me that the judges had messed up and missed Gunter because Shawn Ray had got to Ben Weider and Ben Weider had got to Wayne and Jim Manion, the head judge, and said that he wanted judges on the panel who hadn't judged the Olympia for at least five years. They'd ended up with a lot of inexperienced officials, who, according to Wayne, had missed Gunter altogether in the first round of judging.

'It's because they were in such awe,' said Wayne. 'When you're sitting at that judges' table at the Mandalay Bay, and you look around, there's people in front of you, behind you, all around you in semicircles. There's the Mr Olympia competitors onstage. That stage is 120 feet wide. Some of them lost their cool. They voted on people that they thought should be there. And what woke them up was round two, when Gunter came out and did his compulsories and the crowd started going nuts. But that's what happens with an inexperienced panel.'

Bodybuilding was a small sport with an immovable champ. What Gunter achieved was enough to make him a star within its confines. His physique actually improved a little in the couple of weeks between the O and the Show of Strength. Nascent Guntermania offered him a momentum he'd never had before. His 300 lb of beef hurtled forwards with force behind it. Ronnie Coleman was travelling too, but he was going backwards. He'd weighed around 246 lb onstage at the Mr O. By the Show of Strength, after criss-crossing time zones in a first-class seat to win Dorian's Dutch Grand Prix, he'd weighed 265 when he stepped onstage in New Orleans.

Only 287 people actually watched Gunter Schlierkamp beat Ronnie Coleman in the biggest upset of all time. It was like being at the Rumble in the Jungle or at least the muscle version of it. It made bodybuilding feel like a real sport, one susceptible to the fallibility of the competitors rather than the judges.

Everything was alive with possibilities. Ronnie went back to Texas convinced that he'd been mugged. Gunter returned to California sure that he would become Mr O. Jay Cutler became even more certain that he too had beaten Ronnie Coleman, at the 2001 Mr Olympia.

Almost everyone seemed to think that Ronnie had it coming. He'd survived so many tight contests he seemed punchy. He was nearly forty, gripped by entropy, vulnerable to the first guy who could land enough heavy shots.

Gunter Schlierkamp was the man who had. The next time I saw him was at the Arnold Classic. Whether he really had changed or whether people were just projecting their perceptions on to him, he seemed different; he seemed like Ronnie or Jay, Kevin or Chris, one of the top guys, a player, a star. He seemed *bigger*. At the Arnold, people had flocked around him wherever he went. Gunter had a great way with them. He wore his 'Guntermania' T-shirt. He had a high, sing-song voice that sounded out of place coming from such a man. He smiled all the time. He seemed genuinely delighted with the attention.

There was no artifice in any of it and it was a good feeling for Gunter. For a long time, five years or so, he'd placed badly in the shows he had entered. But his wife Carmen had pointed out to him that he could be successful in bodybuilding without actually winning contests. He had size, and all the crowds loved a freak, and he had warmth: like Andreas Munzer, who had been his friend, he was a good guy. He was uncomplicated in a pure way and there was no sign of any malice in him. On his website, he'd divided up his life story into little sections with titles like

'I Marry My Dream Girl' and 'Our First House and First Dog'. He seemed the least driven of the three: Jay Cutler's iron jaw and Ronnie Coleman's mute hugeness lent them a severity that Gunter did not have in him.

He'd pick up his phone with a cheery 'Schlierkamp!', and then he'd proceed to be so attentive and helpful and at pains to explain himself it was easy to mistake his demeanour. His life suggested otherwise. He was another farm boy, born in Olfen, near Düsseldorf. He got his genes from his mother's side of the family; they were all broad-beamed and sturdy. He'd made all of the classic mistakes in bodybuilding, overtraining through eagerness. He got his pro card in November 1993, when he became Mr Universe. Albert Busek had supported him, just as he had supported Arnold Schwarzenegger and Andreas Munzer. Gunter and Carmen had decided to come to America for three months in the summer of 1996 to see if they could make a life together there. They'd only been in New Jersey for a few weeks when they were conned out of most of their money but they endured and overcame. Carmen gave up her degree in nutrition so that Gunter could try his luck in the IFBB. His placings weren't great, but then he was an outsider. He persevered. He was a big man, 6′ 2″, and it would take years for his frame to balance properly. For a while, as his various body parts lagged or boomed, he looked like a walking wardrobe, but then his shoulders broadened and his waist tapered and his thighs arched outwards and he started to look like a contender.

Now that he was living in California, he'd taken some acting lessons and had some voice coaching and he'd appeared in a few ads and the odd film as an extra. Then it all started happening for him in bodybuilding, and he signed a Weider contract and had a full schedule and he and

Carmen bought a nice house just outside of LA.

For the Mr O and the Show of Strength of 2002, he'd worked with a trainer called Charles Glass, who had sculpted Gunter a new shape, and also with the 'diet' guru Chad Nicholls. Nicholls was the outspoken guy who found himself embroiled in various rows and controversies. Nicholls and Gunter had split after the Show of Strength and Nicholls had begun running Gunter down every chance he got.

Gunter said that he wasn't disturbed by Chad Nicholls. He'd come though worse. He'd do his talking at the Mr O with a body as big as a house. He and Charles Glass were working away, adding and subtracting, and most of all multiplying. When they were done he would be stepping on show stages at 315 lb or so as a matter of course. Then no one could miss him up there. Then everyone would catch Guntermania.

(iii) Big Ron Gets Biblically Big

He was as dense and massive as a night sea. What people didn't know about Ronnie Coleman when he was tucked down there in Arlington, Texas, for eleven months a year, keeping himself under the radar, was just how damn *big* he really was. Only Big Ron knew that. It was odd. A few weeks before every Mr O, pictures of Ronnie Coleman would appear on the Internet or in a magazine, and he would look so amazingly large and muscle-bound everyone would say that he was unbeatable, and then he'd turn up at the show and he'd have got himself down to 260 lb or so and he'd be a bit unbalanced and off and people would shake their heads and wonder what had happened.

But he'd been on a winning run for half a decade and failure had become something that happened to other people. He just went on and on, winning and winning, and it didn't really matter to him by how much or how little. When we were on the bus in Holland going to the Dutch Grand Prix, he'd said to me that he didn't care if he only won shows by one point. It made no difference to him what anyone else thought. The 2002 Mr O had been business as usual. Gunter had made a charge and finished fifth. Kevin Levrone had got it together and had posed charismatically to edge the evening session. But Big Ron had won. He had seen no omens, no portents to suggest to him that something bad was about to happen. Perhaps that's how it always was, though. Defeat came out of the clear blue sky one day, just after you'd looked up and seen nothing on the horizon.

Ronnie's loss to Gunter Schlierkamp soon became a mythic thing: everyone knew someone who'd spoken to someone who'd seen someone who'd been there. And they all said something different: Gunter was awesome, Ronnie was awful; Gunter was gifted it, Ronnie was robbed; Wayne had fixed it; Joe Weider had cooked it up. The GNC had been a deus ex machina for bodybuilding, and everyone had an opinion about it.

Ronnie's opinion was that he'd been stiffed. Word came out of Arlington that he thought the judging may have been racially motivated. Wayne DeMilia knew people who trained with Ronnie. He'd heard the news.

'I know Ronnie is saying stuff down in Texas,' Wayne said. 'I know guys that train in his gym and Ronnie's saying "You fixed this."'

Wayne went off on one of his riffs about Ronnie Coleman and the GNC Show of Strength.

'There was hardly anybody there,' he said. 'But I do know this. I *was* there, and Ronnie is totally confused where his body should be. Gunter was on the money.

'I said to Ronnie, "What you gotta realise is that in '98–'99 you were probably in the best proportion you could be for your frame. Those muscles have gotten bigger. Just cos you're bigger, doesn't make you better."

'And the other thing is, age has come in. Did Gunter beat him there? Yeah, Gunter beat him. Gunter beat him decisively. Then the thing I expected happened of course: what happens every time a white guy beats a black guy, "*Oh, it's racial.*" Any time a black guy loses, it's a racial decision.

'So now the judges have got a problem, right? Jay's blond and white and Gunter's blond and white. What's gonna happen here? If all the judges go that way, Ronnie's gonna win cos they'll split the white vote . . .'

Wayne laughed. He knew that Ronnie was only kidding himself if he thought that he'd lost because he was black. He'd been black in all the shows he'd won, too.

Ronnie said that only God would tell him when it was time to stop competing. His body was on a wide and gentle arc. He'd been a pro a long time before it had been good enough to win anything, so it followed that his decline might be a slow one, too. He had come through in a generation of guys who were the first to get the big magazine contracts and supplement deals and the high prize money. They were the first who could make enough out of bodybuilding not to have to contemplate an entirely new career after four or five years. Ronnie probably made more than half a million dollars per year by competing just once.

He was almost forty and he knew deep down that time would defeat him in the end, but he still had all of this strength and muscle maturity. Perhaps he listened to Wayne DeMilia, perhaps he listened to others, perhaps he just worked out what to do himself: the way to win the Mr O

216

again was to get bigger, not smaller. He ruled the Era of the Freak, after all. If he had body parts that were out of whack with the rest like Wayne said he did, why not bring the others up to match? Big Ron decided to do something he'd never done before: present himself onstage at the Mandalay Bay as huge as he knew he really was.

Being Mr Olympia defined his life. When you called his home number, a little message came down the phone: 'Hi, this is Ronnie Coleman. Mr Olympia . . .' in case anyone didn't know. He wasn't like Arnold or Jay, looking for something after the sport, something bigger and wider and better. For Ronnie it was all about the joy that being Mr O gave him. It was all he really wanted. He wasn't a media-type guy. He didn't go in for self-promotion. He wasn't the gregarious sort. Ronnie Coleman was not flash. He was a God-fearin' Southern man who'd been raised by his mother; he still adored her and brought her to the Mr O with him each year. It seemed pretty obvious that there was no way Ronnie was going to depart gently, not up there at the Mandalay Bay in front of his mom and the biggest ever Mr O crowd.

He was quite a hard guy to get hold of. When you did, he sounded as if he was speaking from inside a baronial hall, with lots of echo and peripheral sound. His voice was measured and quiet. Ronnie didn't speak much. When he did, he spoke like a man who was used to people listening to what he had to say. If he offered a sentence, it was a sentence everyone paid attention to. It was a sentence with muscle. He told me that he was training extremely heavy, with a new intensity. He wasn't worrying about the other guys or what they were doing. When we spoke about the GNC Show of Strength, he was quite dismissive. 'It's all done for tickets for the Olympia,' he said. 'That's just the way it went. If I've won every show for the last five years, or if I've been beaten, what's going to sell more tickets?'

I asked Ronnie why he always got so emotional when he was announced as the Mr O, and he said that it was because he was surprised that he had won. He allowed God to rule his life and he never knew what God had in store for him, so he was never able to presume that he would win. Then when he did, it all came bubbling out and he'd make his speech thanking God and his mom. Every time it happened, it was special, unique. Every time it happened, it gave meaning to his life, it lent strength to his faith, it paid respect to his mother. He wasn't sure how he would feel when he wasn't Mr Olympia any more, but he trusted that it would be God who'd decide on the moment it would happen, and not Wayne DeMilia. That's why Big Ron wasn't worrying about Jay Cutler or Gunter Schlierkamp. That's why he wasn't concerned about the judges or the Weiders. He relied on a higher power and for Him, Big Ron got Biblically Big.

10

Hollywood Ending

Wayne DeMilia had signed a five-year contract with the Mandalay Bay resort and casino to stage the Mr Olympia show, but he was saying long before the term was up that he couldn't imagine the contest being held anywhere else. Vegas and the Mr O were a tight fit: the biggest men on earth competing in the most excessive sport in the world, in a town dedicated to extravagance of every kind. Vegas was all surface, its superstructures were about artifice. Squished into two miles of desert road were bulging replicas of New York, Paris, Rome, Athens, Egypt, medieval England, outer space. Their galactic façades fronted overworked systems. It was the perfect place for bodybuilding. It didn't merely invite excess, it demanded it with its culture of 24/7 gratification. Las Vegas was unreal: it did not make the Mr Olympia show look odd, it made it look *big*. It did not make it stand out, it let it blend in. It accepted it and loaned it the big-time Strip shimmer, too.

The Mandalay Bay and the other hotels nearby were booked out with muscle. Muscleheads had money to spend on their big weekend of the year. At the Excalibur, where we stayed inside a big plastic castle, my room was made up every day by a harassed lady called Rena who had to undertake her duties while dressed as Maid Marian. She told me that her boyfriend was a bodybuilder. Mr O weekend was their favourite of the year. They were big fans of Ronnie Coleman. Muscle was everywhere.

Wayne DeMilia comped all of the Mr O competitors' nice suites at the Mandalay Bay. One of them was Ernie Taylor. Ernie had sat out a whole year of competition since the British Grand Prix to get himself ready for the O. He'd been training at the Temple gym, going in at six each morning to build himself a brand new body for the big one. He'd given it everything. I'd seen him a few times in the months before the O, when we'd been to prison visits and gym seminars with Kerry and Dorian. I thought he'd looked quite majestic, like a younger Chris Cormier. He had the classic X-frame: a nipped waist with muscle pouring outwards from it.

Ernie's big problem had always been his triceps. The big problem was that his triceps were *big*. In fact, Ernie's triceps were *enormous*. They were übertriceps, the triceps from hell. They hung about on the back of his arms, pissing off judges. There was a widely held belief in America, based, like most things, on rumour and supposition, that Ernie had injected them with Synthol, which was a kind of oil that hung around in the muscle tissue and bloated it. Synthol looked very obvious when you knew what to look for, because after a while it would puddle into lumps and make unnatural shapes under the skin. Ernie wished he *had* put Synthol in his triceps. It would have been easy to get rid of. The problem was more difficult, more natural. His triceps were a rogue body part, an unwanted bounty of freakdom. They were genuinely outsized and they had some scar tissue in the muscle that made them look bigger still. He had considered an operation to have the tops shaved away surgically, but then he'd tried to work them less and balance them with a bigger biceps. The physical problem wasn't the worst one, though. The conjecture was destructive, it had become received wisdom: Ernie Taylor has Synthol in his triceps. It seemed like the judges were taking it into account. Ernie had disparaging comments made about him on Internet message boards, too.

Ernie was a sunny character, however. He didn't let anything bother him for too long. Eight weeks before the Mr O, Ernie had fallen off his motorbike. Kerry Kayes told me about it when we were standing in a prison car park in Milton Keynes on a perfect September day, waiting for Dorian and Ernie to turn up.

'I'm sitting at home, six o'clock, Saturday night. Phone goes,' Kerry said. '"Kerry, it's Ernie."

'"All right, Ernie, what's up?"

'"Can you pick me up? I've fallen off my bike."

'"Fookin' hell, Ernie. Where are you?"

'"On the big roundabout by Manchester Airport. The ambulance man's here."

'"Put him on . . ."

'So I'm speaking to the ambulance bloke. He says, "I'll have to take him to Wythenshawe hospital." I says, "All right, I'll meet you there."

'So I go down there. I'm there before the ambulance. Two of 'em get out. They've got Ernie on the stretcher. He's got the collar on. The two of them can't pick him up. Two more paramedics come. They can't pick him up, either. I'm laughing me head off. Two more come and they manage to get him in a cubicle. No joke, there's about six doctors in there, all having a fookin' look. Then they have to cut his clothes off.

221

'The nurse goes to Ernie, "Are you on any other medication?"'

Ernie and Dorian had arrived just as we were laughing at the story. Kerry told it again to Dorian.

'Anyway, I were clean,' Ernie said.

'Tell them what you were doing, Ern,' said Kerry. And then before Ernie could, Kerry said, 'Pulling fooking wheelies with his mate. Eight weeks before the O.'

Ernie grinned. He pulled up his tracksuit to show the grazes on his calf where his motorcycle leathers had rolled up. He'd strained a hamstring, too, but he was going to be all right. 'A two-mile wheelie, it were,' he said, and his eyes twinkled.

'What did I tell you?' Kerry said to me. 'He's a bodybuilder, isn't he . . .'

Ernie was serious about Vegas. He needed the Mr O to be good to him. He was tired and depleted. He was hungry and dry and he wanted it all to be over soon. He'd tried his usual trick on the trip over. He always requested an aisle seat on the plane and when he got on, he made sure that half of him was hanging over in the aisle so the stewardesses couldn't get the trolley past him. Quite often, the purser would come and say, 'Can you come to the front of the plane, sir?' and he'd get an upgrade. It hadn't worked this time, though. The plane was full, front and back. Ernie consumed an aisle and people squeezed past him and stared. It was just a little more pre-show discomfort.

Included in the $600 I'd paid Wayne DeMilia for a VIP ticket for the Mr O was an invitation to Meet the Olympians. It was on a Thursday evening, two days before the contest. Wayne hired a ballroom at the Mandalay Bay and allowed all the VIP ticket holders to come down for drinks with the bodybuilders. After an hour or so, everyone else was allowed in, too. I left the big plastic castle and took a monorail past the fake glass pyramid of the Luxor into the station at the Mandalay Bay. It was one of the nicest places at that end of the Strip, restrained by Vegas standards. Through its deeply air-conned gaming floors and tropical shopping malls, muscleheads cruised incongruously. In the ballroom, Meet the Olympians was underway. Each competitor sat at a high table around the sides of the room. They had their great stacks of 10x8s and they had their vast queues waiting to approach them. Wayne said that he'd set the meet and greet up for a Thursday, 'while everyone still has some money in their pockets', and the athletes could make their share. Wayne made this sound like a grand gesture on his part, and it was, as far as his grand gestures went. He had to hire the ballroom and pay for the union guys to set up the room and hang around to take it down, so there was nothing in it for him.

Jay Cutler had a handwritten sign pinned to the front of his table which said:

Photo $10
T-shirt $20
Video $30
Beanie $20
Hat $10.

The $10 next to Hat had been crossed out and replaced with $5. Jay sat behind the desk in a light blue football jersey. He was already wearing his contest tan. It was hard to describe precisely what colour Jay Cutler was. He was a deep and resinous red, like highly polished wood. He'd have been somewhere between 'ochre' and 'rich mahogany' on a

223

paint chart. It was hard to imagine what being that colour felt like, too, when it was so far removed from his natural state. Perhaps he used it ritualistically, like warpaint, to make himself ready. Or maybe he'd done it so often he didn't realise how exotic he looked. He wore his little half-frown, too, as he signed and allowed people to photograph him. His wife Kerry sat beside him, passing him the pictures to sign and taking the money. Jay looked a little like he had before the Arnold Classic, heavy-eyed and depleted, stripped of mental muscle by the demands of his starving body.

Jay did everything slowly, but not as slowly as Ronnie Coleman, who was a couple of tables away. Ronnie was all covered up, too. It wasn't apparent how big he'd made himself, if he'd come into the show as huge as he knew he was. His great gravitational density was evident, but he'd always had that. He slouched in sloppy workout clothes, obviously wide, obviously deep, but beyond that only he knew. As usual, he wrote very slowly on each photo, with great concentration. His bottom lip poked forwards. He rarely smiled. Ronnie wore a cap that said: 'Mr Olympia Ronnie Coleman'. Jay's just said 'Cuts'. The line for Ronnie's table and the line for Jay's vied with each other for the longest at the back of the room. The longest at the front belonged to Gunter Schlierkamp.

Gunter was less coloured than Jay and he was less depleted, too. He was very approachable and friendly.

He was acting up for photos, smiling, pointing, gurning. His 'Guntermania' T-shirts were still selling well. Dexter Jackson had brown T-shirts with a horrible drawing of him looking like a monster. Lee Priest had a huge line of people waiting for him. He'd either grown his hair or had extensions woven in so he was wearing a weird blond mullet. Kevin Levrone was loitering. Dennis James was sitting and signing and looking confident.

Wayne DeMilia showed up in a slick suit and a candy-striped tie. Someone had told me about the time they'd been invited to Wayne's suite at the Mandalay Bay. It had taken about five minutes to find him in there. There were rooms upon rooms, all deeply luxurious. Wayne shuffled about like Elvis, or maybe Colonel Parker.

Meet the Olympians went on. The competitors filled their boxes and bags with bills. It was another small clue as to where bodybuilding was. Thirty-six hours before the start of the biggest show of the year, in the grip of their dietary agonies, smothered by worries about their condition, seated next to the men who were trying to ruin their professional lives, the competitors had to sit and sign photos for three hours to make some pin money. However big-time Las Vegas made the Mr O look, Meet the Olympians offered an alternative reality.

At the Mandalay Bay Sports Book, Ronnie Coleman was the favourite to win Mr Olympia. Jay was second. Gunter had drifted out. Dennis James and Dexter Jackson had come in. Kevin Levrone seemed to have the equivalent of a puncher's chance – you never quite knew with Kevin. The whirring rumours hummed as usual. Almost everyone in bodybuilding had heard something or seen someone who knew a little or a lot. Ronnie was *huge*. Jay was *on*. Gunter was *off*. Dexter Jackson was twenty pounds bigger. Lee Priest was nowhere near. Dennis James was the real dark horse, this year's Jay or Gunter.

The Olympia issue of *Flex* magazine featured a cover picture of Ronnie Coleman holding his Sandow statue with Jay and Gunter on either side of him, pretending to pull it from his grasp. The three had done a day's photo shoot at

Gold's gym in Fullerton, California, three months before the O. They'd hammed it up for the cameras weighing a combined 935 lb. Jay was 290. Ronnie was 315. Gunter was 330. Ronnie had been the only one to wear a cut-out vest. Jay and Gunter had covered everything except for their arms. Ronnie told people that he hadn't yet started his diet, but it was quite obvious to Jay and Gunter that he had. They'd thrown a few jibes at each other, but it was all pretty good-natured stuff. Ronnie felt he'd scored some points with his condition. Jay remained unworried. Gunter said that he thought that Ronnie didn't like him because he'd won the Show of Strength. Ronnie told them that the Sandow statue he had brought along was from the first of his Mr Olympia wins. He'd said to Jay that the first was the sweetest one, the best. During the shoot, Jay had refused to actually touch the Sandow. He was superstitious. He didn't want to hold one until he'd won it for himself. He didn't want any bad omens halting his ascent on the curve.

I rang Peter McGough soon after the day at Gold's. It was quite a coup for *Flex*, the first time a multi-athlete shoot like that had taken place. Peter said that he slightly favoured Jay Cutler. He thought that Jay's dietician Chris Aceto was very good and that Jay would deliver the kind of grainy and visceral hardness that Dorian Yates had used to dominate the O. Ronnie had looked great too, Peter said, but history showed that he often deteriorated quite badly in the last three weeks before the contest. Gunter had suffered from those attacks by the 'guru' Chad Nicholls. Peter described Nicholls' behaviour as 'squalid'. He felt for Gunter, and he didn't think he could win the show. Nature was also against him. He'd had a big year. This one was likely to be one of consolidation. Muscle, as ever, would take its time.

Chad Nicholls had been working with Ronnie Coleman

and also Dennis James. Dennis lived in Thailand for most of the year, but he'd come to the States a couple of months before the Mr O loaded up with primo beef. He'd been busy in his Thai den, away from the hype. He'd posted some progress shots on Chad Nicholls' message boards and he'd looked incredible: a huge back, a tiny waist, obscene thighs and calves. Peter knew that Dennis could do well, but if he did, it wouldn't be down to Chad Nicholls. The body-builders were getting blind-sided.

Peter had taken a call from Chris Cormier, too. There had been lots of rumours flying around about Chris, which was quite normal given that he lived his random life in a chaotic sport, but he'd been quite firm in saying publicly that he was training for the O and he was going to shock people like Jay Cutler and Gunter Schlierkamp, and maybe even Ronnie Coleman. But then he'd asked Peter if he thought he should skip the O and prepare for the Arnold Classic instead. 'That's not a good sign,' Peter said.

We discussed the judges at the Mr O. They seemed afraid. It was easy to enforce the world order, easier than doing anything else. Peter had raised the issue with Wayne DeMilia. This year things might have to be different.

'I said, "I think you guys just complicate it too much,"' Peter said. '"You get fixated on the names anyway. You should mentally cut these guys' heads off when they come onstage, and go with the bodies."

'Kevin Levrone was fifth in the Arnold Classic. I said to Wayne, "If that had been Kevin Levrone's first contest and his name was Ken Moltone, he would have finished last." He got the first call-out because of the name. Why can't they forget the affinities?'

*

227

It was the same old stuff spinning about. It was a subjective contest, a game of opinions. The only sure thing about the 2003 Mr O was that no one was going to agree about it. It would not end with the right result because there was no right result. This was bodybuilding. This was how muscle was.

There were other rows and scraps going on, other bust-ups and face-offs and scrum-downs. There was always a press conference for the competitors on the Thursday before the show. It was a Mr O tradition. It wasn't just open to the press – aside from the muscle mags and Wayne's Olympia TV crew, there wasn't any press. They were all on the other side of town covering Kobe Bryant's first pre-season game with the Lakers at the Thomas and Mack Centre. Anyone could go to the Olympia press conference, no credentials needed. It was usually unmissable because one or other of the bodybuilders always saw it as a chance to try to publicly humiliate Wayne DeMilia. Wayne already knew what this year's row would be about. It had been hanging around for a while. It was about prize money, or rather the lack of it, for all of the competitors who finished outside of the top twelve places. The top twelve would win a minimum of $1,000 each. The rest got absolutely nothing at all.

Lee Priest, who usually got a high placing, had said he would give away any prize money he won to the competitors who finished outside the top twelve this year. Shawn Ray, who'd twice finished runner-up in the Olympia, had just been elected as the first Athletes' Representative after a ballot of bodybuilders holding pro cards. It was the closest they had got to any sort of union representation. Shawn was on a mission. He had started stalking Wayne DeMilia to demand that everyone got something at the O. He'd been making lots of noise about it in his message-board posts, too.

Just before the Thursday press conference, Kerry Kayes and John Ernster approached Wayne and told him that Dorian Yates Approved would like to offer $1,000 for each athlete finishing out of the places. Wayne accepted, and said that he would match it, too, giving each of them $2,000 for competing. Wayne hadn't suddenly gone soft. He'd just got something to beat Shawn Ray up with.

The prize fund was announced at the press conference. Shawn Ray was late. When the time came for questions from the floor, though, Ray grabbed the mike before anyone else could.

'This is for Wayne DeMilia,' he said. 'Why don't people finishing out of the places get any money when you're making money from the show?'

Wayne waited for a moment and said: 'If you'd been here on time, Shawn . . .'

There was another row, too. Craig Titus, who had a sideline running the official after-show parties at the big contests, was trying to organise a prize for best poser onstage at the Mr O. He'd raised $9,000. He'd asked another bodybuilder, Bob Cicherillo, and also Shawn Ray, Flex Wheeler and Dorian to judge it. Titus and Cicherillo had let everyone know about the prize, too. The fans were already talking about who might win. The one person who Titus hadn't bothered asking was Wayne DeMilia.

Wayne called a meeting of an ad hoc IFBB committee in one of the Mandalay Bay conference rooms to deal with the matter. He asked Kerry to come along. The committee would consist of Wayne, a couple of other IFBB suits, Peter McGough, Kerry and the athletes' rep, Shawn Ray.

Kerry got there early, as always. He'd booked show tickets for Caesar's Palace for himself and Jan and he didn't want to be late. Wayne DeMilia opened the meeting. Bob Cicherillo walked in.

'Get out,' Wayne said, before Bob Cicherillo could sit down.

'What?' Cicherillo asked.

'Get out, I said. You're not the athletes' rep. Shawn Ray has been elected.'

Cicherillo was thrown out. Wayne explained that the posing prize was a non-starter. The judges had to adjudicate on the posing round as part of the contest. What if Titus, Ray, Cicherillo, Wheeler and Yates chose someone different to the winner from the official scorecards?

Craig Titus started arguing. He asked why Wayne DeMilia had accepted money from Dorian Yates Approved for the out-of-place finishers.

'Because he's not asking to judge it,' Wayne said.

The argument went back and forth, but Wayne's point was incontrovertibly true. If the bodybuilders wanted to give out any kind of posing prize, they'd have to do it unofficially, after the weekend was over.

Kerry just sat there. After a while, he looked at his American watch and said, 'Sorry, I've got to go. I've got tickets for Celine Dion . . .'

The Olympia expo opened the next morning at 9 a.m. It was as big as the expo at the Arnold Classic, and just as busy. The cutaway of Dorian's head spun round above the Dorian Yates Approved stand. Someone had also made a life-sized cardboard cut-out of Dorian posing onstage. A craft knife had been used to make a hole where Dorian's face was, and now you could poke your head through the back and have your picture taken. They were also giving away a car in a prize draw. It was parked right next to the stand, a nice convertible.

John Ernster, the octogenarian whey magnate, was there already. 'Hey, skinny!' he said to me. 'Finished writing that book yet?' He was on rambunctious form. Someone introduced himself to John in a Southern accent as 'a lawyer'.

'A *liar*?' John Ernster exclaimed. 'I always wanted to meet one of those,' and everyone laughed.

'Written any nasty stories lately?' he asked me, and before I could say anything, he said: 'I gotta magazine for you . . .' He dug around at the back of the stand and pulled out a copy of *Muscle and Elegance*, a girlie mag that had graphic pictures of nude female bodybuilders. 'Look at that!' he said, opening it at random. 'Looks like she's gotta steak coming outta there . . .'

Kerry had heard from Peter McGough and Kevin Horton, who shot pictures for *Flex*, that Ronnie Coleman had the Mr O sewn up. They'd seen him stripped two days before the show. I was still hoping that it would be Jay Cutler. I didn't really know why, I just felt that Jay wanted it the most. Kerry bet me a dollar that Ronnie had him. I accepted. Kerry had been busy betting. He was betting on Michael Gomez, a super-lightweight boxer who trained at his gym and who he'd begun doing nutrition for. Gomez was fighting a Scot called Alex Arthur in Glasgow. Arthur was a local hero. He was also Frank Warren's next Great White Hope. The bookies had Gomez at four and a half to one, a ridiculous price. Kerry knew how strong Gomez was. He had managed to get a hundred on Gomez by phone.

He showed me the text messages he'd been getting from Gomez. Two days before the weigh-in and four days before the fight, Gomez was at nine stone eight. He had to be at nine stone four on the scales.

'I told him,' Kerry said. 'I said, "Gomez, trust me, you've got to eat . . ."'

231

Gomez was struggling with the great paradox of nutrition known to all bodybuilders. You had to eat to lose weight as well as to gain it: the metabolism was stimulated by regular food, it burned it all up, and the body retained less fat because it wasn't worried about where the next meal was coming from. Gomez ate. The day before the weigh-in, Gomez was at nine stone six and a half. On the morning of the weigh-in he was a touch under nine five. At the weigh-in he was nine stone four bang on and drinking a litre of water. Alex Arthur had to step off the scales three times before making the limit. Gomez had sent Kerry a text that said: '9–4 . . . U R THE DADDY'.

Kerry admitted he would rather have been in Glasgow than Las Vegas. He liked Gomez. Gomez was a rogue. He was a gypsy, born in the back seat of a car. He had no idea when his birthday was. He'd lost five fights, one after being arrested for manslaughter – he was cleared – and two after partying immediately before the fights. In 2000, he'd been thought of as a prospect. Now he was an opponent. He knew Alex Arthur was his last chance. He'd said he would retire if he lost.

His trainer Billy 'The Preacher' Graham and Kerry had got Gomez in shape at Betta Bodies gym. It was a new avenue for Kerry, offering all of those years of knowledge on how to finesse the human body with infinite subtlety to boxers as well as bodybuilders. Boxers needed it. They'd been training the same way for a hundred years, not eating correctly, making themselves weak trying to make the weight. Kerry was demonstrating to them how to do things properly. He said that someone had told him Gomez looked like a little bodybuilder when he weighed in. Kerry was going to the Olympia prejudging to watch Ernie, but he would be stuck to his mobile phone for news of Gomez and Alex Arthur.

Dorian was dealing with his usual queues at the Dorian Yates Approved stand. Dorian liked Las Vegas. He looked bleary-eyed. 'I sleep when I get home, mate,' he said. He was pissed off with Wayne DeMilia. Ever since he'd retired as Mr Olympia he felt that Wayne had failed to treat him with the respect due to a champion. Each year, Wayne would give him a ticket somewhere up in the gods, and the fans would ask him why he was sitting so far from the stage. It wasn't as if there were hundreds of ex-Mr Olympias that Wayne had to give tickets to. Only eleven people had ever won, and one of them was Arnold and another was competing in the show. Dorian had told Wayne that he thought he should sit near the front by the judges' table. The next thing he'd heard was that he could do so, but he'd have to wear an IFBB uniform.

'He said that he thought I wanted to be a judge,' Dorian said. 'He said, "Ah just let him sit on the end and collect the papers up or something . . ."'

Dorian said that he wouldn't be going to watch the show. He was one of the sport's great champions, unbeatable, the first real freak. I didn't blame him at all.

Ernie Taylor was going, though. He came down to the expo to sign some pictures, but he could barely grip the pen. His cheekbones could have cut paper. Ernie slumped forwards over the desk. 'I just want it to be over,' he said. His voice crawled out. 'I just want to eat . . .'

He was already worried about his dining arrangements after the contest. 'I might end up getting room service, and that's going to cost a fookin' fortune for what I want,' Ernie said. He looked disconsolate. He didn't particularly want to talk about food, but he couldn't think about anything else. He said that he might keep eating until he was sick. He sometimes did after a show, just because the taste of any-

233

thing that wasn't turkey or rice or tuna was so exquisite. He'd allow himself one blow-out after the Mr O and then it was straight back on the diet for the European Grand Prix shows. Ernie was entered in the British and the Dutch contests.

At the 2002 Mr O, Ernie had been drawn as competitor number twenty-five. He'd been stuck at the end of the line-up, almost in the wings. At the draw for the 2003 show, Ernie had pulled number one. He would open the whole contest, afternoon and evening. He didn't think too much of that, either.

'I just wanted be in the middle somewhere,' he said. 'And not right after Ronnie or Jay . . .'

Chris Cormier had dropped out of the 2003 Mr Olympia. He'd announced at the press conference that illness would prevent him from competing. No one seemed particularly surprised. I remembered the conversation with Peter McGough. I saw Chris talking to Gunter's trainer Charles Glass. It was starting to look as though Chris would never be Mr O. He'd lost his place on the curve, he'd gone from natural successor to nearly man and it was hard to know exactly when or how it had happened. Jay and Gunter had been behind him; now they were ahead. There would be new stars at this year's Olympia and Chris would have to cede more ground.

The sixteen who were left prepared for the prejudging. It would take place in the arena near the expo hall, in front of five thousand fans. The moment was at hand.

Backstage, they got stripped and oiled and they pumped up. The first hint of order became apparent. Jay Cutler looked very good indeed. He spared no glance for anyone else. Dexter Jackson shone like cut crystal. Dennis James was almost sagging with newly processed muscle. Gunter flicked his legs about and the earth shook. I couldn't see Ronnie Coleman.

The call came for the start of prejudging. Ernie was first up and he wasn't quite ready. He had to go to the stage without the last bits of his oil on him.

I found my $600 seat. It wasn't bad at all, one row ahead of the judges. I had the same view that they had. The sixteen competitors were to come out individually to perform their compulsory quarter-turns. Ernie emerged from the steps at the rear of the stage that brought the athletes into view of the crowd through an arch decorated with the logo JOE WEIDER'S MR OLYMPIA. On the logo, Joe looked about thirty years old. The set was steely and hi-tech. Ernie faced the five thousand and went through his turns, alone on the broad stage. His long year of work began to pay off. Ernie looked tremendous, muscly and big, but finely diced and classically shaped. He was not yet a freak, not yet disconnected from the human race. His triceps played ball. They had been streamlined, trimmed back into proportion. The crowd whooped in surprise. They understood what they were looking at. Ernie had wrestled their respect with his new look. Ernie smiled his bling-bling smile and got a good cheer as he walked off.

After the hype, we would have to wait no longer for Jay versus Gunter versus Ronnie. Cutler had been drawn as number three, Coleman at four. Before them, Claude Groulx, in shape as usual. He'd just won the Masters Olympia, which was for athletes over forty years of age, and the fans gave him a generous hand.

Beside me, just in front of the judges, sat a whole family of freak followers: mom, dad and two strapping sons. They each had a programme. They discussed all of the athletes with great knowledge. They had been coming to the O since the boys were small. They had grown up in the Era of the Freak and they knew one when they saw one. One came towards them now. Jay Cutler had walked up the steps at the rear of the stage and into the lights and the noise.

The screams began before he started his quarter-turns.

'It's your show, Jay . . .'

'You gottem, Jay . . .'

'It's over, Jay baby . . . It's over . . .'

Jay did not react. He steadied himself and looked out from the stage with his thin frown. He began his turns. As he did, each side of his giant body tensed. He released a thin 'shiiiish' of air as he ground himself into the required shape. The deep red oil glowed on him. Jay looked lost in himself. He was detached, apart, distant in his muscle. He finished and walked off.

The fans were not privy to the order of the draw. They did not know who would be next on stage until Wayne announced the name.

'Competitor number four . . .' Wayne said, with some relish. '*Ronnie Coleman* . . .' Despite his pragmatism, Wayne loved these moments, too.

Ronnie came up the steps and bedlam descended on the Mandalay Bay. No one had ever seen anything quite like it. Big Ron was Biblically Big all right. He'd come in huge enough to cause planetary realignment. The most astonishing parts of him were his thighs – they swept outwards for what seemed an immeasurable distance, the kind of distance covered by light alone. But to pick out his thighs was to try and choose the best ride at Disneyland. The rest of him was equally thrilling, equally absurd. The reaction of most people around me was simply to laugh at him. It was an involuntary thing. I realised that I was laughing at Ronnie Coleman as well.

236

'Jesus fucking Christ . . . Look at that . . .' someone said.

The bits of Ronnie's body that he could not grow in any way – his head, his hands, his feet – belonged to another man, not to this inhuman thing. They perched at the extremities of his muscle like children too timid to approach. He breathed effortfully as he turned.

Once the shock of seeing Ronnie died away a little, his methods became apparent. The gut had not gone. When he spun to the rear, it protruded outwards. His lats and shoulders were still monumental but they were offered some proportion by the increased size of everything else. Ronnie had brought up his biceps, he'd promoted his pecs and withered his waist. There was some trickery, some illusion involved in what he was. He swaggered off, sure that he had won already.

Darrem Charles and Art Atwood followed, middle-of-the-pack men. Then Lee Priest with his weird mullet. Lee sent the crowd into shock too. He was a big favourite of theirs, the littlest freak in a freaky town, but he should not have been on the stage. He appeared months away from any sort of condition. Only his trademark arms contained any sort of power. It didn't look like Lee would have too much prize money to give to the lower places after all.

Dennis James brought out his mountain of muscle and put himself into contention. Dexter Jackson wore an extra stone of beef, too, and he'd delivered it shrink-wrapped. Johnny Jackson, Rodney St Cloud and Jonathan Davie came and went. Kevin Levrone had forgotten to bring his legs again. His great torso floundered on its foundations. Then Troy Alves, before Gunter emerged as the penultimate competitor.

Wayne announced Gunter. Gunter walked out. He was not going to win Mr Olympia, that much was apparent.

Here was the true drama of bodybuilding: a year's work over at a glance, a shocking collision of timescales. He was dry and cut, his thighs were mapped with slithered veins, but he had come in flat and small. He'd pulled a Ronnie Coleman, like Ronnie used to before he realised and bit the bullet. Gunter had distilled himself too much. Only the movie-star grin retained its full appeal. Yet even that would prove empty: Gunter's life had become complicated. He'd separated from Carmen just before the show.

Gunter left, and after Melvin Anthony had completed his first compulsories, the line-up came back to the stage. Jay stood next to Ronnie, glancing at him occasionally. Ronnie kept looking up at the ceiling, into the lights. Ernie jigged about on one end of the line. There were some moments of tension as they waited for Wayne to announce the first call-outs.

Then Wayne said: 'Ronnie Coleman . . . Jay Cutler . . . Dexter Jackson . . .'

I looked at Gunter just as Wayne said, 'and *Dennis James* . . .'

Gunter sagged for a second and then stared quizzically, first at Wayne and then the crowd. He pointed at his chest and said, 'Me?'

Wayne ignored him. 'A quarter-turn to the right, please gentlemen,' he said, and the call-outs began.

Gunter got the second call-out, but Ronnie and Jay were already back in line and out in front. Gunter stood in comparison with Dennis, Dexter and Kevin Levrone, and then he had to stay there with Darrem Charles and Troy Alves, too.

Ernie got the fifth call-out, which cheered him immediately. He waved and stepped forwards.

The second round of compulsories began, the order of the

238

seven required poses now deeply familiar, rendered always in Wayne DeMilia's nasal New Yorker: *front double biceps; lat spread; side chest; rear double biceps; lat spread; side triceps; abdominals and thighs.*

They were once more taken individually. Jay Cutler and Ronnie Coleman passed onstage this time, and barely looked at one another. Ronnie was an old king, not quite dead. Jay knew it. Ronnie posed with great power. He watched himself on the big screen as he turned languidly at Wayne's request.

After the second round, the order of the first two call-outs were the same again: Ronnie, Jay, Dexter, Dennis and then Dexter, Dennis, Gunter and Kevin Levrone. The third was a surprise, though: Melvin Anthony, Darrem Charles, Troy Alvez and finally Ernie Taylor. Ernie had nailed it. He was in genuine competition for a top-ten place. He smiled and so did I. It felt good.

There were eleven call-outs but the best was last. Jay and Ronnie were requested again, but without anyone else. They posed very close together, each unwilling to give ground. They kept touching arms and shoulders. They finished and exchanged a nod, and everyone walked off.

I went back to the expo. At one stand I saw Sergio Oliva signing pictures. Arnold Schwarzenegger's nemesis was an old man now. He had a round Cuban face. He was sitting very properly. He wore a white tuxedo with a white dress shirt, slightly old and fraying. He had a black handkerchief, perfectly folded in his pocket. He looked like Havana itself; something once grand and beautiful that was now fading, but proudly. Behind him was an old suitcase, also battered, from which he'd taken the 10x8s that he was signing. He signed his pictures very slowly. They showed him as a young man, when he was known as 'The Myth' and he'd beaten Arnold Schwarzenegger. When he finished, he'd say 'ten', as in dollars. To him, with all that life lived, it must have seemed like easy money.

Kerry waved me over to the Dorian Yates Approved stand. I thought he was after his dollar on Ronnie, who everyone thought had won the prejudging.

'He fucking did it . . .' Kerry said. '*Gomez!* Knocked him out in the fifth. Put him down three times. Apparently it was a war. Frank Warren's totally gutted . . . doing his nut!'

Kerry threw a few air punches in celebration. He showed me the messages on his phone. He'd got round-by-round updates until the third, then he couldn't take it any more. He'd rung a friend of his and Gomez's, Bobby Rimmer, who was also indisposed and watching the fight on TV. He'd had the commentary relayed over and had to leave the prejudging.

Now the phone kept ringing. Kerry was grabbing everyone he knew as they walked past. Then Gomez himself rang. He had five stitches in his eye, a broken hand and broken ribs, but compared to Alex Arthur, who was in hospital, Gomez was tip-top. 'I felt so strong,' he told Kerry. 'I just walked through him. He couldn't hurt me . . .'

Kerry was tip-top, too. Brian Bacheldor, who worked with Kerry and Dorian on the Dorian Yates Approved line of supplements, showed up. He'd managed to get forty quid on Gomez to win, and another ten on a fifth-round stoppage. He'd won about five hundred pounds. The CNP Dorian Yates Approved stand was declared The Only Boxing Stall at the Olympia Expo in honour of Gomez. I told Kerry about Ernie's call-out in the second part of the prejudging. 'Great! He should make top ten . . .'

Kerry smiled and threw some more air punches. A few

minutes later, I heard him saying to himself, 'Fucking *Gomez* . . .'

We killed time, waiting for the evening show. Kerry was telling me and Dorian about the IFBB meeting he'd been to when Wayne had asked him to join the ad hoc committee.

'That Craig Titus . . .' Kerry said. 'He starts off saying, "Shawn Ray forged my signature on the athletes' representative vote." Then Shawn Ray walks in. So Titus says, "I'm not saying that Shawn forged my signature, but someone did . . ." Then at the end, he proposes a vote of thanks for Wayne . . . for all he's done!'

Dorian was non-committal. He'd agreed to co-host Titus's Olympia after-show party at the House of Blues club in the Mandalay Bay, in return for Titus's girlfriend, a fitness athlete called Kelly Ryan, guest posing at the Dutch Grand Prix. He'd agreed to judge the posing prize, too, without having thought about the implications.

'I dunno, mate,' Dorian said. 'I'm not paying attention . . . I'm too stressed out . . .' Dorian was worrying about the European tour. He was promoting the Dutch Grand Prix for a second year.

'Cormier's not doing the European shows now. Dennis James ain't fucking coming. I mean, why are we paying ten grand licensing fees and Wayne isn't guaranteeing any athletes?'

'Because,' Kerry said, 'five years ago when we wanted to put on the Grand Prix, that was the deal. Ten grand licence. It just goes over my head, Doz.' He gestured something sailing by. 'I can't do anything about it . . . so I don't worry about it. That's what it costs, ten grand . . .'

'Yes, but they should be fucking made to do the shows.'

'Doz, when you were a bodybuilder, Wayne used to

241

phone you and ask you to do the shows, and you wouldn't.'

'Yeah, but I said no right off, not two days before. I dunno, mate . . . I'm just stressing . . .'

'Doz,' Kerry said, and made the sailing by gesture again, 'it don't matter. It'll be all right.' Kerry smiled. Dorian smiled, too. They were a good team. They complemented one another. Dorian said that he was going to enjoy the after-show party anyway. At least when he was with other bodybuilders and bodybuilding fans, he was treated with due respect. The afterlife of an athlete was hard, especially for a great one. The rewards of the everyday were less definite, without certainty. Dorian had been Mr O for six years: he would be an ex-Mr O for many more.

We went to the evening show. Within three hours we would find out who Mr Olympia 2003 was. Wayne had asked Kerry to introduce Simon Robinson to the crowd in the same way that he had at the British Grand Prix, when Simon had made his emotional guest appearance. Kerry disappeared to get suited and booted. Before he went, he told me that Arnold Schwarzenegger was planning to fly in from California to surprise the crowd. The Mr O would get some Hollywood shimmer, too. It felt like an ending of a kind, a Hollywood ending in widescreen and technicolor where all the plotlines would be tied up. I sat down in my $600 seat. I was excited about the show. I wanted to know if it would be Ronnie or Jay, or maybe a real upset: Dexter or Dennis. I wanted Ernie to get his top ten. I wanted Gunter to do well. I wanted to marvel at the freaks, to revel in their beef. I wanted the show to be talked about, to be remembered. I wanted all of this even though I understood slightly the cost of becoming what the competitors had become. I wondered if I would still watch bodybuilding when I wasn't writing about it any more, and then I remembered I'd paid $600 to sit where I was sitting and I hadn't ever considered not doing so. My cash fed the freakiness. So did the cash of everyone about me.

Dorian had reminded me that he equated taking steroids with smoking. You weren't going to drop dead after one or two cycles. The damage was incremental, progressive, compounded by itself. It was also random, impossible to calculate accurately. So was the price of the dieting and the effort and the diuretics and the training and all the other stuff that went with it. The bodies of bodybuilders travelled at accelerated speed. Some could take it and some could not. Momo Benaziza and Andi Munzer and the Mentzer brothers were dead. Flex Wheeler had just received his new kidney, donated by a member of his church. Steve Michalik had barely survived Intensity or Insanity. Paul Dillett had frozen. Mike Matarazzo had collapsed. Tom Prince had serious problems. Charles Gaines had decided not to write about bodybuilding any more. He'd lost too many of his friends. Yet Dorian Yates was as strong as an ox, and almost as big. I'd trained with him at the Temple gym. It was like witnessing a machine. Ernie Taylor did two-mile wheelies on his motorbike and had Ultimate Fights. Ronnie Coleman was almost forty and he was the biggest man in the world. Kevin Levrone had run a sixty-metre challenge against Dwain Chambers, the British sprinter, and he hadn't lost by that much.

I was a big boxing fan. I had seen Chris Eubank destroy a section of Michael Watson's brain. I had watched Nigel Benn turn Gerald McClellan into a vegetable. I was there when Mike Tyson bit off Evander Holyfield's ear. During each of those fights, I had been transported by the drama of the event. I still loved boxing. Now I waited for more of the excess that I had paid for and travelled to. I demanded it. So did five thousand others. So did the IFBB and the pay-per-view subscribers. So did the *Flex* readers and the gym rats and the myriad fans of muscle. So did the expo and the supplement companies and the industry. I thought of Peter McGough and his internal debate about his culpability if any of the athletes dropped dead. I thought about mine. We were all complicit in one way or another. As Wayne DeMilia told me, 'We live in a drug society.' We also lived where we had free will. Mike Mentzer's heroine Ayn Rand knew that. Mike had brought it into bodybuilding. He had been explicit about it. Dorian Yates had taken it on and now here we were, in the Era of the Freak, where everything was permitted. People were always asking what sport would be like if everyone was allowed to take whatever they wanted to achieve their ends. Well, bodybuilding was what it was like. The Mr O was what it was like. We settled back and waited for the show to start.

Joe Weider came out with his brother Ben. Chris Dickerson, a former Mr O, sang the national anthem in a rich baritone. We all stood for it. Joe Weider began to speak in his much-imitated voice. He sounded like Vito Corleone on helium. He talked about Arnold Schwarzenegger, the new Governor of California.

'Finally, it is dawning on the world that bodybuilders are smart and brilliant,' Joe said. 'They have stickability and they don't give up.' He spoke about giving Arnold his plane fare to America all those years ago. Joe told us that he had been seventeen years old with seven dollars in his pocket when he started the magazines that he'd just sold for $350 million. He told us that 'people who use weights get better scores in college'. He told us that Arnold was coming, and everyone shouted and cheered for a very long time.

Then Ben Weider spoke. He thanked Joe and Wayne. He

thanked us all. Then he issued us with a challenge: 'If you think it's easy to judge – you judge . . .' I wondered where he had been for twenty years. There were five thousand judges right in front of him, baying for blood, hungry for muscle.

Ernie came out first. I had seen him many times in everyday circumstances. Now here he was in extraordinary ones. The crowd went wild for him. He began with a few slow poses to classical music and then went into some powerful stuff to a rap tune called 'The Dog is Here'. He did his martial arts kicks and then the splits. Things got rowdy. Ernie grinned and waved and walked off.

Jay Cutler brought the house down. Ronnie Coleman finished them off. Jay posed to his own tape. It said he was 'a cut above the rest'. Ronnie had a disco version of the *Carmina Burana* that sounded very dramatic and matched his grandiose routine. He'd carried on posing after the music had stopped. The show went on but the one and two had been decided. Dexter Jackson was this year's Gunter Schlierkamp or Jay Cutler. Dennis James was the freak of choice. Lee Priest cast a sad and noble figure, posing to a song with the chorus 'Heroes . . . live for ever . . .', smiling broadly even though he understood how far he had fallen. It was all over for Lee. Gunter found his charisma again and maybe a few extra pounds and he finished well.

Wayne DeMilia introduced Kerry and Kerry told the story about Simon Robinson losing his leg and almost dying. As Simon came up the steps, five thousand people stood for him. He told me later that when he'd been a doorman many years ago, he used to tell the other lads that one day he'd be on stage at the Mr O and they'd all laughed at him. Well, there he was, after everything that had happened. He chose the perfect music, too, a version of Bruce Hornsby's 'The Way It Is'. It was melancholic and beautiful, sad and redemptive and made for the movies, made for Hollywood, made for America. Many people cried. When Simon was done, Joe Weider came out from backstage and gave him a Mr Olympia competitor's medal. Simon came to the mike and thanked Kerry. And then Arnold came on and the Hollywood ending began for real.

Arnold took the welcome like a pro. I wondered if he felt like a bodybuilder, or a movie star, or a politician. He was on home ground, more so than anywhere else, so I guessed he felt like a bodybuilder. He was the Austrian Oak once more, with a myth that was both vast and deathless. He was reassuring. He said that bodybuilding had given him everything he had. He offered a vague notion of the possible. He pointed out that control of the body was the first step towards control of everything else. We all possessed such sovereignty. He gave Lee Haney a lifetime achievement award. He presented Franco Columbu with a prize, too. Franco, ever the foil, said, 'Finally, I get a prize and Arnold doesn't,' and everyone roared and cheered.

Wayne came to the mike again and thanked Kerry and Arnold and Joe. He called the line-up back to the stage. Claude Groulx, Art Atwood, Jonathan Davie and Lee Priest were eliminated.

Wayne announced twelfth place, which went to Rodney St Cloud. I looked at Ernie, anxious for him to break the top ten. One more place. Wayne said, 'eleventh place . . . winning eight thousand dollars . . . Johnny Jackson . . .'

Ernie looked at his feet. Wayne called him next. He'd broken the ten. He got $10,000, a silver plate and a bowl. Ernie breathed rare air. And now he could eat.

Melvin Anthony was ninth, Troy Alves eighth and

Darrem Charles seventh. The top six remained on stage for the final round. Left to right stood Gunter, Kevin Levrone, Dexter Jackson, Dennis James, Ronnie and Jay. They did the compulsory poses and then the posedown, which was quite chaotic. Jay knelt at the front of the stage. Ronnie and Gunter got up close and compared legs.

Wayne prepared to announce the results. He said that each of the top six would receive a new prize, a Mr Olympia dagger. He paused. 'And anyone who doesn't like their placing can kill themselves with it . . .'

Ronnie Coleman won. He'd been ahead after every round. Jay didn't quite have the muscle to beat him yet. Wayne told me later that he'd seen Ronnie strip off before the show and he couldn't believe his eyes. He'd walked over to him and asked if he could put his hands around Ronnie's upper arms. He hadn't been able to span one with two hands.

'I said to him, "Ronnie, they must be twenty-five inches." He just laughed at me. He said, "I don't know how big they are . . ."'

Ronnie was already talking about beating Lee Haney's record of eight Olympias. That would take him until 2006. He would be forty-four years old. Jay understood that he would have to wait at least one more year. In the meantime, he would make as much as he could out of the second-best body on the planet.

Gunter had come fifth. The crowd howled in protest. He still had some Guntermania going on. He just needed to get even bigger. He knew that he could do it. Dennis James hauled his new body into fourth. Dexter Jackson was this year's Gunter. He had finished third. People were already talking about him becoming Mr O. They said he was the man to end the Era of the Freak, to bring back the classic physique. I didn't think so. Dexter wasn't big enough to turn back time.

Ronnie made one of his emotional speeches. It went on for a very long time, even after the house lights had gone up and people had begun to leave. He brought his mother up on to the stage. He thanked God. He said he loved each one of us, even if we didn't love him. Then he picked up his trophies and his cheque for $110,000 and the keys to the Cadillac car that he'd won and he staggered off the back of the stage, casting a great silhouette.

11

Andi Redux (iii)

Andreas became the first bodybuilder to have a play
written about him. Well, it was part of a play at least,
a very long play by the Austrian writer, Elfriede Jelinek,
best-known for the novel, *The Piano Teacher*, which has
been made into a successful art film. The play was called *Ein
Sportstück*. When it premiered in Vienna it received a fifty-
five-minute standing ovation. Jelinek's themes were intellec-
tual and postmodern. *Ein Sportstück* was about mediated
realities, lives experienced through other mediums: TV,
movies, sport. She used Andi's hollowed body to stress the
primacy of surface over depth. She said that Andi's freaky
frame had been manufactured for rapid consumption and
then thrown away. You had to be patient to get to Andi's
bit though: *Ein Sportstück* lasted for five hours.

And so Andi's body became metaphor, too. He represented something to bodybuilding, and something else to
the wider world. In death, Andi had become someone on to
whom things could be projected: ideas, theories, prejudices.
He could be interpreted, reinterpreted, misinterpreted. By
the time of the 2003 Mr Olympia, he had been dead for

seven and a half years. During that time, no major competing bodybuilder had died. Wayne DeMilia felt that the diuretics problem had been solved by post-contest testing, even though he knew that they were still in use.

My vision of Andi was mediated, too. I had the raw facts of his life and death; they had all been well reported. I had the views of other bodybuilders, some of whom had been Andi's friends. I had some theories of my own about him. But I was unable, or perhaps unwilling, to get any closer. I emailed Albert Busek, who was still editor of *Sportrevue* magazine and an IFBB vice-president, several times and asked to speak to him about Andi's years in Munich. He did not respond, or return my calls. I tried to locate Andi's girlfriend Elisabeth Schwarz. Hers was a very common name in Germany. Eventually, I found a picture of her on a German bodybuilding website. Through a writer called Matthias Penzel I contacted the guy who ran the site. Sure, he said, he knew Sissy. She was still living in Munich with her boyfriend. He suggested that I email Sissy via her boyfriend's address. I did. I explained who I was and why I wanted to write about Andreas. Matthias translated for me. Sissy didn't respond. I could understand that.

The true facts of Andi's death were known only to him. I knew enough about bodybuilding to understand the role of rumour and conjecture. I didn't think that Andi was taking all of the drugs on the list that had been in the newspapers, certainly not in such quantities. No one could say for sure that it even *was* his list. Even his autopsy could not confirm it. Obviously, Andi wasn't clean, either. He'd died an ugly, painful and premature death. He'd lived out his double life, he had kept his secrets.

This is what I thought had happened, my best guess, my hope:

Andi rode the curve. He made the deal. He played the zugzwang. In Munich, he doubled himself. He understood what it would take to make it with a body like his in the earliest years of the Era of the Freak. Andi was a kind man, a nice guy. He did not want what happened in Munich to impact on his real life, on his family in Austria. He hid it well, for the right reasons.

The novelist Timothy O'Grady once wrote: 'The spectacle of greatness is thrilling, alluring, intoxicating. It can make the beholder want to do the same thing, breathe the same air.' From Munich, Andi saw greatness. He saw greatness in Arnold Schwarzenegger, but that was through the simplicity of teenage ambition. Later, as he ascended to become the best bodybuilder in the German-speaking world, he looked at the small gap between his own excellence and that of the five or six men who existed above him. He thought about what it might take to close that gap. Andi was no freak. He could not touch Yates or Dillett for sheer size. He did not have Levrone's charisma or scale. He wouldn't match Shawn Ray for symmetry or approach the perfection of Flex Wheeler's lines. But he could beat them all on condition. He could produce a grain in his muscles that not even the great Dorian Yates could exceed. He could turn his skin into paper and his veins into ringroads around his stripped physique. Andi could take the stage glowing with hardness and he could do it several times a year.

The effort it took was difficult to imagine. Andi had picked the toughest battleground, the most elusive state to appear in and maintain. His USP demanded much of him. But once he had chosen, he could not turn back. There was probably a moment, a tipping point, where he might have pulled out, perhaps when he first became aware of the pains in his stomach and sought a health cure for them. Only Andi

251

would know for sure. But he was a bodybuilder, and bodybuilding was about excess. After a while, you were surrounded by so much of it, it became impossible to see how much was too much: because almost everything was too much. In bodybuilding, the only response to failure was growth. That was the law of muscle. Stressed to failure, it grew. When Andi met failure, he grew to defeat it.

Andi gave it everything because that's what he demanded of himself. He had built an extraordinary body by any standards. He was weirdly beautiful. I had a picture of him in a side-chest pose, a black-and-white shot in which the striations and feathers on him were so deep and defined that he looked like an abstract object, silver and grey.

Andi had decided to find out what was possible for him. He wanted to get as high on the curve as he could, as all of us do. He understood the risks. He took his courage in his hands. He pushed towards his limits. He discovered where they were. In that regard, Andi had lived ferociously, he had strived for the best that he was capable of. I saw it as an act of great bravery to live in that manner.

Andreas Munzer strived and strived, and he found out what he could do. He was able to manufacture one of the ten best bodies from six billion on the planet. In his curious arena, he had almost ascended to the top of the game. He answered every question he asked of himself. He did not die wondering.

I saw unrecognised honour in what he'd achieved. He was more than just a dead guy who'd taken too many drugs. He was not the end of bodybuilding as a sport. Andi was not just a metaphor for postmodern stylings. He was a symbol of what it sometimes took to succeed.

Bodybuilding had not become any less freaky in the years since Andreas had died. Quite the opposite, in fact. In the new millennium, it had assumed a new scale. In 1993, Dorian Yates had become the first Mr Olympia to weigh more than 250 lb. By 2003, Gunter was shaking the stage at over 300 lb. Ronnie Coleman was up around 280. So were Jay Cutler and Dennis James. Gunter and Jay hadn't even finished growing. New freaks were coming. Markus Ruhl would follow Gunter over 300 lb ripped and stripped. Two hundred and fifty pounds only cut it if you were under five foot six. On a frame like that, 250 lb looked the same as 300 lb anyway. Soon someone would become Mr O at over 300 lb and there would never be another one under such a weight. Some day people would look back at Dorian Yates in the same way that Dorian had looked back at Arnold Schwarzenegger, and say, 'Yes, he was a great champion. But he wouldn't make the top fifteen today. He's just not big enough . . .'

When I'd asked George Butler where he thought it would stop, he'd replied that he didn't think it would. 'If they can get to seven feet high and four hundred pounds, then they will, and they'll be eager to do it, too.'

Bodybuilding was not the only drug sport. Every sport was a drug sport. Bodybuilding was the only sport that tacitly acknowledged that it could not go on without them. For all of Ben Weider's efforts, it would never join the Olympic list. It was signed up to all the IOC codes on drug use for its amateur events. The IFBB Pro Rules 'reserved the right' for in- and out-of-contest drug testing. Wayne had halted the catastrophic abuse of diuretics with it. But professional body-builders had taken drugs, and everyone knew it.

At the two major contests in 2003, the Arnold Classic and the Mr Olympia, no drug testing took place. At the Arnold, the testers were detained in Chicago because of the snowstorm on the night of the show. At the Mr Olympia, Wayne said, he'd had to give the room at the Mandalay Bay most suitable for drug testing to Joe Weider instead.

When Wayne told me that, I should have cared, but I didn't. Bodybuilding was mad and weird and fun. It was also dark and obsessional. It was a fantastic story and no one was following it, no one at all. It lacked the commercial cynicism of big-time sport. The people in it were wildly interesting, not unapproachable monosyllabs. It was both glorious and pointless. It contained athletic endeavour and levels of sacrifice that could be matched only by other sports that demanded extremity: cycling, boxing, distance running. Peter McGough had been presenting bodybuilding on the page for half his life. He knew that the bodybuilders wanted one thing and the mainstream another. He'd tried to reconcile the two and he'd often found it impossible to do. 'There's an old argument that says, "*Fuck 'em*". They're never going to accept us, so let's tailor this sport for our community, not their community. They are never going to accept us, so why should we tailor to their community? They don't give a sod about us . . .'

*

Arnold Schwarzenegger, though, had sold bodybuilding and working out. He took it towards the mainstream with the force of his physique and the power of his personality.

Arnold, the great existential force; the king of all kings. Arnold, seven times Mr Olympia. Movie star. Governor of California.

And yet Arnold was a master of double-speak, of subterfuge. During his election campaign, he made a speech about how bodybuilding had been drug testing for years. He held it up as an example for others. He got elected. But even Arnold had to realise how far bodybuilding had come since his time in it, and how it had arrived there. Wayne DeMilia said that he'd been standing with Arnold backstage at the Mr O when Ronnie Coleman walked in front of them, stripped and ready to go out onstage.

'I could see Arnold looking at him and working it out,' Wayne said. 'I said, "Hey, Arnold, look at that. Ronnie's five ten. He's 290 pounds or thereabouts. You were what, six one and about 240 when you won in '75? He's three inches smaller and fifty pounds heavier and more ripped in just under thirty years." Arnold was just shaking his head.'

Arnold had been surrounded by FBI guys and security men during his time in Las Vegas. That was his life now. Kerry was standing about somewhere behind the stage after the show, talking to Simon Robinson. Suddenly a bunch of FBI agents pushed them up against the wall. 'Hey,' they said. 'Arnold wants a photo with you two.' Arnold came and congratulated Simon and Kerry. He stood between them and had a picture done of the three of them together. Arnold understood what it took to be Ronnie Coleman. But he understood what it took to be Simon Robinson, too, and he understood what bodybuilding had given them all.

After the Mr O and the British Grand Prix, I went to see Kerry Kayes at Betta Bodies gym in Manchester. He was working with another of Billy Graham's fighters, a rough and tough light welterweight champ called Ricky Hatton, who was preparing for a hard title defence. Kerry was enjoying himself in the camaraderie of boxing. The gym was full of fierceness and fun. Bodybuilding had something to offer boxing, and lots of sports. Aside from the drugs, it was a giant laboratory churning out priceless knowledge about the human condition. Any athlete would benefit from what men like Kerry knew about training and diet, about cause and effect, about presenting the body in a rarified state.

After Ricky had finished his workout, Kerry and I walked back through his gym. The machines clanked and jangled. There were a couple of bodybuilders working out among the office workers and regular joes.

'See that?' Kerry said to them, gesturing to a TV crew that had been filming Ricky for a piece about his next fight. 'He gets me on Sky TV. The only show you two ever get me on is fookin' *Crimewatch* . . .'

Everyone laughed. Kerry's eyes twinkled.

'That's bodybuilders,' he said, one more time.

Afterword

Wayne DeMilia estimated that 5,097 people had paid to watch Mr Olympia 2003. He had beaten his 4,646. After the show, Ronnie Coleman, Jay Cutler, Gunter Schlierkamp, Ernie Taylor, Troy Alvez, Rodney St Cloud, Art Atwood, Johnny Jackson and Claude Groulx came to Europe for the Grand Prix tour. Dexter Jackson, Kevin Levrone, Dennis James, Darrem Charles and Melvin Anthony stayed in America to prepare for the second GNC Show of Strength. Chris Cormier entered that, too. Ronnie Coleman was flown business-class to Moscow for the Russian Grand Prix. He beat Jay Cutler and won $20,000. He wasn't coming to England for Kerry's British Grand Prix or going to Dorian's Dutch show. Kerry had refused to pay a business-class fare for him. Ronnie was skipping the Show of Strength, too. Perhaps he hadn't yet forgiven them for his defeat by Gunter.

The rest flew from Moscow to England. They arrived two hours before the show began. Jay Cutler won, and Ernie Taylor came second. Gunter was third, a place ahead of a freaky Jordanian called Mustafa Mohammad, who had sent the crowd wild. They slept for a few hours and then flew to

257

Amsterdam the next morning. Jay won again, and Ernie was second again. Ernie was on a roll. He'd qualified for next year's Mr O, and for the Arnold Classic too. Gunter came fourth, behind Mustafa Mohammad.

At the Show of Strength, there was another upset. Dexter Jackson beat Jay Cutler, even though Jay seemed to look better than he had done at the O. Kevin Levrone somehow hauled himself ahead of Dennis James. Gunter finished fifth. Chris Cormier didn't even make the top six. He was placed seventh. Chris knew he was not at his best, but he still felt he'd been shafted.

Kerry sent Wayne an email saying that he would no longer run a British Grand Prix if the Show of Strength continued to take place two weeks after the Mr O. It offered $100,000 to the winner. It had been won twice in succession by an athlete who was not the favourite and who had not travelled to Europe for the tour. The logic was obvious. The Show of Strength had become a force for change to the world order. Wayne moved the date of the Show of Strength. In 2004, it would take place two weeks before the Mr O. That would really shake things up.

Jay Cutler had won $160,000 in two weeks, to go with his early-season prize money. He'd signed new contracts with *Flex* magazine and a supplement company called Muscle Tech. He had probably made more money in one calendar year than any other competitive bodybuilder ever had. He announced that he would be entering the Arnold Classic. He wanted to be the first man to win it three times in a row. It meant that his body would not get too much rest, the rest it might need to grow to a size that could threaten Ronnie Coleman. Perhaps muscle was going to make Jay wait, too.

If anything, Ronnie's ambition had been sharpened by his win. No one knew if he would enter the Show of Strength, but he would sure as hell be at the Olympia, bigger than ever.

Dexter, Gunter, Ernie and Chris Cormier also said that they would do the Arnold. Dexter would now have to live up to his new status. Gunter would be hoping to revive his form after his disappointments. Ernie would take the stage with new confidence. Everyone would be hoping that the real Chris showed up. Other freaks loomed. Markus Ruhl would be back for the Arnold, too.

Everyone would be working away, getting bigger, increasing, multiplying, doubling. There would be no backward steps taken at all.

This was the smoke, this was the fallout from a year of muscle. Kerry found me a number for Grant Thomas, the Welsh Beast. It had been six years since we'd met at his house in Cardiff on the day after Princess Diana died. Grant hadn't made it as a pro. The gap between Universe and Olympia had become too wide, the financial hardship was too great. But Kyle was growing up and Grant was thinking about getting back into training. He wanted to compete as an amateur again, and see if he couldn't give Mr Universe another go, just for the fun of it.

In bodybuilding, there were tigers and there were lambs. The tigers were easy to spot. And it was easy to see the bodybuilders as the lambs, too. But they played it as fiercely as they could for as long as their bodies would allow them to do so. They were entirely committed. They had open eyes. They understood the game. No, they weren't the lambs.

Now I thought that maybe *we* were the lambs; the people who watched, the people who bought the magazines and the VIP tickets and who loved the rumour and the gossip and the intrigue, who wanted Ronnie to get Biblically Big, who fuelled Guntermania, who urged Jay further up the curve, who wanted to see the three of them side by side again, stripped and ripped, high and dry, hard and vascular and brutal, weighing over 900 lb with 5 per cent body fat standing between them and disaster.

Yes, perhaps we were the lambs, living our soft lives and staring up at all that muscle.

Epilogue: May 2005

(i) Freaks and Dinosaurs

Some things in bodybuilding had become just too big. In 2004, the Era of the Freak had got too freaky, even for the people who'd helped create it. If bodybuilding was going to become bigger, the bodies would have to get smaller. And before this evolution could begin, there had to be a time of ruin and collapse. When the ice age came, it blew in fast and no one really saw it coming.

For all of the years that Wayne DeMilia had been promoting the Mr Olympia show, the deal had been done on a handshake between him and Ben Weider. Wayne's sole income came from his piece of the Mr O, and the profits he generated from the other contests he promoted.

When it began it seemed like the usual, just another rumour. In April 2003 someone had rung Wayne to tell him that Ben Weider was trying to sell the Olympia. Then someone else rang and told him the same thing. Wayne called Ben and Ben told Wayne, 'Look, there's no such thing.' Then Wayne was sent the transcript of an online interview with David Pecker, the man who had bought Joe Weider's magazines for $350m. In the interview, David Pecker mentioned some negotiations he'd had with Ben Weider over the rights to the Olympia show.

'I call up Ben and he denies it,' Wayne said, after it was all over. 'I said, "Look, Ben, all I want is not to feel like the wife whose husband is cheating on him. Everyone but me knows."'

Wayne promoted the 2003 Mr Olympia. The crowd was the biggest in history. The expo had five hundred exhibitors and 20,000 people a day passing through. Arnold Schwarzenegger had shown up, just weeks after being elected Governor of California. Ronnie Coleman set a new standard in super-size. Wayne's touch seemed surer than ever.

After the argument they'd had in Canada, Ben had told Wayne that he wanted to formalise their handshake agreement. In December 2003, Wayne received a draft contract. He was unhappy with the terms it laid out. He didn't really want to sign but he felt that he had little choice if he wanted to remain in bodybuilding.

Then David Pecker invited Wayne to dinner and told him that he and Ben had come to a preliminary agreement over the sale of the Mr O. He also told Wayne that he wanted him to run the show, and that he would let him know when the contract was signed.

By the time of the Arnold Classic 2004, the deal between the IFBB and David Pecker had still not been done. Wayne said that he set up a lunch with David Pecker. At the lunch it was proposed that Pecker's company, AMI, establish a new bodybuilding federation. AMI owned the bodybuilding magazines and had all of the athletes under contract to *Flex*. Wayne had the Night of Champions, and the expertise in contest management and promotion. What did they need the Weiders for? They could create their own shows in America and across Europe and Asia.

Wayne offered AMI a crash course in the management of pro bodybuilding. He came up with a name for the contest that would replace the Mr Olympia. It would be called Champion of Champions. The new federation was to be named Pro Division. A website appeared briefly on the Internet. Wayne rang Kerry Kayes and asked if he would be willing to take the British Grand Prix to the new organisation. Kerry told Wayne that he'd go with whoever delivered the bodybuilders.

And then David Pecker went back to Ben Weider and Ben agreed to sell him a controlling share in the Mr Olympia. There was one new condition on the deal: that Wayne have no further role in promoting it.

'So, did I go behind Ben's back?' Wayne said. 'Yeah, I did. Did I get fisted by them for thirty years of loyalty? Did I always take the short end of the stick? Yeah, I think I did.

Wayne had been leveraged. His life and career were the collateral damage from the Olympia deal between the Weiders and AMI. He'd failed to read the signs. He hadn't watched his back. He alone picked up the bill.

Peter McGough put me in touch with David Pecker. I wanted to let him know what Wayne had said. I wrote him an email with a series of detailed questions based on what Wayne had told me. He did not answer them directly. Instead, he wrote: 'I have discovered that bodybuilding is a world filled with people of such passion for the sport that there is a constant tendency for rumors to start and then take on lives of their own. It's really quite amazing. As a result, I never focus on idle chat. To be clear, however, the IFBB, the Weiders and AMI wanted to do a deal on the Olympia and we have an agreement with respect to the development of the Olympia contests and other pro bodybuilding events. The terms are confidential, however, AMI is not a minority shareholder.'

Wayne perished with his eyes open. 'Pecker wanted the event,' he said. 'He doesn't care about me. Who am I? I'm just another employee . . .'

AMI made some changes to the 2004 Mr Olympia. They introduced a challenge round, where the top six body-builders could call one another out to posedown in one of the compulsory positions and the judges would award marks to the winner. The crowd watched the scores unfold on a big screen. Ronnie Coleman won his seventh Mr O by beating Jay Cutler on a rear double biceps pose. Ronnie came over to Europe and cleaned up in Russia, Holland and at the British Grand Prix.

Kerry Kayes seemed sanguine about the upheaval. He'd been around too long to be anything else. At the British Grand Prix, he had a couple of national newspapers and a Sky camera crew running around after Big Ron, and Big Ron delivered a feast of muscle in return. I asked Ronnie how much longer he thought he'd go on for, and he shook his head. 'Dunno, man. As long as I can.' It wasn't apparent how long that would be, but he wanted to break Lee Haney's record of eight Mr Olympia titles. Later, Kerry and Dorian presented Ronnie with his trophy. Dorian looked trim next to Ronnie. It didn't seem possible that anyone could get much bigger. When the pictures came out in the papers and on TV, there was a certain appalled fascination with Ronnie, and with the event. But it was only for one day, and it was only bodybuilding. There were plenty of other freak shows in town.

The sport seemed winded, stilled, the breath knocked out of it. It sat around, ruefully rubbing its injury, apparently unable to move. AMI decided to move the Mr Olympia weekend from the Mandalay Bay hotel, but it took them so long to find an alternative venue and confirm a date for the 2005 show that Kerry and Boris, who ran the Russian Grand Prix, lost the reserve on their venues and the European tour of 2005 was cancelled. Dorian and Lily had broken up before the 2004 Dutch Grand Prix, and afterwards Lily moved to Palm Beach, leaving Holland without a promoter. The Night of Champions was over, too. Wayne owned the contest, and he was staying out of bodybuilding. It was replaced in 2005 by a new show, the New York Pro, which was won by Darrem Charles. The Show of Strength was not allowed to offer prize money to rival the Mr O or the Arnold. Denied its best selling point, the contest that had so disturbed the world order withered on the vine. The 2005 event was cancelled.

Wayne had been through worse things than losing his job. In 1998, he'd discovered that he had prostate cancer. He was forty-eight years old. He described the lowest point, when he'd just been diagnosed and he came home to an empty house thinking, 'What now? Am I going to die?' He applied much of the knowledge he'd acquired through bodybuilding towards his cancer. In particular, he found that the use of antioxidants helped his immune system. After he left the IFBB he set up a supplement company called AO Force. It sold products designed to boost the body. The main one, AO Force itself, was an immediate success. Wayne took it to health expos. He spoke to people who had cancer or HIV and was able to describe to them how it had helped him. More than that, he found that he had a connection with them. He could tell them about the time he thought he'd die. AO Force took off. Wayne expanded the product range. He came up with a muscle builder called Muscle Force and a slimming aid called Slim Force. He came up with something else, too.

'One of the other things about guys who've had prostate surgery,' Wayne said, 'is that they often have to use Viagra. But it don't always work. Or you get headaches after, or blue streaks. So we've developed a natural alternative. It works really good, I'm telling you.'

'What's it called?' I asked him.

'Sex Force.'

It seemed that nothing much was going to keep Wayne down for long.

(ii) 'Everything From A to Z'

In the spring of 2003 *Flex* published a picture of a race between Kevin Levrone and Dwain Chambers, a British sprinter who was ranked number two in the world in the hundred metres. Kevin had spent some time boasting about his athletic prowess. He'd said that he was faster than most pro athletes. In fact, he'd said he was the fastest man alive.

Chambers was living in America, where he'd hooked up with a nutritionist named Victor Conte. Conte was a former musician with the Tower of Power and Herbie Hancock. He got out of the music business and into training and built up a company called Balco advising power athletes like bodybuilders, weightlifters, NFL footballers, baseball sluggers and track sprinters. Loads of West Coast bodybuilders knew of Victor. A few of them even showed up to watch the race. Gunter was there, so was the former pro Milos Sarcev. Chambers and Levrone raced on the track at Orange Coast College in Costa Mesa on 11 December 2002. Dwain looked happy and relaxed. He also looked small next to Kevin, who himself looked withered next to Gunter, who was swaggering around at about 300 lb.

The race was over sixty metres. Kevin began well, but Dwain soon overtook him, like a dad letting his son get ahead before beating him to the line. Chambers crossed in 6.64 seconds, Levrone in 7.9. Afterwards, they posed for *Flex*. Chambers stood in line with, among others, Gunter Schlierkamp and Milos Sarcev. The picture struck me as remarkable: I couldn't think of too many Olympic athletes who would be keen to be seen with bodybuilders in the pages of a muscle mag. Yet the photo in *Flex* turned out to be more than just a curio. Within two years, it would be at the heart of the biggest doping bust in the history of pro sports in America.

Balco was turning over hundreds of millions of dollars through Conte's nutritional supplements, which were endorsed by some of America's most famous sports men and women. Along with Remi Korchemny, who had coached the 1972 Russian Olympic 100m and 200m champion Valerie Borzov, Conte had formed an elite track club, which he'd named after his best-selling ZMA supplement. Among its members were Dwain Chambers, Tim Montgomery, Marion Jones and Kelli White. Under Conte and Korchemny, Chambers and Montgomery had become the world's top-ranked 100m runners. Kelli White was a double World Champion, and Marion Jones remained the brightest star in womens' athletics. Tim Montgomery wasn't just benefiting from Conte's nutritional nous either. Milos Sarcev had devised his weight-training programme.

Dwain Chambers and Kelli White fell first. Chambers tested positive for a previously unrecognisible designer steroid called tetrahydrogestrinone, known to the athletes who used it as THG or 'the Clear'. He was banned for two years in February 2004. White's ban, when it came, was more significant. She'd got herself jacked up on the Clear too, but she hadn't been caught by a drug test. Some of the evidence against her was obtained from documents seized at the Balco offices during a Federal Grand Jury investigation that had begun in 2003.

After Tim Montgomery appeared before the Grand Jury, his testimony was leaked to the *San Francisco Chronicle*. In it, he too admitted using the Clear. The United States Anti-Doping Agency announced that they would seek a life ban against him and another Conte sprinter, Chryste Gaines. On the basis of emails and paper trails, two more Balco athletes, Michelle Collins and Alvin Harrison, received bans of eight and four years respectively. Marion Jones denied any drug use. She threatened legal action against the USADA if they prevented her from competing in the Athens Olympics. She went, but failed to win a medal of any sort.

The Balco investigation might have eluded the wider public consciousness had it stuck to track and field, which was still a minor sport in America. It didn't. Tim Montgomery told the Grand Jury that Victor Conte gave steroids to Barry Bonds, an iconic baseball player. Victor Conte had told an Internal Revenue Service investigator called Jeff Novitsky the same thing: he had provided Bonds with the Clear, the steroid Winstrol and a testosterone cream. Novitsky's memo on his interview with Conte noted that Conte named a total of twenty-seven athletes 'from professional football and baseball players to track and field stars' to whom he had supplied the Clear.

He hadn't been too discreet either, according to Montgomery, who told the Grand Jury, 'Any sport there is, Mr Conte got someone in it. He would brag on Barry Bonds. He would brag on Ronnie Coleman . . .'

Pro baseball had introduced random drug testing in 2003. Under the Major League players' union agreement, penalising athletes for steroid use could only begin when more than 5 per cent of the League's annual anonymous tests came back as positives. That threshold was exceeded for the first time in the 2002 season. Barry Bonds had never tested positive. His Grand Jury testimony was leaked to the press. He denied any deliberate doping. He said that he 'might have unknowingly taken steroids'. At a press conference in February 2005, Bonds was asked if he could explain his 'tremendous growth in muscle strength, getting stronger as you get older? Can you finally put to rest...'

'Can I?' he said. 'Hard work, that's about it. Now it's to rest.'

Kelli White told a World Anti-Doping Agency hearing that she was treated 'like a guinea pig' by Balco. The THG she took helped her to add muscle 'very quickly', but at a cost. 'My menstrual cycle was completely disturbed. I had acne and my voice changed incredibly. And probably the worst thing was, my blood pressure shot up. It took a long time to stabilise.'

In February 2004, Victor Conte, Remi Korchemny, Greg Anderson – a personal trainer to Barry Bonds – and a Balco vice-president named James Valente were indicted on steroid conspiracy charges. They were also charged with, variously, possession of human growth hormone, money laundering and the misbranding of drugs with the intention to defraud. They all pleaded not guilty. The trial is due to begin in September 2005.

What damned many of the Balco athletes was the same thing that damned pro bodybuilders: the way they looked. Dwain Chambers could probably have held his own at an amateur bodybuilding show. Kelli White was jacked. Baseball was full of ripped and shredded jocks, blasting away home-run records that had stood for decades. NFL players looked like Marvel comic heroes. As Balco offered up its secrets, the country at large faced up to the obvious: American sport was juiced. All sport was juiced. Not everyone did it, but lots did. Even George Bush became exercised by the matter. The only sport that no-one seemed surprised about was bodybuilding, of course.

By the Classic of 2005, the issue had become personal for Arnold Schwarzenegger. In addition to the Arnold weekend, he was now the official 'editor-in-chief' of *Flex* and *Muscle and Fitness* magazines. Drugs in sport was political, and Arnold was a politician with business interests in the most notorious of drug sports. It was messy, and Arnold didn't like mess. And yet he thought too much of bodybuilding to step away from it. It was too central to his perception of himself, too responsible for the course of his life for him to do that. Arnold was still the most famous muscleman on earth.

Jay Cutler decided not to defend his Arnold Classic title in 2005. He'd won three times. He wanted to be ready for Ronnie Coleman and the Mr Olympia show. Markus Ruhl was absent. Gunter Schlierkamp was taking a break. Big Ron didn't need the Arnold Classic, either. By accident or design, the 2005 show was slimming down. Dexter Jackson won. Dexter had become the poster boy for smaller physiques – not that anyone outside of bodybuilding would have noticed. He weighed almost 230 lb. To the wider world, he was still a heavy load, hulking about the stage dripping muscle. His body, with its great peaks and its spectacular crevasses, made only one comment to the people of America: freak.

Arnold Schwarzenegger stood next to Dexter Jackson and presented him with his prize. When he made his usual speech to the crowd, Arnold told them that bodybuilding needed to address its drug problem. He didn't hold back. 'Even though every sport is struggling with the drug issue,' he said, 'we have to do even more in order to get rid of drugs from our sport once and for all. We have to do everything from A to Z.'

Some people booed Arnold, onstage at the Arnold Classic. Afterwards, Dexter told a journalist that 'it would be good' if Arnold carried out such plans. Dexter added that he didn't take steroids himself.

Two months before the show, in his capacity as Governor of California, Arnold had gone to meet the editors of the *San Francisco Chronicle*. The *Chronicle* was important to Arnold, and Arnold and bodybuilding had become a story for the *Chronicle*. They challenged him over his ongoing interests. They said that the sport had 'endemic' drug-abuse problems, and that his close proximity presented him with an ethical dilemma. Arnold was ready for them though. He said that his editor-in-chief role 'allowed him to present a valuable message about . . . the dangers of abusing steroids and other performance-enhancing drugs'. Afterwards, he told reporters, 'I'm going to continue promoting health and fitness. I've made it very clear that I want to weed out all of the problems that they write about that is unhealthy for anybody'.

Arnold's press secretary, Margita Thompson, added, 'It's who he is. It goes to his core. He sold bodybuilding and made it more mainstream. He sold working out and physical fitness. Now he's shifted into selling California'.

So perhaps that's what Arnold was after all: a salesman. No longer a bodybuilder, no longer an actor, not really a politician in any conventional sense. He was an icon, an image, an idea. He was Arnold, and you either bought what he was selling or you didn't.

AMI had committed to paying Arnold's non-profit-making Governor's Council on Physical Fitness $1.25m over five years for Arnold's services. Doug Heller, who ran a website called ArnoldWatch, said, 'These magazines are where Arnold the Brand meets Arnold the Politician. You've got this venue for Schwarzenegger to essentially improve his own stature in the public – and he's using it freely.'

Willie Brown, the former Mayor of San Francisco, said, 'He's a whole franchise. He's always been a franchise. He's very good at it, the public loves it and they don't view his attention to his franchise responsibilities as being in conflict with his job as Governor. So he's really, really lucky. The rest of us would be barbecued . . .'

The benefits for David Pecker and AMI were obvious, too. Arnold legitimised bodybuilding. He dragged it a little way from its ghetto. He gave the sport a face that Ronnie and Jay and Gunter and the rest could not. As with many things in his life, Arnold offered the situation some spin.

Peter McGough felt that Arnold was serious in his intent. *Flex* began to tackle the matter. Peter ran editorials that called for the end of the drug bellies. Arnold pressed his harder line on steroids. The IFBB issued a directive to judges to penalise inflated guts. Mustafa Mohammad, the freaky Jordanian, collapsed twice – at the 2004 Mr Olympia and the Dutch Grand Prix – after using the diuretic Aldactone. He was warned by the IFBB that he would be banned if it happened again. Peter said that there would be 'a discussion period' on more meaningful drug testing, including out-of-competition testing. He felt that it had to be introduced gradually. David Pecker said that there was a 'widespread acknowledgement of drugs in our sport. Now we have to address the problem of eliminating them.'

To prosper in its third century, it seemed, bodybuilding would be glancing backwards through time for its new ideal. Arnold had a vision of how things might look and he was pushing it through. The freak of the future would have tons of muscle, but a waspish waist in the shadow of giant shoulders. He would have proportion and symmetry. He would have classical lines. He would be beautiful and Elysian, a vision of human perfection that had thrummed through the centuries. In all, he would look very much like Arnold Schwarzenegger indeed.

Acknowledgements

Kerry Kayes, Dorian Yates:
Their generosity, counsel and friendship made this book possible.

And:
Ernie Taylor, Ronnie Coleman, Jay Cutler, Gunter Schlierkamp, Chris Cormier, Wayne DeMilia, Peter McGough, George Butler, Charles Gaines, Dianne Bennett, Kenny 'Flex' Wheeler, Dexter Jackson, Simon Robinson, Matt Lors and Lors Communications, Grant Thomas, Gary Phillips, Jan Kayes, Debbie Kayes, John Ernster, John Hodgson and all at CNP/Dorian Yates Approved, the Temple Gym, Arnold Schwarzenegger for being Arnold-esque at the right times, the estimable *Flex* magazine, James Phillips.

The other competitors at the shows and events reported:
Dennis James, Kevin Levrone, Markus Ruhl, Claude Groulx, Tommy Thorvildsen, Jaroslav Horvath, Paco Bautista, Giovanni Thompson, Lee Priest, Milos Sarcev, Art Atwood, Paul Dillett, Johnny Jackson, Nasser El Sonbaty, Shawn Ray, Bob Cicherillo, Rodney St Cloud, Troy Alves, Quincy Taylor,

Vince Taylor, Mike Matarazzo, Ahmad Haidar, Mustafa Mohammad, Stan McReary, Eddie Abbew, JD Dawadu, Craig Titus, Peter Brown and Elisabeth Schwarz.

Andreas Munzer and Mohamed Benaziza.

Those of us without the muscle:
Tristan Jones, Rachel Cugnoni, Beth Coates, Mick Wall, Matthias Penzel, George Hotten, Maureen Hotten, Julie Simpson, Caroline Cope, Simon Kanter, Simone Hotten for the transcriptions, Scott Morgan.
Thank you Yasmin Hounsell.

I'd like to acknowledge the following books, articles and publications:

Pumping Iron by George Butler and Charles Gaines
Arnold Schwarzenegger: A Portrait by George Butler
A Warrior's Story: A Portrait of Dorian Yates by Dorian Yates and Peter McGough
Arnold by Wendy Leigh
Gorilla Suit by Bob Paris
Pumped by Cynthia Kuhn, Scott Swartzwelder and Wilkie Wilson

'The Power and The Gory' by Paul Solotaroff, from *Village Voice*
'Size Matters' by Erik Hedegaard, from *Details*

Flex
Der Spiegel
Bild
Muscle and Fitness
Muscular Development